Visitor Management

Visitor Management
Case studies from World Heritage Sites

Edited by **Myra Shackley**

Centre for Tourism and Visitor Management
Nottingham Trent University

OXFORD   AUCKLAND   BOSTON   JOHANNESBURG   MELBOURNE   NEW DELHI

Butterworth-Heinemann
Linacre House, Jordan Hill, Oxford OX2 8DP
225 Wildwood Avenue, Woburn, MA 01801-2041
A division of Reed Educational and Professional Publishing Ltd

℞ A member of the Reed Elsevier plc group

First published 1998
Paperback edition 2000

British Library Cataloguing in Publication Data
Visitor management: Case studies from World Heritage sites
    1. Sightseeing business   2. Historic sites – management
    I. Shackley, Myra
    338.4'791

ISBN 0 7506 4783 3

Composition by Scribe Design, Gillingham, Kent, UK
Printed and bound in Great Britain

Contents

Contributors

All contributors to this book are, or have recently been, affiliated to the Centre for Tourism and Visitor Management at Nottingham Business School, Nottingham Trent University (Burton Street, Nottingham NG1 4BU. Phone +44 (0) 115 941 8418, fax +44 (0) 115 948 6512. Contributors can be contacted at this address, unless otherwise stated.

David Airey, now Professor of Tourism Management at the University of Surrrey, was formerly Professor of Tourism at the Centre for Tourism and Visitor Management, Nottingham Trent University. His particular research interests currently include the development of tourism in transitional economies, together with tourism education and careers. Contact: d.airey@surrey.ac.uk

Sheena Carlisle completed an MA in the Social Anthropology of Tourism at the College of St Mark and St John, Plymouth and has since been a part-time fieldwork assistant examining tourism issues in Ethiopia.

Katie Evans was formerly a Lecturer in Tourism at the Centre for Tourism and Visitor Management and is now a Senior Lecturer at the University of Derby, where she runs an MA in Tourism Management. Her current research interests relate to the management of monumental World Heritage Sites. Contact: C.M.Evans@derby.ac.uk

Lindsay Fielding is a research student at the Centre for Tourism and Visitor Management working on the use of Information Technology for the management of Protected Areas, particularly GIS (Geographic Information Systems) and Internet resources.

Alexandra Muresan is a research student at the Centre for Tourism and Visitor Management whose areas of interest are focused on issues concerning tourism development strategies, tourism management and marketing in Eastern Europe.

Sophie Turley is a lecturer in Tourism and Visitor Management at Nottingham Trent University with research interests in the management and marketing of visitor attractions, particularly at sites seeking to satisfy multiple and potentially conflicting objectives.

Jenny Rivers has just completed an MA in Tourism Planning and Management at the Centre for Tourism and Visitor Management and also works as a leader of heritage tours in southern Egypt.

Chris Ryan formerly taught tourism and marketing at Nottingham Trent University and is now Professor of Tourism at Northern Territory University, Darwin, Australia and editor of the journal *Tourism Management*. Contact: cryan@business.ntu.edu.au

Myra Shackley is Professor of Culture Resource Management at Nottingham Trent University and Head of the Centre for Visitor Management. She is particularly interested in the management of visitors to historic sites and Protected Areas. Contact: myra.shackley@ntu.ac.uk

Figures

List of tables

Preface

It is now almost twenty years since the first cultural properties considered to be of universal cultural significance for all humankind were inscribed upon the World Heritage List, a list which now contains 380 cultural sites, 107 sites of natural significance and nineteen mixed sites including both cultural and natural resources. The World Heritage List is the modern equivalent of the Seven Wonders of the World; a series of sites, monuments, landscapes and buildings each of which has, in some way, made a unique contribution to human history. Although many visitors may not realize the complexities of the processes by which locations are added to the list (which is administered by the World Heritage Centre at UNESCO headquarters in Paris), the term 'World Heritage Site' is instantly recognized as designating something very special, in tourism terms a definite 'must see'. The List contains universally recognized sites, like the Pyramids or the Great Wall of China, but it also includes smaller, less well-known properties and monuments whose significance is universal and which transcend existing cultural values. Needless to say, such sites are magnets for visitors and the enrolment of a new property on the World Heritage List, with the concomitant publicity, is virtually a guarantee that visitor numbers will increase. The original purpose of the World Heritage List was to provide a mechanism whereby sites of universal value could be protected within a management framework and allowing access to conservation funding. Many sites are fragile, threatened not only by natural erosion but also, increasingly, by the large numbers of visitors who wish to see them. Visitor management has become a new and as yet inexact science which aims to balance the needs and requirements of the visitor with the potential impact that the visitor may have on fragile buildings or artefacts. Each World Heritage Site has to solve the problems posed by the visitor management dilemma in its own way, and has done so with varying degree of success. However, the sheer size of many of the sites and the need to cope with annual visitation levels which may run into the millions has necessitated the development of visitor management strategies, some formalized and some existing purely by custom.

In 1995 the Centre for Tourism and Visitor Management was set up at Nottingham Business School with the express purpose of providing a focus for the study of visitors, particularly in relation to sites of cultural significance or where tourism involved significant impact upon natural resources. Since that time staff and students at the Centre have been involved in a wide variety of research projects within this general area, which have, most recently, concentrated on cultural World Heritage Sites. The results of some of this work are presented in this book in the form of a series of ten case studies which examine very different World Heritage Sites throughout the world, looking at visitor management issues within a general framework of cultural tourism and resource management. The sites are immensely varied, from the Pyramids of Giza with more than 2 million visitors per year, to a small island off the west coast of Canada with less than 1000. Some sites, such as Easter Island, are very isolated whereas others, like the Old City of Cracow, are complex multi-use urban centres. Some, like the rock-cut churches of Lalibela in Ethiopia, are of great religious significance and others, like Kakadu National Park in northern Australia, play a seminal role in the lives of the indigenous people who live there. Each case study takes a different approach. The Lalibela case looks at the social impact of visitor pressure whereas at Luxor the issue under the spotlight is traffic management and the visitor experience. Whatever the site, wherever the location and however the site is managed, certain issues appeared which were common to all localities, and these are collected and discussed in the final chapter. What has emerged is not only the desperate need to manage visitors for the benefit of sites, as well as the other way round, but also to find ways to manage the quality of the visitor experience which should, at sites of this type, be something very special and not descend to the mundane. The case studies in this book present some ideas about the ways in which this might be done.

Myra Shackley

1   Introduction – World Cultural Heritage Sites

Myra Shackley

The World Heritage List designates unique cultural sites of outstanding universal value, values measurable in both cultural and economic terms. At the latest update (December 1996) there were 506 properties inscribed on the List, 380 cultural, 107 natural and nineteen mixed. Ten World Heritage Sites are discussed in detail in this book, examples chosen to illustrate the range of different properties which have received World Heritage designation, from all over the world. No two World Heritage Sites are (by definition) alike but all share common problems such as the need for a delicate balance between visitation and conservation. All are national flag carriers, symbols in some way of national culture and character. Most are the major cultural tourism attractions of their country and some (such as Stonehenge, the Pyramids, the Great Wall of China) are powerfully evocative symbols of national identity, universally recognized. World Heritage is a fragile non-renewable resource which has to be safeguarded both to maintain its authenticity and to preserve it for future generations. Visiting a World Heritage Site should be a major intellectual experience, on a different scale from visiting some theme park. The majority of visitors to such sites are, predictably, motivated by an interest in heritage and culture although this motivation may not be matched by any prior knowledge of the site concerned, making the provision of adequate information and interpretation doubly vital.

The World Heritage Convention

The Convention Concerning the Protection of the World Cultural and Natural Heritage (UNESCO, 1972) is one of three UNESCO conventions related to cultural heritage. The others include the Convention for the Protection of Cultural

Property in the Event of Armed Conflict (usually known as the Hague Convention, adopted in 1954) and the Convention on the Means of Prohibiting and Preventing the Illicit Import and Transfer of Ownership of Cultural Property Conventions (1970). All three Acts are relevant for the protection of significant cultural sites, but the first (usually abbreviated to the 'World Heritage Convention') has determined, to a large extent, the preservation of the most significant cultural sites since it was passed in Paris in 1972. In March 1997 148 States ('States Parties') signed an instrument signifying their acceptance, accession to or ratification of the document. At present this does not include the United Kingdom which (despite having sixteen World Heritage Sites) is not currently a member of UNESCO, although there seems a strong likelihood that it will rejoin within the next few years. Lack of UNESCO membership does not disqualify a country from submitting a nomination to the World Heritage Committee which manages the World Heritage Convention, although, of course, it does mean that the country is not contributing funding to UNESCO from which, ultimately, finance to administer the World Heritage Committee is derived.

The World Heritage Committee, assisted by the UNESCO Secretariat and the World Heritage Centre, is located in offices in Paris. This Centre holds the World Heritage Archive, publishes a newsletter and journal, operates a WWW site (UNESCO, 1997) maintains a mailing list and acts as a coordinator for national and regional governments and for all the numerous organizations involved in the management of World Heritage Sites. The Centre is understaffed and underfunded, probably because when it was initially set up more than twenty years ago the level of governmental interest in World Heritage Sites was grossly underestimated. One result of this is that World Heritage designation does not automatically carry with it routine financial support although, as is frequently demonstrated by the examples discussed in this book, nomination generally improves the ability of a country or site to access conservation funding. There are different ways of accessing emergency funding, mentioned below, but after designation a World Heritage Site which is not recognized as being at risk receives no UNESCO funding and is left to generate the necessary financial support from governmental and other sources. Nomination to the list confers status, but not cash, and that status is dependent upon the site satisfying a complex set of criteria including the submission of a detailed site management plan.

The World Heritage Committee has three basic functions:

- To identify, on the basis of nominations submitted by national governments, cultural and natural properties of outstanding universal value which are to be protected under the Convention, and to list those on the World Heritage List (Appendix 1)

- To decide which properties on the World Heritage List are to be inscribed on the List of World Heritage in Danger (for properties which require major conservation assistance requiring funding under the Convention)
- To determine how and under what conditions the resources in the World Heritage Fund can best be used to assist governments in the protection of their World Heritage Sites.

There is a set of official UNESCO guidelines for the operation of the Convention (*Operational Guidelines for the Implementation of the World Heritage Convention*) written in 1977 and revised in 1992, as well as more specific information (Feilden and Jokilehto, 1993), published jointly by UNESCO, ICOMOS (International Council on Monuments and Sites) and ICCROM (International Centre for the Study of the Preservation and Restoration of Cultural Property) which presents management guidelines specifically for cultural World Heritage Sites. There is also the *World Monuments Watch*, an annual list of one hundred most endangered sites. This new programme is on its first 5-year plan (1996–2000) supported by grant aid from American Express and other sponsors. However, the sites included on this need not necessarily have received World Heritage nomination but similar criteria are recommended. Sites enter the list on the basis of the significance, urgency and viability of actions proposed for their conservation and the list currently includes one archaeological site discussed in this book (Orongo, on Easter Island: Chapter 5).

The World Heritage List

All the relevant criteria for nomination to the World Heritage List are found in the *Operational Guidelines* (UNESCO, 1992). The list consists of cultural sites, natural sites (often, but not always, National Parks) and a new category called 'cultural landscapes' which was added in 1993 (von Droste *et al.*, 1995). The procedure for designation is complex but basically involves the submission of a dossier for a particular site, by a national government and on standard forms which must be accompanied by archive information, which is then considered by a committee who decide whether the site warrants World Heritage status. The process of nomination, evaluation and decision making takes at least a year and a half. Since the conditions include the submission of detailed historical and archaeological records as well as management plans considerable expense is often involved. In the case of a developing world nation this may frequently involve the use of outside consultants. Lack of know-how and finance are the reasons that many countries containing significant cultural sites have not yet applied for their elevation to World Heritage status. Other reasons may be political, and it is significant that the majority of sites recently added to the list come either from the former Soviet bloc, Eastern Europe or from Central and South America. Having a few World Heritage Sites confirms nationhood in some cases, although it can also be used (in the case of newly created countries) to create a slightly spurious cultural history.

The cultural sites are divided into two categories:

1   Monuments, groups of buildings and individual sites
2   Groups of urban buildings

These categories produce very different visitor management problems with much attention being currently focused upon the second, urban, category. The two major groups are broken down into several subdivisions, and World Heritage Sites may be included under several different subcategories (as are most of the examples discussed in this book, shown in parentheses).

Criteria for inclusion under the first category are that the site must:

- Represent a unique artistic achievement or a masterpiece of creative genius (Thebes, Giza, Lalibela, Easter Island) or
- Have exerted great influence over a span of time or within a cultural area of the world on development in architecture, monumental arts, town planning or landscape design (Hadrian's Wall) or
- Bear a unique or at least exceptional testimony to a civilization or cultural tradition which has disappeared (Ninstints, Thebes, Giza, Lalibela, Hadrian's Wall, Easter Island) or
- Be an outstanding example of a type of building or architectural ensemble or landscape which illustrates a significant stage or stages in human history (Biertan, Hadrian's Wall) or
- Be an outstanding example of traditional human settlement or land use which is representative of a culture (or cultures) especially when it has become vulnerable to the impact of irreversible change or in exceptional circumstances or in conjunction with other criteria (Kakadu, Easter Island) or
- Be directly and tangibly associated with events or living traditions, with ideas, or with beliefs, with artistic and literary works of outstanding universal significance (Thebes, Giza, Lalibela).

The second category refers mainly to historic towns (including cities and other urban sites) and again has several possible subdivisions:

- Towns of a specific period or culture almost entirely preserved and largely unaffected by subsequent developments
- Towns which have preserved spatial arrangements and structures typical of successive stages in their history – the historic part takes precedence over the contemporary environment
- Historic centres which cover exactly the same area as ancient towns but are now enclosed within modern cities
- Sectors, areas or isolated units which preserve coherent evidence of the character of an historic town which has disappeared.

Within this book it is easy to see how most sites are good examples of these categories and how, despite their differences, they each represent something unique, a monument or location of outstanding significance to humanity. Examples are the churches of Biertan or Lalibela as distinctive architectural styles or the abandoned Native American village of Ninstints with the world's most significant *in-situ* collection of carved totem poles. Easter Island is certainly a unique testimony to an all-but-vanished civilization, and the pyramids and tombs of Giza and Thebes in Egypt are some of the ancient world's most significant and familiar monuments. Not all World Heritage Sites are as well known and they vary considerably in size. Some (Ninstints, Easter Island) are in quite inaccessible locations while others (Bukhara, Cracow) are large complex urban centres. One (Hadrian's Wall) is an immense linear feature connecting groups of significant buildings. Others (Easter Island, Thebes, Giza) are spread out over extensive areas. Kakadu National Park in Australia is an especially interesting case since it was designated as a site containing features of both natural and cultural significance. Bukhara and Cracow here provide examples of the difficulties encountered in managing visitors to historic urban centres, having taken very different attitudes to their World Heritage designations.

As well as conforming to one or other of the categories above, all potential World Heritage Sites must also meet tests of authenticity in design, material, workmanship or setting and, in the case of cultural landscapes, their distinctive character and components (Shackley, 1997). This is not always easy. It is relatively easy to prove authenticity for all features of an isolated archaeological site, long since abandoned (Shackley, 1997) and comparatively easy to control access and conservation. Dealing with a complex, living and inhabited city centre such as that of Cracow or Bukhara is a very different matter, producing problems frequently related to the conflicting demands of conservation and the requirements of the people living there.

World Heritage Sites, because of the formalities required before designation, have adequate legal protection and/or traditional protection and management mechanisms to ensure the conservation of the nominated property or landscape. This means that a government which does not have established (and effective) protective legislation and management mechanisms is not eligible to submit its site for nomination. It is also required that the government can provide proof of the ways in which it is proposing to administer the World Heritage Site, including ways of managing visitors, conservation and public access. Once a site is inscribed on the list it is (theoretically) periodically inspected and the World Heritage designation can be withdrawn if the management criteria are not being met. There are recent examples of countries which have nearly lost World Heritage designation for several major sites when the World Heritage committee felt that recommendations for conservation and pollution control were not being followed. However, in the case of extremely remote sites (such as Ninstints) visits from representatives of the World Heritage Committee would be a rare event although representatives of the sponsoring country could (theoretically) apply for the nomination to be withdrawn if designation criteria were not being met.

World Heritage designation can also be withdrawn if the site has deteriorated to the extent that it has lost those criteria which qualified it for inclusion in the first place, perhaps by lack of effective conservation, over-restoration or some natural disaster.

If a World Heritage Site is under some sort of threat (either natural or human) its nominating government can also apply for it to be placed on the List of World Heritage in Danger which aims to provide international financial assistance. This comes from the World Heritage Fund, which in 1996 had a budget of a mere US$3.4 million and may be called upon to provide technical help, training and emergency aid. The Fund draws on UNESCO member state dues and voluntary contributions.

Managing the world's heritage

Each World Heritage Site has a management plan which details its policy towards visitors, addressing such issues as entry charges, local tourism business development, potential damage to the heritage resource, congestion, reduction of visitors at peak times, dealing with specific types of visitors (school parties, coach tours, visiting experts). Sites should also be well maintained (litter free and with adequate visitors' facilities such as the provision of information, catering, guides, lavatories). They should have information available about the significance and (if relevant) the chronological development of the site in a format that can be understood at different levels, and in different languages, and there should be adequate on-site information to enable visitors to orientate themselves while avoiding intrusive signage. This is almost never done and most World Heritage Sites, particularly those in developing countries or where tourism and visitor management policies are poorly developed, have a very basic level of on-site interpretation (or even none at all). The significance of a World Heritage Site is such that it will act as a magnet for visitors, meaning that issues of accessibility, transport, accommodation and other service provision have to be tactfully dealt with in order to avoid swamping the site itself with commercial outlets while still providing for visitor needs. This, also, is extremely difficult. In many cases there is direct conflict between a site manager who wants visitor numbers restricted in order to avoid damage, local people (who wish to generate cash from visitors) and national governments (who may wish to use the site image as a marketing device).

Many World Heritage Sites charge no entry fee, either because it would be impossible to collect one (as in the case of an urban centre) or because it is felt to be culturally inappropriate. When such a fee is collected it often contributes little to the site conservation but disappears into some government budget. Few World Heritage Sites have admissions queues but some can become seriously congested in peak season, and many (like Stonehenge) have grossly inadequate visitor facilities. Lastly, when managing a World Heritage Site for tourism it is essential to consider the long-term interests of the people working and living in the host community. Challenges to the management of World Heritage Sites include:

- Who has the day-to-day responsibility for management? This is often complex, needing local management control and trained staff who understand the significance of the site. The site manager has responsibility both for visitor safety and the safety of the site, to ensure that visitors have a high-quality experience with no negative impacts on the site.
- Designation of a World Heritage Site implies change (Fielden and Jokilehto, 1993), increased visitor numbers, more traders, governments seeking to enhance the site by over-restoration and damage to landscape by intrusive

development such as landscaping or mineral extraction – all issues covered in the cases discussed in this book.

- Large visitor numbers create problems; crowding can lead to frustration and thus to vandalism. There need to be mechanisms for clearing litter, repairing paths, and considering site ecology as well as the welfare of visitors.

Visitor management

There is a surprising paucity of evidence connecting the results of visitor pressure with definite physical impact on cultural sites although several cases discussed here stress the ways in which visitor pressure exacerbates conservation problems which are already present (Cleere, 1989). These may be stresses on the fabric of monuments from pollution or traffic vibration, or on included artefacts and decoration from exhaled gas, abrasion by touching, walking or defacement by souvenir hunting or the application of graffiti. Many such visitor impacts can be avoided by a combination of restricting numbers with visitor-education policies (instructing visitors where to go, how to behave, why to avoid flash photography) but any such policy is only as good as the degree to which it is enforced and policed. The presence of on-site guardians does not guarantee the effectiveness of visitor management policies, any more than the presence of a guide guarantees that the visitor will receive adequate and appropriate information. Other visitor management issues which will frequently recur in the course of these cases include the control of parking, the necessity for avoiding self-styled guides and training official ones, and the elimination of souvenir vendors or beggars from major heritage sites or wherever else they can harass the visitors. World Heritage Sites need basic facilities like litter bins as much as they need complex ones like visitor centres, and the needs of individual visitors who may be elderly or disabled are a prime consideration. Each World Heritage Site should have interpretative signage, guides, an associated exhibition or museum, perhaps listening posts, portable tape players, audiovisual displays and ample written material to aid the visitor in discovering its history, but such tools are often expensive and difficult for a developing world government to finance. It is frequently impossible to buy so much as a simple guidebook on the site.

Visitors need to be managed so that the sheer weight of numbers neither distracts from the enjoyment (and education) of individuals nor has any adverse effect on the historic resource. If properly applied visitor management techniques can also reduce maintenance costs and increase income (Fielden and Jokilehto,

1993). The World Heritage Committee feels that visitors should be allowed to view such sites at their own speed rather than having to follow a compulsory guided tour, and that visitor numbers should always be controlled, especially where such numbers could have a potentially damaging effect on fabric. There are well-known ways of managing visitor behaviour, including the natural tendency of people to turn left when entering any space, and ways to spread visitors out by drawing their attention to less well-publicized routes or features but these are seldom applied to any except the best-managed (and best-funded) attractions. Despite these drawbacks, World Heritage Sites continue to be the mainstay of the global heritage tourism industry, and their possession is a pearl of inestimable value for a national government. It is therefore hardly surprising that the World Heritage List is growing quite rapidly, and that visitor awareness of the significance and location of World Heritage Sites is certainly at an all-time high.

References

Cleere, H. (ed.) (1989) *Archaeological Heritage Management in the Modern World*, London: Allen and Unwin

Feilden, B.M. and Jokilehto, J. (1993) *Management Guidelines for World Cultural Heritage Sites*, Rome: ICCROM

Shackley, M. (1997) 'Tourism and the management of cultural resources in the Pays Dogon, Mali,' *International Journal of Heritage Studies* **3** (1), 17–27

UNESCO (1972) Convention Concerning the Protection of the World Cultural and National Heritage, Paris: UNESCO

UNESCO (1985) Conventions and Recommendations of UNESCO concerning the Protection of the Cultural Heritage, Paris: UNESCO

UNESCO (1992) Operational Guidelines for the Implementation of the World Heritage Convention (revised version), Paris: UNESCO

UNESCO (1997) *World Heritage Newsletter* and quarterly *World Heritage Review*. http://www.unesco.org.whc.welcome.htm

van Droste, B., Plachter, H. and Rössler, M. (1995) *Cultural Landscapes of Universal Value*, Stuttgart: Gustav Fischer Verlag

2 Bukhara (Uzbekistan)

A former oasis town on the Silk Road

David Airey and Myra Shackley

The blacked aridity all around oppressed me inexplicably, as though the city was dying instead of being restored (Thubron, 1995, p. 60)

Keywords: Bukhara   Silk Road   Uzbekistan   Central Asia

Location grid reference: 39° 47'N   64° 26'E

World Heritage List inclusion date: 1993

Summary

This former Central Asian trading hub of the medieval Silk Road is now a medium-sized city trying to reconstruct its former architectural glories in the context of Uzbekistan's post-Soviet market economy. World Heritage designation has facilitated extensive reconstruction programmes for major Bukharan Islamic monuments dating mostly from the sixteenth century. Development of a pedestrian zone has minimized the effect of traffic vibration and fumes but monuments are still threatened by rising saline groundwaters. Uzbekistan has a thriving heritage tourism industry combining Bukhara with the neighbouring ancient cities of Samarkand and Khiva.

Over-reconstruction of the ancient city centre has created a sterile tourist zone failing to match the original vibrancy of Central Asian urban life. Although the quality and nature of the tourist services and facilities are changing they still strongly reflect their Soviet origins.

Introduction

Bukhara is a medium-sized city (population approximately 250 000) located at the edge of the Kizyl-Kum desert in what is now the Republic of Uzbekistan (Figure 2.1). In its tenth-century heyday it was the market centre for Central Asia, whose 27 acres of bazaars traded furs, amber and honey travelling east along the Silk Road from Russia for silk, jewellery, glass, jade and ceramics travelling west to the ready markets of Europe. The name 'Bukhara' was once synonymous with trade in high-quality silk carpets, abandoned in favour of cheap factory-made products when Uzbekistan came under Soviet domination seventy years ago but now re-emerging with other aspects of a market economy after the country gained independence in 1991. The old city contains a series of significant monuments dating mainly from the sixteenth-century Sheibanid empire but little remains of the earlier city destroyed by Genghis Khan in AD 1220. Today, Bukhara forms part of an Uzbekistan heritage tourism 'milk run' (Figure 2.1) in conjunction with the neighbouring Silk Road cities

Figure 2.1 Location of Bukhara and the main tourist route in Uzbekistan

of Samarkand and Khiva. Many of its monuments have been heavily reconstructed, most in the Soviet period, with early work of dubious quality. More recent projects include implementation of a pedestrian area within the urban core to minimize traffic vibration and pollution. This has been successful, but the extensive reconstruction has imparted a sterile quality to the visitor experience giving Bukhara the feel of a stage set. Major conservation difficulties still remain, particularly with combating rising saline groundwaters. Heritage tourism is now increasing again, facilitated by easier air access and improving ground-handling services. Many Western tour companies are developing international tour ideas based around the Silk Road theme which provides potential for dramatically increased numbers of visitors to Bukhara over the next decade. Whether this potential is realized will depend in part on the quality of the facilities for tourists which at present strongly reflect the Soviet legacy.

Tourism in Uzbekistan

The development of tourism since independence

Although modern Uzbekistan is a twentieth-century Soviet invention (Figure 2.1) it is both the most heavily populated and ethnically diverse country in Central Asia. The many contradictions evident in contemporary Uzbekistan only emphasize the ways in which it is trying to create a post-Soviet identity, rediscovering in the process a glorious history dominated by its position as the focus of the Silk Road. Dry, landlocked Uzbekistan was one of the poorest states of the former Soviet Union with 60 per cent of its population living in overpopulated rural communities, but it is the world's third largest cotton producer and is also a major producer of gold and natural gas. Uzbekistan has two World Heritage Sites; Bukhara and the inner town (Ichen-Kala) of Khiva. These, combined with Samarkand, are the foci of its heritage tourism industry. The centre of Samarkand contains the three great blue-tiled madrassas around the Registan Square, as well as the fifteenth-century observatory of Emir Ulug Beg, Tamerlane's grandson. Tamerlane himself is buried in Samarkand in the city which was the focus of his empire around AD 1400, as is a cousin of the prophet Mohammed whose tomb provides one of the many significant places of Islamic pilgrimage in a country which is gradually rediscovering its Islamic faith.

Against a background of economic dislocation and privatization, following independence in 1991, attention has been turned, *inter alia*, to the service sector

(United Nations Development Programme, 1995, p. 19) and within this, tourism is identified as 'one of the major and important directions' (Akhmedov and Saidaminova, 1995 p. 144). Clearly tourism is important as a source of economic development and job creation. In addition, for a newly independent country with a rich cultural heritage, such as Uzbekistan, tourism has the potential to create a (spurious) image of long-term stability and provide a basis for establishing a national identity. The importance of tourism is confirmed by a Presidential Decree issued in 1995 on 'measures towards the revival of international tourism in Uzbekistan'. This sets out a range of measures to encourage tourism including an investment incentive framework, actions to reduce barriers, such as visa requirements, as well as encouragement for the development of the supply of tourism facilities, including cultural centres.

The development of tourism since independence has been marked by attempts to restore the connections which were broken when the country separated from Moscow and by efforts to build upon the legacy left by the Soviet period. Restoring the connections has included the creation in 1991 of a state airline, Uzbekistan Airways, and re-establishing links with the tourism markets which formerly were conducted through Moscow. Uzbekistan Airways now (1997) provides flights to Tashkent from nineteen international destinations and has modernised its fleet. Similarly the national tourist organization, Uzbektourism, has opened international offices in Western Europe, North America, Russia and other key markets and has maintained representation at the major tourism fairs. Even so, it is taking a long time for Uzbekistan to recapture the level of demand which it achieved through Moscow before independence.

Apart from its role as a promotion agency, Uzbektourism, which was created in 1992, has also played a central role in building on the legacy left by the Soviet period. In the first place it has acted as the Ministry of Tourism and it took over the operation of key components of state-controlled tourism including international hotels, transport and guiding operations and tourist centres. Subsequently it has led the commercialization of these operations in some cases as a prelude to privatization. It has also acted as the licensing authority for emerging private tourist operations. As a result, while much of the tourism provision remains in state hands there is a burgeoning private sector particularly among small-scale operators. Indeed, tourism enterprises have been among the leaders in the development of a private sector.

In spite of these developments the legacy of the Soviet period still shows clearly in much of the supply of tourism facilities, particularly in the international hotels. Most have their origins as state-run enterprises controlled from Moscow. They are on a large scale and a lack of recent investment means that they compare poorly with modern Western hotels. Recent privatizations, new developments and the emergence of small, private accommodation operations are changing the picture but, at least in the medium term, the supply of accommodation will be more suitable for large tourist groups accustomed to Soviet-style operations than to modern independent tourists.

Patterns of tourism demand

Despite the fact that Uzbekistan became a member of the World Tourism Organization (WTO) in 1994 no internationally recognized tourism arrival statistics have yet been issued and the definitions used for **tourists** and **visitors** do not follow the WTO conventions. It has been estimated (Agzamov and Tashmuratov, 1995, p. 21) that during the period 1980–95 the numbers of visitors to Uzbekistan doubled from about 250 000 to 500 000 (Table 2.1).

It is difficult to reconcile these figures with the more detailed (and probably more reliable) breakdown of figures for visitor arrivals at Samarkand and Bukhara which totalled less than 70 000 for 1990. The disparity may be accounted for by

Table 2.1 Tourist arrivals in Uzbekistan 1970–95

Year	Tourist arrivals
1970	165 787
1975	222 290
1980	287 771
1985	329 636
1986	340 808
1987	366 708
1988	393 865
1989	427 884
1990	455 594
1991	455 100
1992	475 580
1993	461 000
1994	434 400
1995	500 000 (estimate)

Source: Agzamov and Tashmuratov (1995)

the suggestion (Agzamov and Tashmuratov, 1995, p. 22) that about 90 per cent of arrivals quoted in Table 2.1 are business visitors, not counted in any more detailed analysis. Thus, if 90 per cent of the 1990 455 594 are commercial visitors the remaining tally of 45 560 visitors accords far better with the Bukhara and Samarkand data. Other verbal estimates (Fazullayev, personal communication) indicate that around half a million visitors arrived in Uzbekistan during 1995, with a possibility that the number may double in 1996. There is some doubt about the accuracy of these general arrivals figures since no arrivals/departure forms are completed by visitors and such data must therefore be gathered from visa applications or hotel registration forms.

Tourism in Bukhara

Visitor attractions

Visitors to Bukhara are attracted by its history and significant monuments, although after the architectural wonders of Samarkand the city may be something of a disappointment. Bukhara, described by Curzon (1889) as 'the most interesting city in the world', is located at the edge of the Kizyl-Kum desert with Central Asia's only inhabited intact historic core – hence its World Heritage designation. It was founded around 3000 years ago, conquered by Alexander in 329 BC and fell successively within the Achaeminid, Greek, Seleucid, Parthian, Kushan and Sassanian empires before the Arabs arrived. Bukhara's heyday was in the tenth century when its empire covered most of modern Uzbekistan and Tajikistan plus much of Iran and Afghanistan as well. It was a famous centre of Islamic learning whose 250 madrassas attracted students from as far away as Moorish Spain. The city was destroyed by Genghis Khan in the twelfth century (with the exception of the Kalyan minaret) and passed under the shadow of Samarkand until the late sixteenth-century when it was a thriving focus of eleven separate trade routes but had a reputation for being unhealthy. The old city includes more than 350 monuments, many heavily restored. World Heritage designation was confirmed for the whole of the old city in 1993, and has been the key to obtaining conservation funding and implementing a visitor management scheme.

All Bukhara's monuments are located within the historic core within walking distance of each other (Figure 2.2). They are dominated by the ancient fortress (or Ark) on an artificial hill 20 m above the city square. It was the centre of the

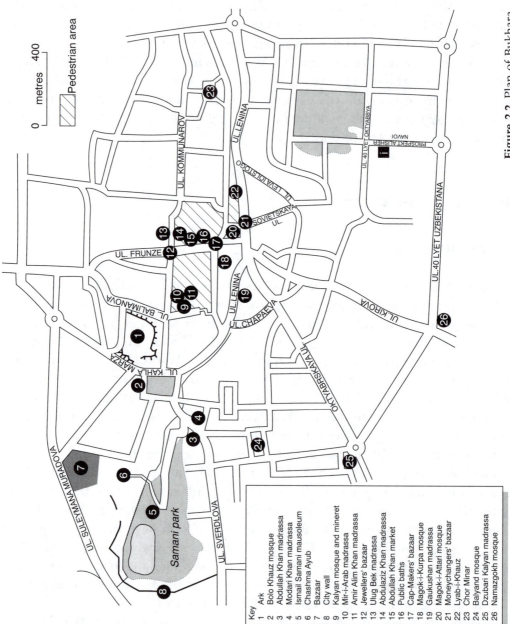

Key
1 Ark
2 Bolo Khauz mosque
3 Abdullah Khan madrassa
4 Modari Khan madrassa
5 Ismail Samani mausoleum
6 Chashma Ayub
7 Bazaar
8 City wall
9 Kalyan mosque and mineret
10 Mir-i-Arab madrassa
11 Amir Alim Khan madrassa
12 Jewellers' bazaar
13 Ulug Bek madrassa
14 Abdulaziz Khan madrassa
15 Abdullah Khan market
16 Public baths
17 Cap-Makers' bazaar
18 Magok-i-Kurpa mosque
19 Gaukushan madrassa
20 Magok-i-Attari mosque
21 Moneychangers' bazaar
22 Lyab-i-Khauz
23 Chor Minar
24 Balyand mosque
25 Dzubari Kalyan madrassa
26 Namazgokh mosque

0 metres 400

Pedestrian area

Figure 2.2 Plan of Bukhara

Shrakristan quarter, formerly inhabited by artisans and aristocrats, which has been very extensively restored, mostly for tourism, as part of a UNESCO project. Other significant sites include the extraordinary brick-built Ismail Samani mausoleum (AD 907), one of the world's oldest monuments to famous Muslims and the nearby Chashma Ayub (Spring of Job), both sites of pilgrimage. The most frequently visited monuments include the Kalyan mosque and minaret which also acted as a lighthouse to help caravans crossing the desert at night. It is nicknamed the 'Tower of Death' since Genghis Khan and his successors threw criminals off it and it was the tallest building in the world (47 m high) when completed in AD 1127. Many of the city's original multi-domed bazaars have been reconstructed and integrated into the pedestrian area, such as the Taq-i-Zargaran (jewellers' bazaar) and Taq-i-Telpaq Furushon (capmakers' bazaar). They now cater mostly for tourists and many of the internal shop units are empty because of a combination of high rents and the slow development of the market economy. A standard tour of Bukhara also includes the Magok-i-Attari, Central Asia's oldest mosque, and the pool Lyab-i-Khauz surrounded by 4000-year-old mulberry trees and flanked by the great Nadir Divanbegi and Kukeldash madrassas.

Uzbektourism is trying to broaden market appeal by developing cultural tourism. One recent development has restored and opened the house of the nineteenth-century wealthy merchant Fayzail Hoodayev in a suburb of Bukhara. Here visitors can tour the house, see a historical exhibition and take tea in the beautifully restored rooms while watching a demonstration of traditional costumes. Other efforts to promote wildlife watching, hunting and activity tourism in the surrounding region have been less successful and at present tourism to Bukhara is almost entirely motivated by an interest in its history and monuments.

Tourism organization, transport and accommodation

Uzbektourism in Bukhara plays a central role in the marketing and provision of tourism facilities. It currently operates the three main international hotels as well as restaurants and guide services. It is also responsible for providing ground-handling services, package and individual travel arrangements and maintains marketing contacts through attendance in international travel fairs and sales missions to the major Western markets. With more than 350 staff it is by far the biggest component of the tourism sector.

In many ways Uzbektourism in Bukhara, which is one of twelve regional organizations of the national Uzbektourism organization, represents a continuation of the former centrally controlled provision of tourism services. However, in line with the national move to commercialization and privatization it has, since 1995, been operating as a joint-stock company. Presently one-third is state owned and controlled by the national Uzbektourism organization, 45 per cent is in the collective ownership of the employees and the remainder is owned privately. In theory, this gives a measure of freedom for the organization to develop its own approaches to operating and marketing tourism to the city. In practice it is still early days and apart from a few initiatives such as support for the merchant house described above, it is substantially following the tradition of tourism based on ancient monuments.

The three international hotels in Bukhara between them provide about 1000 beds. As in the rest of Uzbekistan they have their origins as state-owned enterprises and, although they are now no longer government controlled, they still retain the essential characteristics of their origins which makes them most suitable for large, standardized groups. The opening of a new large hotel in 1996, under the ownership of the national Uzbektourism organization, improved the overall quality of the accommodation stock but it did little to change its nature. It will also create potential occupancy problems given that the average annual occupancy for the existing hotels is only 50–60 per cent. Arguably more interesting changes are taking place in the accommodation stock through the development of small private bed and breakfast type establishments. Some of these are now gaining international publicity (Time, 1996) and potentially they will play an important role as the market for tourism to Bukhara moves away from the large standardized group arrangements. But while the Bukhara Uzbektourism organization controls both the hotel stock and is the major marketing organization for the town it is difficult to see how such small independent operations will have a substantial impact on the patterns of tourism.

Visitors to Bukhara

Table 2.2 examines the pattern of visitors to Bukhara and neighbouring Samarkand between 1990 and 1995. A distinction is made by Uzbektourism between **tourists** and **visitors**. A **tourist** is defined as someone who is travelling with an organized group purchasing ground-handling services either directly from Uzbektourism or from a private organization licensed by Uzbektourism. A **visitor** is someone who has arrived in the country independently and made his or her own travel and visa arrangements. Business visitors are not listed under either category.

Table 2.2 Visitor arrivals at Bukhara and Samarkand 1990–95

Year	Bukhara		Samarkand	
	Tourists	Visitors	Tourists	Visitors
1990	32 485	1885	24 000	9700
1991	27 004	714	12 300	4100
1992	26 492	2141	9400	3200
1993	8217	7827	10 100	2600
1994	9729	9268	5700	3000
1995	11 941	7225	14 500	5000

Source: Samarkand Tourist Information Centre and Uzbektourism, Bukhara

Since most group tourists to Uzbekistan will visit both Samarkand and Bukhara (via Tashkent) it is reasonable to conclude that fewer than 15 000 cultural tourists arrived in 1995, less than half the figure for 1990. Tourist arrivals to Bukhara have steadily declined since 1990, quite dramatically so over the past three years. A similar pattern may be seen at Samarkand although the 1995 figure looks more optimistic. Independent visitors to Samarkand also declined but now may be recovering, whereas independent visitors to Bukhara dropped to 714 during 1991 (the year of independence) but have subsequently recovered. The discrepancies in these arrivals figures may reflect the fact that until 1994 it was necessary for a visitor to have a separate visa for each city, as well as the fact that Samarkand is much more easily accessible from Tashkent attracting those visitors staying only a short time. Unfortunately, no data are available on length of stay or visitor spend although interviews suggested that the majority of hotel guests stayed two or three nights in each locality with a further two or three nights in Tashkent (Yacubov, Satyvaldyev, personal communication).

Tourism to Bukhara is strongly seasonal (Table 2.3) with an autumn peak (August–October), low season from November to March and a second peak in spring (April–May). June and July, when temperatures can reach 47°C in the shade, are unpopular months for a visit and the lack of well-developed facilities for winter sports does not give any indication that this seasonal pattern is likely to change.

In both Bukhara and Samarkand the tourist market is dominated by Japan, France and other European countries whereas the majority of independent visitors come from Europe and the USA. Indonesian and Malaysian visitor arrivals may

Table 2.3 Seasonality of tourist arrivals to Bukhara and
Samarkand 1994–5

Month	1994		1995	
	Bukhara	Samarkand	Bukhara	Samarkand
January	659	280	691	400
February	428	340	684	520
March	400	798	800	738
April	820	750	1127	2000
May	1043	900	1265	2800
June	653	500	799	1300
July	729	320	808	530
August	1132	350	1557	890
September	1172	700	1681	2300
October	1066	600	1164	1800
November	624	350	812	720
December	605	290	655	540

Source: Samarkand Tourist Information Centre and Uzbektourism, Bukhara

be growing in connection with business interests. There is a disparity between the quoted number of visitors from CIS countries, 20 per cent in the case of Bukhara but not recorded for Samarkand. No figures are available for visitor origins prior to 1991, although it cannot be assumed that these were largely from the former Soviet Union or nearby states. Many Uzbektourism officials (e.g. Danilov, personal communication) commented that before the disintegration of the Soviet Union international arrivals from Europe and America were considerably greater than today, due to easier air access (via Aeroflot routings through Moscow) and perceived internal stability. The task for today's Uzbektourism is not merely to create a European market where none existed before but rather to recapture one which has shrunk.

The origin of today's visitors (Table 2.4) is closely related to the routings of Uzbekistan Airways with its direct flights from Frankfurt, London and Istanbul and connections to India and Pakistan. Some changes were observed in 1995 with the start of charter flights now available from Japan to Bukhara, for example, bringing in 120 tourists on each trip accompanied by Japanese-speaking guides. There is a small but discernible increase in visitors from the Gulf States motivated by pilgrimage and facilitated by Uzbekistan Airways flights from Dubai.

Table 2.4 Origins of tourists and visitors to Bukhara and Samarkand 1995

Country	Bukhara		Samarkand	
	Tourists %	Visitors %	Tourists %	Visitors %
Japan	25	5	30	5
France	25	5	20	1
Italy, Spain, Germany, EU	22	30	20	30
USA	10	17	4	24
Indonesia	3	5	6	15
Malaysia	5	2	5	10
Asia–Pacific	3	6	9	4
Other	7	10	6	11
CIS	–	20	(not recorded)	

Source: Samarkand Tourist Information Centre and Uzbektourism, Bukhara

Visitor management

During the summer of 1996 the writers had the opportunity to visit not only Bukhara but also neighbouring Silk Road cities and, by a series of field visits and structured interviews, to obtain an overview of existing visitor management and conservation strategies for Uzbekistan's cultural heritage. The low numbers of visitors to Uzbekistan have produced few visitor management problems although it is conceivable that this might change if promotions such as the 2500th Anniversary of Bukhara or the Silk Road project stimulate interest in the country. Today's tour party generally spends two to three days in Bukhara and employs a guide from Uzbektourism (via one of the hotels) for at least one half or full day tour. Since the city centre is so compact it is perfectly possible to find all the major monuments without a guide and many independent visitors do so, utilizing one of the two available Western guidebooks (Whittell, 1993; Lonely Planet, 1996) or locally available information.

Guides, interpretation and conservation

In many ways the quality of the guiding service in Bukhara benefits from the Soviet legacy. Until the break-up of the Soviet Union the incoming tourist agency Intourist operated a sophisticated training system for local guides. This included training not only in knowledge about the destination and in languages but also in guiding techniques. Guides had opportunities to develop their skills in Bukhara as well as in Tashkent and Moscow. The result is a cadre of twelve guides, employed by Uzbektourism who demonstrate a high level of technical and inter-personal skills relevant for group visits to the historic sites. The problem for the next generation is to replicate this knowledge and experience and, at the same time, equip guides with abilities to deal with different types of tourist groups, including possibly more independent tourists.

At present there are adequate numbers of guides available although the development of Japanese charter flights to Bukhara did create some visitor congestion. This was solved by Uzbektourism guides who divided the large parties into small groups and started tours from a different part of the city, avoiding overcrowding at important sites. No over-visitation problems have been recorded at any historic sites although difficulties are sometimes experienced with domestic visitors and Muslim pilgrims who occasionally remove tiles or pieces of plaster as souvenirs of holy places. However, such visitor pressure is a minor matter compared with the problems historic buildings are experiencing from rising saline groundwater, air pollution and traffic vibration. The last is especially troublesome in Samarkand but has been solved in Bukhara by the development of what is effectively a pedestrian precinct around the major monuments, started some seven to ten years ago while still under Soviet rule (Figure 2.2). The pedestrian zone encompasses most of the monuments with the exception of the Ark and Samani Park, allowing visitors to walk between them on a brick-paved network of paths.

The foundations of Bukhara's monuments are threatened by alterations in surface drainage such as the filling-in of many of the city's ancient canals. Conservation work has involved replacement of damaged brickwork and the construction of new foundations, but difficulties with saline groundwaters are compounded by the fact that the new bricks used in restoration are made from local clays, also heavily saline. The only bricks exempt from the problem seems to be those made to a traditional recipe involving eggs and camel milk which cannot now be replicated but which have survived intact in the Kalyan minaret and Ismail Samani mausoleum. The Uzbek government is unable to match the money and conservation expertise of the former Soviet Union (although some of the earlier Soviet restoration projects are of dubious quality), but money has been raised from overseas sources including the Arab League and UNESCO. Twenty-six of Bukhara's monuments are to be restored in the future by a UNESCO programme and one of the great benefits from World Heritage Designation has been to facilitate access to conservation funding.

Despite the best attempts by Uzbektourism and the private sector there is a lack of on-site information for visitors, with the exception of that provided verbally by guides. Little interpretative signage exists and no waymarked trails have been constructed. Some written information is available in different languages but there is ample scope for improvement. Some major monuments such as the Nadir Divanbegi madrassa include handicrafts and souvenir stalls within the premises although there is little aggressive salesmanship or pressure to buy. Few items have been developed especially for the tourist trade and there is some evidence that the development of a market economy has actually stimulated ancient crafts such as the manufacture of silk carpets and textiles in Bukhara as well as a revival of silver and coppersmithing.

Conclusions

Since independence Uzbekistan has sought to promote tourism as an important source of income and employment, mainly based around its 7500 historic sites and ten major towns, many of which are associated with the ancient Silk Road. Bukhara forms one of the three pegs in the heritage tourism 'milk run' which has developed for international visitors between the cities of Tashkent, Samarkand and Khiva, an industry which has been helped by strong presidential interest in the conservation of Uzbekistan's heritage plus financial aid from the European Union, GTZ and Arab League. Advisers from the UN and UNESCO have initiated conservation schemes since Uzbekistan achieved independence and liaison between Uzbektourism and the Ministry of Culture has been helpful in promoting the image of the country as the centre of the ancient Silk Road. Relatively low visitor numbers have minimized visitor impact at ancient sites and permitted the tourist a high quality of experience, although this is marred by a lack of on-site interpretation.

At present the type of tourism offered by post-independence Uzbekistan is substantially the same as that operated under the Soviet regime. It is substantially based on group visits, staying in large hotels and visiting historic monuments. Some developments in the supply, such as small private accommodation units, are being established and these will lend themselves to more independent tourism, but so far these developments are relatively minor.

Most visitors see Bukhara after they have visited Samarkand, but the quality of the visitor experience is curiously different (Table 2.4). Unlike Samarkand, where magnificent monuments are dotted throughout a busy urban core and surrounded by dusty building sites, Bukhara's monuments are enclosed within a pedestrian precinct (although still surrounded by building sites). This should, in theory, greatly improve the quality of the visitor experience but in practice it tends to have the opposite effect. The pedestrian zone was constructed with the twin objectives of minimizing the impacts of traffic pollution and vibration on Bukhara's monuments and replicating the effect of an open-air museum. The result is more like a film set than a living, breathing town. The tourist can be under no illusion that here is a project which has been carried out for tourists; few local people stop at the highly priced shops and the real life of the city is restricted to the bazaars and maze of dusty alleyways south and west of the tourist area. Bukhara has been divided into two, with the sterile core area undeniably preserving all its major monuments but completely failing to replicate the original atmosphere. No one visiting Bukhara could fail to be impressed by the magnificence of its ancient buildings but it requires an almost impossible leap of imagination to recreate their original setting. The busy, noisy, dirty markets which would have filled the centre have been replaced by empty pavements, and a heritage tourist accustomed to the life and bustle of cities such as Damascus or Xian at either end of the Silk Road could not but be disappointed. Despite the splendour of individual buildings and the praiseworthy attempt to remove traffic pollution, Bukhara has the feel of an open-air museum, the over-restoration eliminating much of the original atmosphere.

Acknowledgements

We are most grateful to the following individuals and institutions who provided information, access and assistance during the fieldwork for this chapter. V. S. Danilov, L. N. Sherchenko (Uzbektourism, Samarkand), T. Tashmuratov (International Tourism Department, Tashkent State Economic University), A. Satyvaldyev (Chief Executive, Hotel Uzbekistan), S. O. Fazullayev, K. Shaacramov, O. S. Khodjaev (Uzbektourism, Tashkent), L. B. Kouzminskaya (Uzbektourism, Bukhara), M. A. Yakubov (Executive Director, Hotel Afrosiab, Samarkand), T. Kuziev, First Deputy Minister, (Ministry of Cultural Affairs, Tashkent), S. S. Akhmedov and A. Mirzaakhmedov (Uzbektourism, London), and Siroj Loikov (who acted as guide and interpreter). Fieldwork funding was provided under Research Enhancement Funding by the Nottingham Trent University and both figures were drawn by Linda Dawes, International Studies (the Nottingham Trent University).

References

Agzamov, S. and Tashmuratov, T. (1995) *Perspectives of Development of International Tourism in Uzbekistan*, Tashkent: Tashkent State Economics University

Akhmedov, E. and Saidaminova, Z. (1995) *Republic of Uzbekistan, reference book* (3rd edition), Tashkent: Uzbekistan Press

Curzon, G. (1889) *Russia in Central Asia*, London: Blackwell

Lonely Planet (1996) *Central Asia*, Melbourne: Lonely Planet Publications

Thubron, C. (1995) *The Lost Heart of Asia*, London: Penguin

Time, 'Bukhara, Uzbekistan', 20 May 1996

United Nations Development Programme (1995) *Uzbekistan, Human Development Report*, Tashkent: UNDP

Whittell, G. (1993) *Central Asia*, London: Cadogan Books

3 The Fortified Church of Biertan (Transylvania)

Alexandra Muresan

Biertan has retained its medieval elements which include the church, built in the sixteenth century, a number of old houses around the central square and the triple layer fortification of the church, one of the best preserved in Europe, which still stands in its original urban context (World Heritage List, 1996)

Keywords: Biertan   fortified church   Transylvania   Romania

Location grid reference: 46°8'5"N   24°31'18"E

World Heritage List inclusion date: 1993

Summary
The Fortified Church of Biertan, which was once the most important Protestant Episcopal centre in Transylvania, is now a valuable religious, architectural and historic monument of European cultural heritage. The Cathedral displays some of the best-conserved elements of painting, sculpture and decorative art in Transylvania and stands as evidence of the centuries-old German colonization of Romanian territories.

Restoration work encountered financial difficulties towards the end of the 1970s, when the Romanian organization in charge of heritage sites was dissolved by the Communist regime. The 1993 World Heritage designation brought new sponsors for restoration work and new roads were built, making the old German village more easily accessible to domestic and international visitors. However, the Fortified Church is in danger of losing more visitors every year due to poor marketing, reflecting former Communist policies.

Introduction

Biertan is a village with approximately 3000 inhabitants, located in the heart of the Tara Vinului region (Wineland) in Transylvania (Figure 3.1). Biertan was first officially mentioned in 1283, when it was included in the large family of fortified churches built by the *'hospites saxones'* (Saxon guests) on the Romanian territory of Transylvania. Before that in the twelfth century the Hungarian King Geza II brought Secui (Turkish–Magyar population) and Saxons (Germanic population) from Flandra, Luxembourg, Saxonia and the Moselle valley, to colonize his conquered territories, where the Romanian population was defending its own institutions and way of life. Most of these colonists were farmers, but among them there were also artisans and merchants. These colonists were offered large privileges within the Romanian territories, in exchange for military and fiscal duties. They organized themselves judicially, administratively and religiously and added their contribution to the economic and cultural development of Transylvania (Constantinescu, 1969). In order to fulfil their obligations towards the Hungarian Kingdom, and at the same time to ensure their protection, the Saxons invented a defence system which was focused on fortified churches (Fabini and Fabini, 1985).

Later, between the sixteenth and the seventeenth centuries, Biertan was known as the most important Protestant Episcopal centre in Transylvania. The Saxon Bishop of Biertan was responsible for all the rural communities of Transylvania, with the exception of Cluj, and for all the Evangelical communities populated with Catholic Croatians and Bulgarians. Until 1940 the rural community of Biertan survived through natural growth and immigration. During Communism the process of immigration increased, drastically affecting the continuity of this German minority in Biertan. After the fall of the Communist regime in 1989, numerous negative ethnical, social and cultural factors that appeared within the Germanic community generated the feeling that they were no longer wanted in Biertan (Derer, 1993).

Today Biertan is both a cultural symbol and part of the turbulent history of Transylvania, and a monument of unique religious architectural value in Europe. The Episcopal Cathedral of Biertan, dedicated to the Holy Virgin, contains some of the best-conserved elements of painting, sculpture and decorative art in Transylvania. The restoration work became necessary after an earthquake in 1977, and was fully supported by the community and the Evangelical Episcopacy of Sibiu, due to the fact that the organization in charge had been dissolved by the Communists. After Biertan's inclusion in the World Heritage List in 1993, the works of reconstruction and restoration ceased to have financial difficulties as

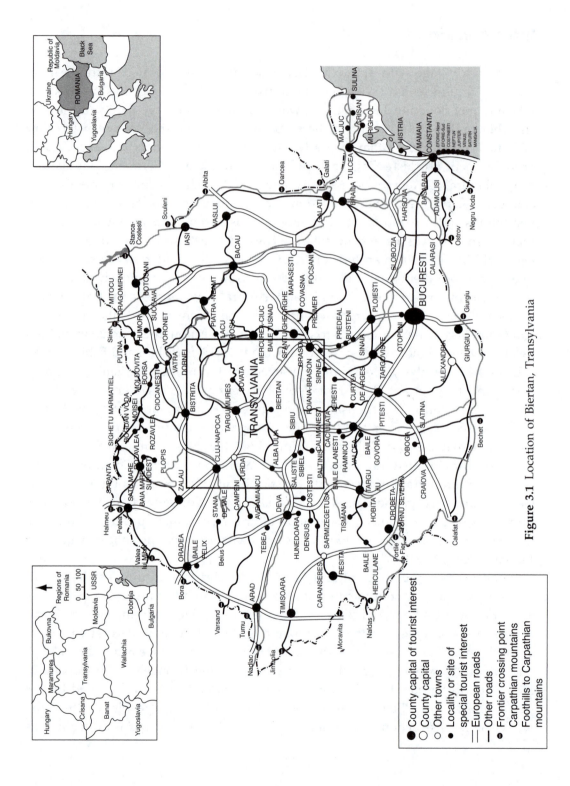

Figure 3.1 Location of Biertan, Transylvania

sponsors offered support. New main roads have since been built, making the village of Biertan easily accessible to domestic as well as international visitors. Biertan was included in cultural package tours in the past, but now, with increased interest in Romanian heritage tourism, there is great potential for attracting and accommodating more visitors throughout the year. Whether this will be achieved relies on exploring ways of improving the marketing and interpretation of the Episcopal Cathedral of Biertan.

Tourism in Romania

The post-Communist development of tourism

Romania has enormous potential for tourism, its natural resources lying in extremely favourable climatic and topographical conditions (Hall, 1991). With almost one third of the country comprising mountains and one quarter of the land area covered by forests, Romania has major potential for both winter and summer tourism. The Black Sea Coast line is made of a southern section of approximately 70 km of sandy beaches, ideal for recreation, and of a northern deltaic zone, the mouth of the Danube river, comprising one of Europe's most distinctive ecosystems (Turnock, 1991). Romania has rich resources of mineral water and therapeutic mud, which, together with local climatic characteristics, have formed the basis for the development of over 160 spas. One third of all European sources of thermal waters are concentrated in Romania. Other attractions include cultural assets lying close to major tourist resorts, especially in the Carpathian zone which was long acknowledged as the cradle of the Romanian nation (Stanley, 1991).

Prior to the mid-1960s, tourism development was focused on health spas and a limited number of traditional resorts in the Carpathian mountains and on the Black Sea Coast. Government investments in international standard tourist facilities have been complemented by a welcoming attitude on the part of the Romanian people towards international tourists. From the mid-1960s to the early 1980s, tourism became a development priority with rapid results. At the beginning of the 1980s, due to a serious economic crisis, lower standards of service and heightened state security created considerable tourist dissatisfaction. Tourism ceased to be a priority and its products declined because of Communist restrictions. The number of foreign entries to Romania dropped seriously towards the end of 1990, as a consequence of the country's economic situation after the 1989 Revolution and the poor standard of services offered to both domestic and international tourists.

In order to stop tourism decline, the Romanian government set as a main objective for the year 1992 to 'treat tourism as an activity of indirect export and thus doubling the revenues made' (Government of Romania, 1996). The Ministry of Tourism elaborated a ten-year 'Strategy for Restructuring, Consolidating and Developing Tourist Demand' encouraging privatization and foreign capital investment in the tourism industry. Substantial foreign assistance came from the European Bank for Reconstruction and Development (EBRD) and the European Union (EU). The EBRD's long-term plan of investment in the infrastructure was aimed at modernizing the roads and ports, the railway system, and Bucharest's international Otopeni airport, while the EU contributed to training workforce for the tourism industry through the PHARE assistance programme. The Romanian leadership became aware of the importance of the service sector to the national economy, of the fact that the Romanian tourist industry could contribute to reducing unemployment and to attract the world's attention towards the country as a new cultural destination.

Since the Revolution, the development of Romanian tourism has been manifested through the promotion of new forms of tourism, such as: rural tourism, ecotourism, cultural tourism, new laws encouraging small-scale privatization, and a better supply of tourism facilities throughout the country. More destinations were included in tours and package holidays for domestic and international tourists. By 1996, seven major foreign hotel chains opened in Romania, together with foreign franchises such as Western fast-food and soft-drink retailers who found a profitable market for their products. In the same year, 320 travel agents registered with the National Association of Travel Agents (NATA) out of approximately 800 in the country which were currently promoting tourist and visitor destinations to travel fairs worldwide. TAROM Airlines, the main Romanian air transport company, has expanded its fleet and now serves forty-two destinations on four continents. In the opinion of Dan Matei, the Tourism Minister, 41 per cent of Romanian tourism was privatized by the beginning of September 1996, with high hopes that the figure would reach 70 per cent by the end of the year (Lazar, 1996).

There is undoubted potential for further development of the Romanian tourism industry, despite the fact that the remains of the Communist regime tend to slow the process. Tourism has a new cultural dimension, which had not been promoted before the Revolution. Between 1991 and 1993, some of the most beautiful Romanian churches and monasteries, (e.g. the Fortified Church of Biertan, the Monastery of Horezu and the painted churches of Moldavia) were added to the World Heritage List as well as the Danube Delta. Since then, the promotion of new historic, cultural sites and private accommodation, where small groups of tourists are introduced to traditional Romanian culture, has become a potential tool for ensuring long-term tourism development in the country.

Tourists and visitors in Romania

The number of tourist arrivals in Romania increased from 2.3 million in 1970 to 6.7 million in 1980 and then experienced a massive 215 per cent decrease in the 1981–91 period, a reflection of the country's unattractive social, economic and political environment. When the 'Iron Curtain' opened up in 1990, the number of tourist arrivals increased suddenly to 6.5 million (Table 3.1). The immediate effect of this was that tourists from the former Soviet Union, who were no longer restricted to the Soviet bloc, abandoned their post-war Black Sea Coast holiday resorts for new Western destinations. However, advantageous business deals offered by Romania to foreign investors raised the number of tourist arrivals to 6.4 million in 1992, an increase of 1 million on the previous year. Many Western

Table 3.1 Foreign arrivals in Romania 1970–95

Year	Foreign arrivals (millions)
1970	2.3
1975	3.7
1980	6.7
1985	4.8
1986	4.5
1987	5.1
1988	5.5
1989	4.9
1990	6.5
1991	5.4
1992	6.4
1993	5.8
1994	5.9
1995	5.4

Source: National Commission for Statistics, 1995 and 1996

firms were allowed 100 per cent ownership of Romanian companies, with low taxes to pay in their first year of business. Once those deals ceased to be available, fewer business and transit tourists entered the country. In consequence, the statistics show a significant decrease in tourist arrivals in 1993, 1994 and 1995. Approximately 38 per cent of the post-1989 arrivals quoted in Table 3.1 represent business and transit tourism.

Slight inaccuracies in the tourist arrivals statistics seem to occur from the fact that, before 1989, these statistics were not calculated following the World Tourism Organization (WTO) conventions. The first official publication comprising internationally recognized definitions for tourists and visitors appeared only in 1994, despite the fact that Romania has been a member of the WTO since January 1975.

Even if the Romanian tourist authorities applied the WTO concepts in 1996, the problems of delays in centralising national statistics would still remain unsolved. As much of the tourism industry has been privatized after the Revolution, some of the hotels and travel agents, for example, no longer report their figures to the national authorities in charge, making the process of gathering and collating data a very complicated one.

What seems to have changed radically after the Revolution is the country of origin of the foreign tourists and visitors to Romania. Before 1989 substantial numbers of tourists came from countries such as: Germany, Yugoslavia, Portugal, the United Kingdom, Poland, Spain and Czechoslovakia. As a consequence of the revolutions which took place in Europe at the end of the 1980s, those numbers were replaced with tourists coming from countries such as: Republic of Moldova, Italy, Turkey, Ukraine, Canada, the United States. The number of visitors from Bulgaria, Israel, Hungary, France and other EU countries remained more or less the same (National Commission for Statistics, 1995).

Tourism in Transylvania

Visitor attractions

To most visitors, Transylvania is associated with haunted castles, werewolves and vampires, thanks to Bram Stoker's novel and to Francis Ford Coppola's blockbuster *Dracula*. Even though the ruins of the Bran Castle, hidden in the forests of the Carpathian Mountains, might appear to be the perfect home for a bloodsucking count, Transylvania has much more to offer to visitors than just ghost tours.

Situated inside the arc of the Carpathian range and having a 200 km diameter, Transylvania, 'Land beyond the Forest' from the Latin *'trans silva'* (Constantinescu, 1969), is one of the travel frontiers of Europe. International visitors can easily access it from Hungary on daily trains, buses or on any of the eight European highways crossing Romania, their entry visas being issued at the border. Transylvania is the most romantic Romanian province, and the richest in natural resources (Ministry of Tourism, 1995), offering visitors natural parks and reservations, (e.g. Retezat National Park and the Piatra Craiului region), unique species of flora, glacial and crater lakes, karst scenery and the opportunity to observe traditional crafts and drink excellent wines (Ministry of Tourism, 1995). Domestic and international tourists are fascinated by the well-preserved old traditional villages, Dacian and Roman citadels, churches and monasteries, medieval castles and historical monuments. The City of Brasov, featuring the Black Church, the most representative monument built in the Gothic style in Romania, and the Saxon Town Hall, as well as the medieval citadels of Cluj, Medias, Alba Iulia, Sighisoara and Sibiu, are a cultural proof of over 700 years of cohabitation between the Romanian and German communities.

Fortified churches – a new visitor destination

The most impressive cultural attractions of Transylvania are its fortified churches. These fortifications originate in the Dacian fortresses built throughout the country during the Roman domination, in the period AD 101–106. Even though they were designed as defence systems with walls reaching 2 m in thickness, sentinel passages, towers and surrounding trenches, most fortified churches have significant religious value as well as demonstrating their builders' skills in architecture, astronomy and the science of war. Moreover, Transylvania is unique in the world for being the region with the highest concentration of fortified churches. Their number is close to 300, but only half are still in good condition (Fabini and Fabini, 1985). The rest are now in an advanced state of deterioration or nearly ruined, mainly because of the lack of interest and funding on the part of the Romanian Communist regime. It is only since the World Heritage designation of the Fortified Church of Biertan in 1993 that more fortified churches are offered money for restoration every year, from various non-governmental sources. Unfortunately, it takes more than just money to develop these visitor attractions, and the Romanian government has left it up to the communities to raise funds and struggle with the difficulties.

The way Biertan is being managed as a visitor attraction is representative of all heritage attractions of the same type in Romania, and the only difference lies in the fact that more international visitors stop annually at Biertan since its inclusion in the World Heritage List. Also, compared to the rest of the Transylvanian fortifications, Biertan still stands in its traditional urban context and has retained the original church with a triple-layer fortification system. This system is considered to be one of the best preserved in Europe (UNESCO, 1996).

Visitor attractions at Biertan

When arriving at Biertan, visitors are impressed by both the size of the construction (Figure 3.2), situated on a hill in the heart of the village, and its relationship with the village itself. Once they enter the fortification, they experience the feeling of travelling back in time, as not much has changed inside apart from the fact that it is now a museum.

Figure 3.2 The Fortified Church of Biertan (photo: George Dumitriu)

Architecture and style

The Church was built between 1492 and 1522, and features a unique combination of the late Gothic style and elements of the Renaissance. The defence system with three towers was added later, in the fifteenth century (Dragut, 1976). The fortified ensemble has plenty of unique works of art, with most valuable and attractive elements such as: the great polyptych altar, the door of the vestry and the original octagonal construction of the triptych arch. The gold-plated polyptych altar (Figure 3.3), is the richest decorated altar in Romania and of a unique design in Europe. Built in Medias, the altar belongs to the late Gothic style and consists of twenty-eight icons glorifying the Holy Virgin to whom the Church was dedicated in 1524. The wooden door

Figure 3.3 The gold plated polyptych altar at Biertan (photo: George Dumitriu)

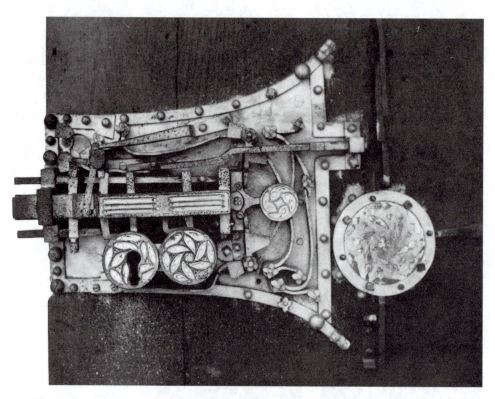

Figure 3.4 The lock on the vestry door, Biertan (photo: George Dumitriu)

of the vestry, made by an artisan from Sibiu, impresses through the sophisticated closure system(Figure 3.4) which is unique in the world. The mechanism comprises seventeen iron bolts activated only by two keys and was created just before 1515 as a means of protecting the sacred vessels, jewellery and money belonging to the Church (Fabini, 1971). The pulpit, pews and portals, suggesting the transition from Gothic to Renaissance, are placed among the most valuable sculptures of Transylvania and reflect the fantastic skills and knowledge of geometry, architecture and religion possessed by the medieval masons and artisans.

Religion and traditional practices

In the south-eastern side of the Fortified Church visitors discover the history, traditions, and old practices of the community, all displayed in a small museum which was once a detention room for married couples. One of the old Catholic practices consisted of locking up the married couple who attempted to divorce until the two settled their misunderstandings and abandoned the idea of separation. The museum also displays original documents signed by famous local leaders concerning the rights the community had in those times.

The Defence Tower situated in the south of the Fortified Church, also known as the Catholic Tower, once hosted Catholic worship which was still allowed at Biertan even after the adoption of the Protestant ideology by the community in the sixteenth century (Vatasianu, 1959). Now deserted, its frescoes cannot be restored for both financial and technical reasons. In one of the other towers visitors can enter the secret room where all the major decisions of war concerning Biertan were made. The room has been transformed into an archive and displays valuable objects such as old music instruments, the official stamp and the heraldic sign of the state.

Cultural events in Biertan

The main cultural events in the region of Biertan which are currently being marketed nationally and internationally to attract visitors are the Annual German Gathering, taking place in the second week of September, and the Annual Medieval Fair of Sighisoara, in August. On these occasions, Germans from different foreign countries gather in Biertan to celebrate together. Many domestic and international tourists book package tours in order to watch the traditional costume parades, dances, plays, concerts and other street performances, as well as to take part in the religious worship together with the Saxon villagers. These events are most likely to attract more tourists to Biertan in the future. Apart from them, the religious worship held in the Cathedral of Biertan on alternate Sundays is the only potential tourist attraction for the rest of the year.

Visitors to Biertan

Tourist transport

Tourists and visitors can easily reach Biertan by road as the village is situated approximately 80 km away from the medieval citadel of Sibiu and 140 km from Brasov, the second largest city and tourist resort of Romania. There are regular bus services between Medias and Biertan, and many national and international trains stop at either Sibiu or Medias daily. The main road leading to Biertan is of a European standard. The rest were repaired since its World Heritage designation in 1993.

Lately, quite a few international tour operators and companies, mainly German, have looked at ways to include Biertan in their heritage tours. Unfortunately, these foreign agents face obstacles even when trying to establish long-distance contact with the site, by telephone or fax. For a worldwide acknowledged destination like Biertan, these problems of communication are a real handicap to tourism and visitor management.

Tourist accommodation

The Church of Biertan is administered by the Episcopacy of Sibiu, the same religious establishment which supervises the Parochial House where fifteen beds are sometimes available for overnight stays. However, domestic and international tourists prefer the 'Guesthouse', a former nursery school belonging to the Evangelical Church, which is also the only good standard tourist accommodation in Biertan. The house is open throughout the year, with thirty-nine bedspaces. It caters for singles, families and groups and it also provides good standard facilities for conferences and other business trips.

Nevertheless, tourists find significant inconveniences in the services provided by the Guesthouse, such as:

- No self-catering facilities
- There are no food markets, snack bars or restaurants in the area
- Expensive accommodation prices, comparable to the rates of a three-star hotel on the Black Sea Coast
- Telephone connections with foreign countries may take hours
- Payment can only be made in cash.

There is no doubt that foreign tourists are restricted in their choice of accommodation and the available accommodation does not meet their expectations. The village is very small and surrounded by hills with cultivated land, leaving no space for building hotels or leisure centres. On the other hand, any of these facilities catering for mass tourism would spoil the charm and the culture of the place.

Visitor arrivals

There are no official records of the number of annual arrivals to Biertan, before or after the Revolution. Tourists and visitors never needed to register to enter the village and the host families who administered the fortified church never kept any record of the number of entrance tickets sold. The only records of tourist arrivals available to the author were the ones registered in the Guesthouse reception book, and even those were only a few years old. During the visit at the site, the author gathered more information from the staff in charge of the Guesthouse, from the administrators of the Church and from tourists and visitors themselves.

Figure 3.5 shows the annual estimations of the numbers of domestic and international tourists staying at the Guesthouse. They were gathered from interviews, the tourists' 'Comments' book of the Guesthouse and the author's twelve–day observation period spent at the site. According to the records of the Guesthouse, the number of overnight and short breaks increase every year in the months of December and August, the busiest months of the tourist season in Romania. The numbers increase in August mainly because of the cultural events taking place in the area.

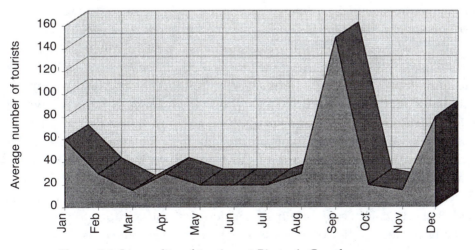

Figure 3.5 Seasonality of tourism at Biertan's Guesthouse

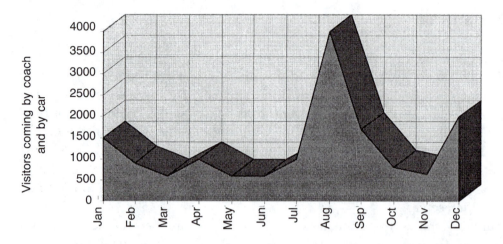

Figure 3.6 Approximate annual number of visitors to the Fortified Church of Biertan

Figure 3.6 illustrates the approximate number of visitors to the site. According to the administrators of the Church, the numbers vary around the same monthly figure every year, although this more than doubles in the month of August when the Medieval Fair takes place. There were no major changes in 1996 from previous years. However, before the Revolution more organized tours included Biertan, and they involved groups of scholars and young people (Weinrich, 1996, personal communication).

More domestic than international visitors stop at Biertan every year, but more Romanian government officials, foreign diplomats and organized foreign groups stay overnight or for short breaks. This reflects the overpriced accommodation which middle-class Romanian families can no longer afford. Although there are no official records of the international visitors to Biertan, the majority of them are known to come from Austria and Germany (Onweiller, 1996, personal communication). Usually they are mature citizens coming on package holidays which include tours of Romanian heritage sites. Other groups visiting Biertan include German students doing their fieldwork at the site or in the area. The rest of the visitors come by car from other parts of Europe, such as Italy, Belgium, France and the neighbouring countries, and stop at Biertan in their attempt to make the most of their trip to Romania. At the end of her study period at Biertan, the author concluded that the country of origin of the tourists and visitors to Biertan is proportionally related to the countries where Biertan is marketed as an international heritage attraction.

Marketing Biertan

The main aims of marketing visitor attractions vary with the type of attraction. In the case of man-made phenomena that have not been designed to attract visitors (castles, churches) or natural features of the landscape the aim of marketing is to manage demand so that the attraction is not damaged by over-use. On the other hand, with attractions such as special events and festivals, and attractions like theme parks, the aims of marketing are to raise the number of visitors, revenue, and to increase attendance to maximize the economic benefits of tourism for the local economy (Horner and Swarbrooke, 1996). In the case of the Fortified Church of Biertan, the aim of marketing is to increase visitor numbers. Unfortunately, the concept exists only in theory in Romania. Very little is being done by the local authorities in charge to fulfil this aim. Being administered by a public authority, the lack of funds and initiative influence the development of the attraction in a negative way. Due to the low demand and the few financial takings since the opening of the Guesthouse, the administrators had no other choice than to contact prospective foreign sponsors and travel agents themselves, so as to attract their attention towards Biertan and the fact that it has been included in the World Heritage List. Otherwise, distribution is little developed in the Romanian attraction sector, including Biertan. There is very little advance planning to visit Romanian heritage sites, many visitors finding out about these places as they accidentally pass them on the highway. The same happens in the case of the Fortified Church of Biertan. Visitors stopping at Biertan are astonished by the fact that they cannot see any promotional material of this internationally recognized heritage site. There are no maps of the location, tourist leaflets or brochures available, no souvenirs or postcards of Biertan or the region. The shops cater for villagers only, being open early mornings and late afternoons. Some information about the significance of the place and its history is summarized in leaflets printed in German and handed to visitors at the entrance. The information available at the entrance of the Church is also only written in German, which makes it very difficult for Romanians and other nationalities to understand.

Ways of marketing Biertan nationally and internationally need to be looked at by the government authorities as a priority, otherwise the lack of awareness of the site is most likely to influence visitor numbers negatively in the future. At present, Biertan and its fortified church are being promoted through external organizations, mostly German. These agents are under pressure because of the growing international competition, and are always in search of new destinations to offer to their customers. Within the country though, the main way of promoting the site to potential visitors is by word of mouth (Onweiller, 1996, personal communication).

Visitor management at Biertan

The Romanian tourism industry suffers from a series of constraints which prevent its development, such as:

- The country's lack of experience in marketing and promoting tourism
- The poor investment in tourism infrastructure (Franck, 1990, p. 335)
- The low-quality services compared to the western expectations (Rafaelsen, 1995, p. 12)
- The lack of staff training programmes
- The lack of an appropriate supporting legal framework for tourism.

Apart from these problems, there are also gaps with an immediate impact on the management of Romanian heritage sites. During the author's visit to Biertan and the neighbouring County of Brasov, serious gaps were identified in the areas of the on-site information, services provided by the travel agents, and interpretation and conservation of the Church. In spite of the numerous staff-training schemes introduced by the Ministry of Tourism after the Revolution, there is still an inadequate number of guides at heritage sites throughout the country. In fact, Biertan has none. The tourists coming on package holidays accompanied by guides or guidebooks are the only ones fortunate enough to find out about the historical and religious significance of the site due to poor on-site interpretation. Otherwise, the total lack of on-site information and guidance for independent tourists and visitors stand, as a barrier to tourism development. Visitors heading towards Biertan find signs referring only to the village, with no other interpretative signage about the Church and its significance. However, as a result there are no discernible adverse impacts from visitors to Biertan.

Several problems do occur with the area of the conservation of the site. The work of restoration has suffered financially since the national organization in charge was dissolved by the Communist regime in 1977. The local German community and the Evangelical Episcopacy of Sibiu managed to cover the costs involved in the restoration of the altar, the pulpit, the arch, the mural paintings and the frescos of the Church. During the restoration work a system of metal scaffolding was inserted into the arch as a means of support, the arch windows were replaced with stained glass, and the lime was removed carefully. Some of the elements such as the fourteenth-century frescos of the Catholic Tower required more advanced techniques which the local community could no longer afford. The tower as well as other valuable elements of the fortified ensemble are left in a deplorable condition since the clergy and most of the German families left the village. Sadly, Biertan loses more and more German families every year since the Revolution, further lowering the quality of the tourist experience at the site.

Conclusions

Although substantial changes have occurred in the perception of tourism in Romania, the resorts still cater for the same purposes as before the Revolution, i.e. to attract large groups of visitors to major hotels and organize tours at heritage sites from there. The prices foreign citizens paid for accommodation, meals and entertainment in Romania just after the Revolution were far higher than those that applied to the Romanians. That reflected the government's policy orientated towards attracting as much foreign currency into the country as possible. In 1996, some of the major resorts adjusted their prices to a common figure for both Romanian and foreign citizens, with the obvious result that Romanians paid more and a consequent decline in levels of domestic tourism.

A number of interesting developments in Romanian tourism, particularly the development of small privately run accommodation, mean that the Romanian tourism industry will soon be able to cater for larger numbers of independent tourists. This will inevitably result in competition within the tourism accommodation sector and, hopefully, should result in higher levels of service quality reflecting traditional Romanian hospitality and culture.

The Ministry of Tourism considers the management of heritage sites a priority, but there has, as yet, been no significant improvement in the quality of the visitor experience. However, Biertan is one of the fortunate sites where the community itself has made a difference, rather than relying solely upon the state which is chronically short of capital. At other more popular Romanian heritage sites visitors often have to cope with the lack of drinking water, petrol or proper lighting, and even poor road access, pollution and low standard accommodation. At Biertan adequate, though simple, accommodation is available, access is relatively easy (except during the winter months) and the visitor gains a brief glimpse of Romanian village life as well as Romanian cultural history.

There is a general tendency on the part of the local authorities in charge to claim that lack of money is the cause of the slow development of visitor attractions, including the conservation and interpretation of major heritage sites. This situation is not helped at Biertan by the lack of systematic charging, or of the availability of catering or merchandise outlets which might contribute much-needed funds. The small number of visitors will never generate much money, and at present those visitors contribute virtually nothing to the financial resources of either the Church or the community. However, despite the rise of interest in Biertan after World Heritage Site designation the Romanian government will not continue to attract visitors unless information about the site is more widely available, particularly by marketing to overseas. The fortified churches of Transylvania will always attract small numbers of regular visitors, because their advantageous geographic position makes them easily accessible and their historical and cultural significance is widely recognized. At present they are unable to develop any further as tourist attractions but, as a result, there are no adverse impacts of visitor activity, but few positive ones, either.

Acknowledgements

I wish to express my sincere gratitude to the following individuals for the information provided and for their assistance during the fieldwork period in Biertan: G. Dumitriu (National Commission for Historic Monuments, Romania), E. Weinrich and her family (caretakers of the Cathedral of Biertan). N. Onweiller and the management of the Guesthouse in Biertan.

References

Constantinescu, M. (1969) *Istoria Romaniei*, Bucharest: Editura Didactica si Pedagogica

Derer, P. (1993) 'Some aspects concerning the preservation of fortified churches of Saxons of Transylvania', in International Conference on Biertan – Important Evidence of the Saxon Civilization of Transylvania

Dragut, V. (1976) *Dictionar enciclopedic de arta medievala româneasca*, Bucharest: Editura Didactica si Pedagogica

Fabini, H. (1971) 'Andreas Lapicida – ein siebenbürgischer Steinmetz und Baumeister der Spätgothik', in *Österreichische Zeitschrift für Kunst und Denkmalpflege*, Vienna

Fabini, H. and Fabini, A. (1985) *Kirchenburgen in Siebenbürgen*, Leipzig: Kochler and Amelag

Franck, C. (1990) 'Tourism investment in Central and Eastern Europe', in *Tourism Management*. **11**(4), December

Government of Romania (1996) Governance Programme 1997–2000. [Online] at http://www.guv.ro/

Hall, D. R. (1991) *Tourism and Economic Development in Eastern Europe and the Soviet Union*, London: Pinter

Horner, S. and Swarbrooke, J. (1996) *Marketing Tourism Hospitality and Leisure in Europe*, London: International Thomson Business Press

Lazar, R. (1996) 'Turismul romanesc este privatizat in proportie de 41 la suta', *Libertatea*, 10 September, Bucharest

Ministry of Tourism (1995) *Romania, come as a tourist, leave as a friend*, leaflet, Paris: Barry Maybury Conseil

National Commission for Statistics (1995) *Romanian Touristic Yearbook*, Bucharest: Ministry of Tourism

Rafaelsen, B. (1995) *Investment Promotion, Export Development and Tourism*, Brussels: European Commission

Stanley, D. (1991) *Eastern Europe on a Shoestring*, London: Lonely Planet Publications

Turnock, D. (1991) 'Romania', in: Hall, D. R. (ed.), *Tourism and Economic Development in Eastern Europe and the Soviet Union*, London: Pinter

UNESCO (1996) *Biertan and its Fortified Church*. [Online] at http://www.unesco.org/whc/sites/

Vatasianu, V. (1959) *Istoria artei feudale in tarile române*, Bucharest: Editura Didactica si Pedagogica

4   Cracow (Poland)

The former capital and 'national shrine'

David Airey

You will find a city of hallowed store;
to this treasure the guardian bards will lead;
lo, their hands point through the dingy light,
bringing bygone times back into sight

(Stanislaw Wyspianski)

Keywords: Cracow   Poland   market economy

Location grid reference: 50° 03'N   19° 55'E

World Heritage List inclusion date: 1978

Summary

Cracow is the former capital of Poland. For 700 years it was the coronation and burial site of Polish kings and it is still the final resting place of Polish heroes. It is also the seat of many Polish institutions including the Catholic Church and the Jagiellonian which is Poland's oldest and leading university. With this background it is a kind of national shrine for Poles described by a former bishop of the city, Pope John Paul II, as 'a summary of the history of Poland'. Yet Cracow reflects more than Poland. Centuries of invasion and conquest have left a legacy of many periods and regimes.

   Today Cracow presents a rich history of monuments, churches and other buildings which was relatively unscathed by the Second World War. It is now a major centre for Polish and international tourism. Following the collapse of Communism in 1989, Poland has made a successful transition to a market economy. For tourism in Cracow, this has meant the development of services and facilities to meet and encourage a growing tourism market. However, the pace of change is, in places, running too fast for the planning and control mechanisms. As a result, problems of visitor crowding and visual pollution are appearing.

Introduction

Cracow is Poland's third largest city (population approximately 750 000). It is located on the country's main river, the Vistula, just at the point where the flat European plain to the north begins to rise towards the Tatra Mountains in the south (see Figure 4.1). But it is more than just a third city. In many ways, although

Figure 4.1 Map of Poland

it is located in the very south of the country, it is the centre of Polish culture, religion and history. Its first appearance in historical record was in AD 965 and from AD 1040, until the seat of government was moved to Warsaw in 1597, it was the capital of Poland (Zamoyski, 1987, pp. 20 and 192). However, although it ceased to be the capital and although, in the meantime, the Polish state was conquered and partitioned more than once, Cracow has retained its position as 'a kind of national shrine' (Rozek, 1996, p. 24). For long it has been a place of pilgrimage for Poles. One former minister of tourism has commented that 'young people's curriculum always includes a visit to Cracow' (Paszucha, 1995, p. 44). It has also been a popular destination for foreign visitors and Poland's re-entry to the global tourism marketplace after 1989 has brought Cracow new opportunities as an international tourist destination.

The current character of the city of Cracow as a tourist destination is strongly influenced by three factors. The first is its long history. Although evidence of some of the earlier phases of its past has been obliterated by invasion and replacement, it nevertheless retains buildings, artefacts and other reminders from the pre- and Romanesque periods onwards. It is particularly its Gothic and Baroque design, buildings and churches that set the tone of the town. Cracow is reckoned to have 300 historic town houses, fifty-eight churches (Dziedzic, 1996), 6000 historic buildings and monuments (Fitt, 1992, p. 51) and thirty museums containing more than two million exhibits. These account for about one quarter of Poland's museum resources. The second factor is that Cracow has always been a major centre of Polish institutions. It was the coronation town and burial place of kings and national heroes. It is a centre of the Catholic Church in Poland. Most recently it was the place from which Pope John Paul II was called to the Holy See in 1978. It is also the home of Poland's oldest and most renowned university. The Jagiellonian University was founded in 1364 and today it remains Poland's major seat of learning with 20 000 students. These together, in their various ways, provide a powerful attraction both to Poles and to foreigners for visiting the city. The third factor is the extent to which Cracow has absorbed and been influenced by, willingly or otherwise, a range of foreign influences. As a result, as one commentator has put it, 'this most Polish of Poland's cities...is the most European of all the Polish cities' (Dziedzic, 1996). Its location and the turbulent history of Poland have combined to expose the town to all types of settlers and invaders. At one extreme these include the Mongol invasions from 1241 that the city still commemorates daily by a trumpeter sounding the alarm from the tower of St Mary's church. At the other they include the influence of Italian architects who, for example, turned the Gothic Wawel Castle into a magnificent Renaissance palace.

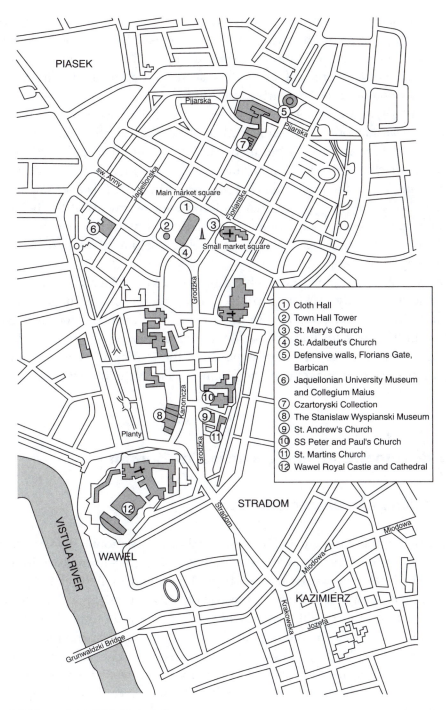

Figure 4.2 Plan of the Old City of Cracow

They also include the Jews who settled in the town from the thirteenth century and from the mid-fifteenth century became established in a Jewish quarter in the town's Kazimierz district. The Jews were an integral part of the town until the Nazi invasion of 1939 brought an end to six centuries of history but in turn created history of a sombre type in nearby Auschwitz.

In summary, these factors have created a city that is rich in attraction for tourism, an attraction that is enhanced by a number of other features. Many of the individual attractions are grouped within walking distance in the city centre whose compact, geometric design dates back to the medieval period and which is set round one of the largest market squares in Europe. It is also surrounded by a ring of parkland (the *Planty*), that replaced the town walls at the beginning of the nineteenth century (see Figure 4.2). These along with the fact that the centre is a lively and thriving area for living as well as visiting gives Cracow a particularly strong tourist appeal.

Cracow was among the first twelve designated World Heritage Sites in 1978. A key issue for the city now is to protect and preserve this heritage at a time of transition to a market economy. Tourism is just one of the current influences on the city. In the years since the fall of Communism there is plenty of evidence that there is an effective response to the needs of the tourist market. The question is whether the visitor management and planning controls will do justice to the city's past.

The development and patterns of demand

Dimensions and characteristics

According to the Institute of Tourism (1996), international visitor arrivals to Poland as a whole have shown a remarkable and consistent increase in the years from 1986. Total visitor arrivals rose from 3.7 million in 1986 to 17.8 million in 1990 and to 82.2 million in 1995. Of these about 19.2 million in 1995 can be considered as tourists (overnight visitors) according to the definition of the World Tourism Organization. In the region of 60 per cent of such inbound tourism is considered by the Institute as city tours. Domestic tourism has been rather less resilient over the same period. Participation by Polish residents in tourism of one night or more fell from 53 per cent in 1990 to 46 per cent of the population in 1994. In 1995 there was a recovery to 54 per cent. These national figures provide

Table 4.1 Arrivals in Cracow 1987–96

Year	Domestic arrivals (staying and day visitors) (000s)	International arrivals (staying and day visitors) (000s)	Total arrivals (staying and day visitors) (000s)	Total arrivals (staying visitors only) (000s)
1987	2340	260	2600	n.a.
1988	2315	335	2650	n.a.
1989	2200	400	2600	n.a.
1990	1790	418	2160	n.a.
1991	1376	424	1800	740*
1992	1500	505	2005 (2050)*	833*
1993	1680	600	2280 (2600)*	962*
1994	2300	700	3000	1181*
1995	2600	800	3400 (3500)*	1352*
1996	2700	1000	3700*	1800*

Sources: Urzad Miasta Krakowa oraz Urzad Wojewodski w Krakowie (1987–93), Urzad Wojewodzki w Krakowie (1994–5), personal communication (1996). Figures marked with an asterisk are from the Cracow Branch of the Institute of Tourism.

a background to the information collected at a regional and city level for Cracow given in Table 4.1. These figures, which include day trippers as well as staying visitors, demonstrate a similar consistent upward trend in international arrivals. There was an annual average growth of 20 per cent between 1987 and 1996. Domestic arrivals in the city declined significantly after 1989 to a low point in 1991 but have now more than recovered to their pre-1989 levels. Together these provide an increase of more than one million arrivals, or an annual average growth of more than 4 per cent over the ten years. Of these figures, as also shown in Table 4.1, tourists staying for one night or more increased from 740 000 in 1991 to 1 800 000 in 1996, an annual growth of nearly 30 per cent. Approximately 55 per cent of staying visitors in 1996 were from outside Poland, accounting for 52 per cent of tourist nights spent in the town (Burzynski, 1997).

A further breakdown of the key characteristics of the arrival figures is given in Tables 4.2–4.5. Table 4.2 shows the main countries of origin of the international tourists. Germany, the USA and the UK account for about one third of all arrivals. These, together with four other West European countries, provide more than one half of the city's international visitors. Romania, Ukraine and Russia also provide

Table 4.2 Origin of international tourists to Cracow 1996

Country	Nights (%)	Average length of stay (nights)
Germany	13	1.88
USA	11	1.98
UK	8	1.92
Romania	7	1.20
Ukraine	7	1.70
France	6	1.86
Italy	5	1.84
Netherlands	5	2.00
Russia	4	1.77
Austria	3	1.87
Other	31	—

Source: Institute of Tourism, Cracow, 1997

a substantial number of visitors. However, it is noticeable that these have a significantly lower average length of stay. This may suggest that they include visitors who are in Poland for business rather than leisure reasons. Table 4.3 provides further information on length of stay. More than 57 per cent of visitors stay in the town for three nights or fewer with the figure for domestic visitors being 63 per cent. According to the Cracow Branch of the Institute of Tourism, the average length of stay in 1996 of international tourists was 1.79 nights and of Polish tourists was 2.02 nights. Table 4.4 shows the purpose of visit to Cracow. Not surprisingly, sightseeing and culture feature high on the list and account for about

Table 4.3 Length of stay in Cracow 1996

Length of stay (nights)	Domestic (%)	International (%)	Total (%)
1–2	53	26	44
3	10	18	13
4–5	13	16	14
6–7	7	11	9
More than 7	16	29	20

Sources: Borkowski K *et al., Monitoring Zjawisk Turystycznych, Badania Diagnostyczne Turystow Odwiedzajacych 1994–1996*, Krakow Instytut Turystyki AWF-Krakow, Instytut Turystyki oddzial w Krakowie

Table 4.4 Purpose of visit to Cracow 1996

Purpose of visit	Domestic (%)	International (%)
Sightseeing, culture, leisure	51	47
Visiting friends and relatives	13	15
Education	10	9
Visiting places connected with the family	5	8
Shopping	4	5
Business	8	4
Religion	2	2
Sport	2	1
Health	1	1
Other	4	8

Sources: Borkowski K *et al.*, *Monitoring Zjawisk Turystycznych, Badania Diagnostyczne Turystow Odwiedzajacych 1994–1996*, Krakow Instytut Turystyki AWF-Krakow, Instytut Turystyki oddzial w Krakowie

50 per cent of all the reasons for visiting the town. Table 4.5 gives information about the accommodation used by the tourists. A much higher proportion of the foreign visitors stay in hotels while for the Poles a significant number stay in hostels. The latter may reflect the large number of people of school age visiting the city. A final key characteristic for which detailed information is not available is month of visit. However, evidence from other sources (Pytlarz, Kruczek,

Table 4.5 Accommodation used by tourists to Cracow 1996

Accommodation	International tourists (nights) (%)	Domestic tourists (nights) (%)
Hotels	57	41
Motels	2	2
Pensions	1	1
Tourist houses	11	13
Hostels	6	21
Private homes	0	2
Seasonal accommodation	7	8
Camping	7	1
Other	9	12

Sources: Institute of Tourism, Cracow Branch

personal communication) and the fact that more than 90 per cent of visitors to the Royal Chambers arrive in this time (Urzad Wojwodzki w Kracowie, 1996, p. 109) suggest that the bulk of visitors arrive between April and October with May, June and September as peak months.

Main tourist groups

This brief analysis of arrival data helps to establish the pattern of the demand for tourism to Cracow. The key features are that it has recently been relatively buoyant; if day-trippers are included the domestic market accounts for the overwhelming proportion of arrivals but of those staying at least one night, the majority are from outside Poland; a relatively few countries provide most of the international arrivals; the length of stay is relatively short; culture and sightseeing dominate the reasons for being in the city; hotels are the most popular form of accommodation, with hostels being important for the Polish tourists; the demand is very seasonal.

Against this background it is possible to begin to establish further patterns of demand in and for Cracow. There are a number of clear groups of tourists to the city. Excluding those on business and visiting family, and excluding those who are thought to be traders from the East, the tourists can be grouped into about three broad categories. First are the Poles, particularly groups of young people of school age, who are visiting the city as a part of their national heritage. The seasonal peaks in May, June and September, and the popularity of hostel accommodation may be partly explained by these groups. The second are the foreign tourists who are mainly in Poland for sightseeing and related cultural reasons. Many of these are on tours, mostly by car or coach, of Poland or of Central and Eastern Europe. More than forty tour operators provided such tours from the UK in 1995/6 and about one half of these included Cracow (Wasilewska, personal communication). From neighbouring countries, particularly Germany, such tours are more normally self-arranged and by car. The fact that many such tours visit Cracow as one stop on an itinerary which may include Warsaw, Berlin, Prague, Budapest or Vienna helps to explain the relatively short average length of stay. So far, partly because of the relatively limited number of direct flights into the local airport from major Western cities, Cracow receives few 'city break' tourists. The final group are those who are in Cracow for special reasons such as religion, ancestry, cultural events. These include the Jewish groups for whom Cracow is an important stop on a tour of an area of the world that played such a major part in the recent Jewish past. Again these typically stay in Cracow for a relatively brief period.

Main tourist routes

Each of these groups has its own demand patterns within the town (Figure 4.2). The typical pattern for the Polish tourists is a route that takes in the Market Square, including St Mary's Basilica, the Cloth Hall, the City Hall Tower and St Adelbert's church. Together, these form an impressive collection of Gothic and Italian Renaissance architecture. St Mary's represents a particularly important part of Polish heritage and culture partly because of the Gothic altar of 1489. Also all Poles will know about the hourly bugle call from the tower which is interrupted in mid-note as a reminder that the original bugler, who gave the warning, was shot in the throat by a Mongol arrow during an early invasion. From the Market Square the route includes St Florian's Gate and the Barbican which are virtually all that remains of the city's defences, the Jagiellonian University and the Gothic courtyard of the Collegium Maius, before heading via Grodzka and Kanonicza streets to the Wawel Hill. With 2 million visitors (Urzad Wojewodzki w Kracowie, 1996) this is the most visited place in Poland. Here the main sites are the Royal Cathedral and the Royal Castle. Beyond these, the many museums and galleries offer further attractions including the Czartoryski Collection which includes work by Leonardo da Vinci and Rembrandt.

In many ways the route taken by the international visitors to Cracow concentrates on the same area from the Market Square to the Wawel Hill. Typical guided tourist routes in the city centre are three-hour walking tours with or without entrances to the major sites (St Mary's Basilica, Royal Cathedral and Royal Castle). More recently, and particularly since the release of the film *Schindler's List* in 1992, which dealt with the destruction of the Cracow Jewish community and which was mostly filmed on location in the area, more international visitors have ventured beyond the immediate Old City to the adjacent district of Kazimierz. In addition to major Roman Catholic sites, this most notably contains the former traditional Jewish quarter where many Jewish buildings, synagogues and reminders have been restored. These include the former Old Synagogue which is now a historical museum. It is also the location of many of the scenes from the Spielberg film. So-called 'Schindler's list tours' are now included in the itineraries offered by many of the guides, and guidebooks are on sale dealing with the film and the events that it portrays. These cover the locations from the film, as well as the actual location of the Nazi-created Jewish ghetto and concentration camp that are, in fact, across the river from Kazimierz itself. In the confusion between film and reality many tourists prefer to see the film locations. In the process they, at least, gain some insight into this aspect of Cracow's recent past and tourism is spread beyond the Old City. As a commentator in a British newspaper wrote in 1994 '"Schindler's tourism" may have come just in time to save the district's crumbling buildings from terminal decay, but in return Kazimierz has had to swallow some pride and sell itself as a recently used film set. When it comes to attracting the crowds, six centuries of history count as little compared to a couple of hours of screen time' (*The Guardian*, 1994). During their average stay of just under two nights international visitors also visit nearby attractions. In particular they visit the salt mine at Wieliczka and the former concentration camp at Auschwitz–Birkenau. Both of these also hold World Heritage Site designation.

Given that the final group (those in Cracow) are concerned with special interests it is more difficult to identify particular tourist routes. However, included in these is one particular group which does follow a fairly common pattern, the Jewish groups. They are primarily interested in the Jewish heritage of the town and for this reason Kazimierz plays an important part in their stay. Included in this are visits to the former and present synagogues as well as the Jewish cemeteries. More recently, it is reported that these groups are also visiting the Catholic areas of the Old City including the Royal Cathedral.

The development and patterns of supply

The development of the supply

Since the change from Communism, Poland has become a predominantly market-driven economy. Around three quarters of the economy is now in private hands and further privatizations of state-owned companies are imminent (World Report, 1997). This change is evident in the tourism sector. Apart from parts of some of the major former state companies, such as Orbis and LOT Polish airlines, which have been commercialized but not yet privatized, much of the provision of tourism services is now in private hands. As far as Cracow is concerned, 98 per cent of business establishments are now operated privately (Municipality of Cracow, 1997). The town centre is full of privately owned, small tourism and hospitality businesses from bars and restaurants, to street sellers and souvenir shops. The 1997 *Cracow Tourist Guide* lists a total of thirteen tourist agencies that provide travel and sightseeing arrangements in the city and there are as many as 400 free-lance tourist guides (Pytlarz, personal communication). Some of these small entrepreneurs have been at the forefront of developing the tourist services. This includes the development of the 'Schindler tours' in Kazimierz.

According to the City Council (Municipality of Cracow, 1997), as shown in Table 4.6, Cracow in 1995 had a total supply of ninety-six establishments offering 21 840 beds for tourist accommodation. Of these more than one third were in hotels. This gives Cracow the highest proportion of hotel beds to inhabitants of any town in Poland. It has 11.43 per 1000 inhabitants compared to Warsaw's 8.54 (Municipality of Cracow, 1997). There are no five-star rated hotels. Three are in the four-star category and sixteen are three-star rated. All the larger hotels are located outside the Old City itself. Five are in the state-owned Orbis chain with the others owned by companies and individuals. Within the Old City there are some smaller hotels in generally successful conversions of attractive property which mainly took place before 1989. Annual average occupancy is estimated (Municipality of Cracow, 1997) to be about 54 per cent for hotels with that of four-star hotels being the highest at nearly 60 per cent.

It is surprising that there has been so little new hotel development as only three new hotels have opened since 1993. Currently it is reported that there is a shortage of hotel accommodation in Cracow which the City Council estimate to be about 1500–2000 beds (Obara, personal communication). In response to this the

Table 4.6 Tourist accommodation in Cracow 1995

Type	Establishments	Beds
Hotels – four star	3	794
Hotels – three star	16	2641
Hotels – two star	17	3207
Hotels – one star	13	1876
Total hotels	49	8518
Seasonal hotels	n.a.	1965
Tourist houses	n.a.	1530
Camping	n.a.	1964
Youth hostels	n.a.	1310
Other	n.a.	6552
Grand total	96	21 840

Source: Municipality of Cracow (1997, p. 9)

Council has been actively seeking the development of four- and five-star properties and has included a specific section on hotels in its investment guide (Municipality of Cracow, 1997). This gives background information as well as existing and proposed locations for hotels. So far, five international chains are pursuing investment opportunities and have identified potential sites, although problems of multi-land ownership are among the factors creating delays. None of the new developments, or proposed locations, are within the Old City itself although some sites are located just outside the *Planty*. Within the areas enclosed by the *Planty* the Council are encouraging small-scale bed and breakfast-type accommodation. They are also supporting hotel developments in the ring of Austrian forts that surround the town. So far, one of these is operating as an independent hotel.

As far as transportation is concerned, the adequacy of the links is mixed. The Cracow International Airport at Balice has recently reopened after a complete overhaul in 1995. Annual passenger traffic is about 450 000 with a capacity of about one million (Municipality of Cracow, 1997). Currently there are regular flights to Warsaw as well as to eleven major cities in Western Europe. These are forming a basis for 'city break' visits to Cracow. There is a fast rail link to Warsaw and the rail station is being extensively renovated as part of the creation of a communications hub. However, international rail links south remain poor. Road links still need to be improved. In particular the new highway to Warsaw is still a long way from completion. Transport weaknesses are identified as a factor in the slow take-up of hotel investment opportunities (Obara, personal communication).

Problems with transportation also lie in the city itself. Traffic congestion is already high at peak times and the city authorities have introduced park and ride schemes. Access by traffic and parking in the Old City is strictly limited and entry by tourist coaches is forbidden. A tourist coach park near the Royal Castle provides the closest access. Obviously these restrictions have a very positive influence on the overall amenity of the Old City. However, they have a number of other effects. The fact that many tourists, particularly the elderly, are reluctant to walk anything more than short distances concentrates the tourists' visits into a relatively small area near the coach park. The provision of small electric chauffeured 'buggies' provides some assistance but there are relatively few of these. The prohibition on coaches also restricts access to the hotels with the consequence that tour groups stay mainly in the hotels outside the Old City which in turn leads to the need for transportation to the main sights. The local tourist and coach companies provide regular transport to the major centres outside Cracow, particularly to Wieliczka and Auschwitz–Birkenau, but it is less easy for tourists to get public transport to other parts of the town itself such as Kazimierz.

Restoring and developing the attractions

The attractions of Cracow particularly focus on the historic buildings, monuments and museums. Most of these are in the ownership or control of the public sector or the Church. For the most part, in the Old City, they are in an adequate state of repair and recent and current renovation is greatly enhancing their appearance. Following the designation as a World Heritage Site in 1978 a special fund was created by the National Government specifically for restoring the monuments of Cracow. Currently this fund stands at the equivalent of US$10 million per year and it is normally supplemented by joint funding. This money has provided an important resource to protect and improve the Old City and to provide tourist amenity. One of the conditions for receipt of the funds is to provide access to visitors, for at least part of the year. In 1978, after a few decades of pollution from the steel-works which the authorities located just outside the city boundaries, the fund was of particular importance. In the intervening years it has been used to good effect and Cracow Old City is in a better state of repair than many equivalent Polish towns. The case of neighbouring Kazimierz is less happy. The absence of any special funds plus a lack of clarity about property ownership mean that this part of the town is in a very poor state of repair. Individual churches, synagogues and other buildings have been restored and individual small restaurants and museums have been developed but on the whole it presents a very poor appearance.

In addition to the physical attractions, Cracow is also a major centre for arts, culture and other events. The development of this cultural heritage was an early decision of the city authorities after 1989 with the creation of the International Cultural Centre and associated activities such as the first European Cultural Month designated as such by the European Commission held in June 1992 with support from the Polish Ministry of Culture, the Italian government and other bodies. This was seen as 'an important element of Cracow's new development strategy' (Purchla, 1993) Subsequently Cracow has been designated as one of nine cities of European Culture for the year 2000 and leading up to this, starting in 1996, is a series of festivals and events that celebrate local and international culture. This is in addition to regular and annual performances and events such as the Jewish Culture Festival or the International Short Film Festival.

The public authorities in tourism

Apart from the national government itself there are two levels of government involved in tourism in Poland. The regional government or *Voivod* is a branch of central government and covers the region. The city government or *Gmina* is locally elected and covers the town or local area. Within both organizations there are responsibilities for tourism development and promotion. At the *Voivod* level, tourism in Cracow falls within the Department of Culture and Tourism and the Department of Economic Policy. The former carries out tourism promotion. At the *Gmina* level a separate tourism section was closed in 1993. Tourism is currently the responsibility of the Promotion and International Cooperation Bureau although a Department of Sport, Leisure and Education, a Department of Strategy and Development and the Monuments Protection Department are also involved in tourism and related issues. A more recent development has been the creation in 1997 of the Cracow Organization for the Development of Tourism (KART). This is a joint initiative supported by the *Gmina*, the national tourist promotion body for Poland, the Cracow Regional Development Agency, which represents the *Voivod*, and other local organizations including the Cracow branch of the Institute of Tourism which is a research organization, and the Chamber of Tourism which represents about seventy local companies. KART has been set up as a registered company and is taking on the role of promoting tourism to Cracow and operating the local tourist information offices. This clearly reflects an increasing shift away from state control.

Impacts and issues

The impacts of tourism

The unemployment rate in the Cracow region in 1995 was among the lowest in the country, 8.7 per cent compared with the national figure of 15.4 per cent (Municipality of Cracow, 1997). Up to 1989 economic strategy for Cracow was based on manufacturing and the local steelworks formed a mainstay of the economy. After 1989 the local strategy has placed a greater emphasis on culture and tourism (Beiersdorf, personal communication). An estimate of employment in tourism in Cracow is given in Table 4.7. This gives a total of about 23 000 employed of whom up to 20 per cent may be in part-time work. On a rough calculation this represents about 5 per cent of the local workforce. Perhaps more significantly, at least in symbolic terms, it is comparable to the current employment in the local steelworks where employment has been declining. Against this

Table 4.7 Employment in tourism 1996

Sector	Estimated number (full-time and part-time)
Hotels and accommodation	3200
Travel agencies and offices	1500
Catering	5000
Attractions	1600
Transport	5600
Guides, tour leaders	950
Administration	100
Retail sector	5000
Total	22 950

Source: Kruczek *et al.* (1996)

background it is perhaps not surprising that policy toward tourism has been influenced by economic development issues.

Apart from crowding at certain points and at certain times, so far, the physical impact of the tourists themselves has not created major problems. Some problems of humidity affecting the tapestries in the Royal Castle are reported but not on a major scale and there are reports of vandalism to monuments. A more significant impact is created by the tourist enterprises, particularly, and most noticeably, from poorly placed and inappropriate advertising. In many places the cluster of signs, banners and sunshades not only detracts seriously from the visual amenity of the Old City they also obscure each other. The effects of the move to a market economy and the associated deregulation have clearly caught up with the city's powers to control such developments. The powers of control appear to be more in evidence as far as developing the premises in the Old City is concerned. Here, the combined work of the City Conservator, the City Architect's Office and the *Voivod* successfully control many of the developments. For example, a planning application by McDonald's to open an outlet in the main square was accepted only with severe restrictions. So far the new McDonald premises have not been developed. Apart from the vigilance of the Conservator the limited development in the Old City and beyond might also be explained by the ownership by the Church and City and the complex rights of sitting tenants introduced after 1989 as well as disputes of ownership.

Visitor management and policies

With one notable exception, the approach to visitor management is relatively under-developed. The exception is at the Royal Castle where for the past three years a timed booking scheme has been operating. This limits the size of groups and their time of entry. Groups must be booked in advance and even individuals cannot be sure of entry at times to suit themselves. Elsewhere there are no sophisticated systems of control and as a result particular areas of crowding are developing. One of these, the Royal Cathedral, is a particular pressure point. This is adjacent to the Royal Castle but being under separate control (the Royal Castle is a national museum while the Cathedral is part of the Church) there is little coordination between them.

Also, except on the Wawel Hill, and again developed by the Royal Castle, there is little signposting for tourists and little apparent encouragement to go to the less-visited parts of the Old City or other parts of the town. The city brochures now include Kazimierz and festivals and activities are promoted in that part of town but little guidance is provided on the ground of how to get there. In many ways the spread of tourists out of the Old City into Kazimierz has resulted from a combination of the Spielberg film and private initiatives to exploit its potential, rather than as part of a visitor management strategy. So far the signposting in Kazimierz itself is almost non-existent. Similarly, little attention is given to visitor interpretation. Other than in some of the museums there are few explanatory labels or signs.

Beyond a broad aim to increase tourism for economic reasons and to protect the city's monuments there appear to be four strands of policy for tourism. The first is to encourage visits to sites away from the Old City. In addition to the production of publicity material, plans are in hand for the development of a major site on the other side of the river from the Royal Castle. This will include a cultural centre and an opera and conference centre. At this stage land is being acquired and applications are being made for state funds. The second is to increase the town's hotel stock although so far no new hotels are onstream. The third is to lengthen the stay of visitors. This will require the development and promotion of additional attractions and visits. Finally there is an aim to encourage conference tourism.

Conclusions

There are two important elements to the background of tourism in Cracow. The first is that Poland as a whole has quickly, and generally successfully, made a transition to a market economy. The speed of change in Poland is such that it is easy to forget just how great the change has been from a system where central planning was dominant. The second is that its history, monuments, culture and location mean that it is almost inevitable that Cracow will be a magnet for tourists. With this background it is not surprising that a thriving market-led tourism has taken over from the former state-controlled tourism and in many ways it has been successful. Bars and restaurants are busy, the tourist guides are in high demand and in the peak season it is difficult to get a hotel room. In their ways these are all measures of success. However, the rapid process of change has also exposed some gaps and tensions which need to be addressed if Cracow is to keep its heritage intact.

There are clearly some weaknesses in the controls over the private sector. At a superficial but very noticeable level advertising signs now detract from the visual amenity of the Old City. However, beyond this there are other, potentially longer-lasting problems associated, for example, with the change of use of premises and land. At present a number of factors, such as the disputed ownership of land, the security of tenants provided after 1989 and ownership by the Church and City, act as a brake on developments. But there is a need for robust planning and control measures if the pressures for development are not to conflict with and change the character of the town.

The systems for visitor management have also not kept up with the growth in tourism demand or the change in the regime. So far the introduction of visitor management controls has been piecemeal or non-existent. The emergence of Kazimierz as a second centre to visit has in some ways happened by the accident of a successful Hollywood film. This has given Cracow a new opportunity and breathing space. The next step must be to ensure a more coordinated approach to visitor management in the town, both to enhance the visitors' experience and to ameliorate some of the immediate problems and congestion. It could also contribute to goals of increasing the length of stay.

For more than forty years from 1945, Cracow, as a heritage site, was both threatened and protected by the regime. It was threatened by pollution from neighbouring industry and by the fact that, as a focus for nationalist interpretation, it was treated with suspicion. But it was, at the same time, protected by controls over development and restrictions from what Ashworth (1996) called the 'neighbouring West European culture tourism market'. Now this world has changed. Poland and Cracow have responded well to these changes in terms of meeting market needs. It is clearly important, as Cracow once again becomes a focus for visitors, to 're-establish the legitimacy of conservation' (Hammersley and Westlake, 1994, quoted in Ashworth, 1996).

Acknowledgements

I am most grateful to the following individuals and institutions who provided information, access and assistance during the fieldwork for this chapter:

Dr Zbigniew Beiersdorf (Director, Monuments Protection Department, Municipality of Cracow), Dr Krzyzstof Borkowski (Academy of Physical Education), Dr T. Burzynski (Institute of Tourism, Cracow), Stanislaw Dziedzic (Director of Culture and Tourism Department, Cracow Voivod Office), Jerzy Gajewski (Promotion and International Cooperation Bureau, Municipality of Cracow), Mr Kodura (Municipality of Cracow), Dr Zygmunt Kruczek (Academy of Physical Education), Maria Lichota (State Sport and Tourism Administration, Warsaw), Maciej Obara (Promotion and International Cooperation Bureau, Municipality of Cracow), Professor Jan Ostrowski (Director, Royal Castle, Wawel), Dorota Plader (Academy of Physical Education), Professor Jacek Purchla (International Cultural Centre, Cracow), Elzbieta Pytlarz (Art Historian and Guide), Mr Pytlik (Institute of Tourism, Cracow), Bogna Siwadlowska (Department of Culture and Tourism, Cracow Voivod Office), Miroslaw Sulma (Municipality of Cracow), Agnieszka Wasilewska (Academy of Physical Education) and Dorota Wasik (Cracow Academy of Economics).

References

Ashworth, G. J. (1996) 'Holocaust tourism and Jewish culture: the lessons of Cracow–Kazimierz', in Robinson, M. *et al.* (eds), *Tourism and Cultural Change, Conference Proceedings*, Newcastle upon Tyne: University of Northumbria at Newcastle

Burzynski, T. (1997) *Statistics*, Cracow: Institute of Tourism (information provided privately)

Dziedzic, S. (1996) *The Cultural Heritage of Cracow*, Cracow: Cornelius

Fitt, J. (1992) 'Historic cities and tourism: A message from Cracow', in *Managing Tourism in Historic Cities*, Cracow: International Cultural Centre

The Guardian, 16 May 1994, London. p. 24

Institute of Tourism (1996) *Polish Tourism 1995*, Warsaw: Institute of Tourism

Kruczek, Z. *et al.* (1996) *Analiza Zatrudniena i Kwalifikacj Kadr Turystycznych w Regionie Krakowskim*, Cracow: Instytut Turystyki Oddzial w Krakowie

Municipality of Cracow (1997) *Proposed Locations for the Objects in Cracow – Hotels*, Cracow: Municipality of Cracow

Paszucha, M. (1995) 'Managing places – Cracow', in *Historic Cities and Sustainable Tourism*, ICOMOS UK Conference, Bath 4–6 October

Purchla, J. (1993) *European Cultural Month in Cracow, June 1992*, Cracow: International Cultural Centre

Rozek, M. (1996) *Cracow, City of Kings*, Warsaw: GeoCentre

Salter, M. and McLachan G. (1991) *Poland, the Rough Guide*, Bromley: Harrap Columbus

Urzad Wojewodzki w Krakowie (1996) *Wojewodztwo Krakowskie 1995*, Cracow

World Report (1997) *World Report, Poland*, London: World Report Ltd

Zamoyski, A. (1987) *The Polish Way*, London: John Murray

5 The cultural landscape of Rapa Nui (Easter Island, Chile)

Myra Shackley

In the middle of the Great Ocean, in a region where no one ever passes, there is a mysterious and isolated island; there is no land in the vicinity and, for more than eight hundred leagues in all directions, empty and moving vastness surrounds it. It is planted with tall, monstrous statues, the work of some now-vanished race, and its past remains an enigma (Pierre Loti, 'L'Ile de Paques', 1872)

Keywords: Rapa Nui   Easter Island   Polynesia   Archaeology   Chile

Location grid reference: 109° 26'W   27° 09'S

World Heritage List inclusion date: 1996

Summary

Rapa Nui (Easter Island) is a 180 km² Pacific island, the most distant point in the world from other dry land. At the time of its colonization by Polynesians around AD 400 the island supported lush subtropical forests but less than 1500 years later these had disappeared, triggering the complete destruction of the island's ecosystem. At the peak of its prosperity Rapa Nui supported a complex, stable political system whose clan groups carved gigantic stone statues (*moai*). Uncontrolled population growth and the cutting of forest to transport *moai* resulted in the extinction of most native plant and animal species accompanied by civil war, cannibalism and social disintegration. Today, some 3000 people live on Rapa Nui (now part of Chile) supported almost entirely by heritage tourism. Seventy per cent of the island is a National Park designated as a World Heritage Site (cultural landscape category) in 1996. Tourism is seasonal, entirely controlled by Rapa Nui people and dependent on air access. World Heritage designation has met with some local opposition by restricting development opportunities but others welcome it as a means to access conservation funding.

Introduction

Rapa Nui (Easter Island) is famous for its gigantic stone statues (*moai*) whose abundance and distinctiveness has generated many theories about how and why they were made and moved. The island became well known in the West as a result of the theories of Thor Heyerdahl (Heyerdahl, 1952) who suggested, on the basis both of Rapa Nui stonework and his own trans-Pacific voyage on the *Kon-Tiki* balsa wood raft, that it was colonized from South America. The bleak island and its extraordinary statues have become the focus of a significant tourism industry based entirely on heritage, which supports the entire population. Speculation about the origin of the Rapa Nui people and the society which carved the *moai* therefore fuels popular interest, although comprehensive archaeological work has provided extensive documentation about the prehistory of the island from its colonisation by Polynesians around AD 400 (Bahn and Flenley, 1992; van Tilburg, 1994). Easter Island is a unique heritage tourism destination, difficult to reach, expensive to visit and presenting the visitor with a powerful visual experience of striking landscapes combined with controversial mythologies. Seventy per cent of the island is included in a National Park which was designated as a World Heritage cultural landscape in 1996. However, it seems doubtful whether this designation will have much effect on Rapa Nui tourism. This is entirely at the mercy of the Chilean airline LanChile which provides the only access. Rapa Nui is part of Chile although enjoying a certain degree of autonomy because of its remoteness, but this access route ensures that the future of the island is closely linked to the soaring economic fortunes of Chile which is experiencing remarkable tourism growth.

Tourism in Chile

Chile, a long narrow country with an extraordinary variety of natural landscapes (Figure 5.1) enjoys the most solid and best-managed economy in South America with a dozen years of sustained economic growth at annual rates exceeding 6.5 per cent, single-digit inflation and a commendable budget surplus. The free-market economy has flourished under democratic rule (currently a coalition) since 1989 with tourism representing a major growth area. In 1994 over 1.6 million tourists visited Chile (SERNATUR, 1996) which now has an annual tourism growth rate of 17 per cent. Businesss tourism is also flourishing and the Chilean national tourism agency SERNATUR is heavily promoting ecotourism, activity, and adventure tourism. Most international tourists enter via Santiago, a sophisticated and cosmopolitan capital, where entry formalities are minimal (no visas are required from most countries). Chile is Spanish-speaking although English is widely understood and Santiago has a wide range of efficient and well-organized travel agencies and an excellent range of hotels arranging tours both to Easter Island and elsewhere. Chile's offshore possessions include not only Rapa Nui (Easter Island) but also the remote Juan Fernandez islands famous for their wildlife and for inspiring Daniel Defoe's *Robinson Crusoe* based on the story of Alexander Selkirk who survived alone there for four years. These islands may shortly also receive World Heritage designation.

In 1994 1 622 800 tourists visited Chile (an increase from 50 000 ten years ago) but only 10 per cent of these were from Europe and 2 per cent from the rest of the world, with neighbouring Argentina contributing 55 per cent and other South American countries 21.2 per cent (SERNATUR, 1996). Tourism contributes 5 per cent of Chile's GDP representing 7.2 per cent of export income. The growth rate of 17 per cent is one of the highest in the world, due partly to heavy investment in marketing and partly to the economic situation of Chile which encourages business and leisure travel from neighbouring countries. The relatively low arrivals rate from Europe and North America is attributable to flight time (eight hours from Miami, eleven hours from New York), distance and expense. A visitor to Easter Island from the UK will take a minimum of 21 hours' flying time (plus stops) to reach there via Santiago, usually flying via Miami or direct with a refuelling stop in Argentina or Brazil and connection at Santiago.

Rapa Nui

Easter Island is the most distant inhabited point in the world from other dry land, 3700 km from mainland Chile and 4050 km from Tahiti. Its early Polynesian settlers called the island '*Te Pinto o Te Hunua*' (navel of the world) and it was 'discovered' by the Dutch explorer Jacob Roggeveen on Easter Day, 1722. He described the island as a wasteland of barren rock and grass without a single tree or bush over 3 m high, yet it had once supported lush tropical forest and a large

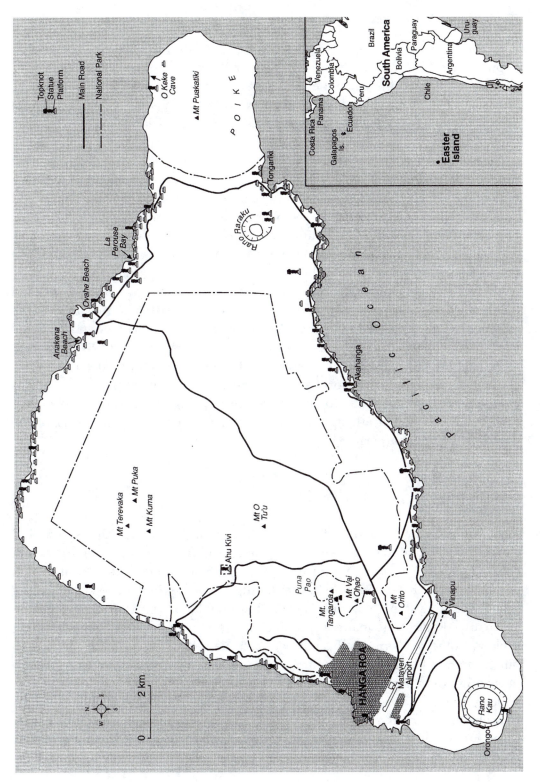

Figure 5.1 Location and plan of Rapa Nui (Easter Island)

population. The few remaining islanders that Roggeveen saw had no native animals larger than insects, not even a native species of bat, bird, snail or lizard. The island is remarkable today for an almost complete absence of wildlife except for a few birds, in complete contrast to other Polynesian islands such as Tahiti or Hawaii. Today the land, people and language are all referred to as Rapa Nui.

The island is best known for its gigantic stone statues (*moai*), standing on raised rectangular platforms (*ahu*) although its archaeological heritage also includes numerous petroglyphs, the remains of ancient houses and burial cairns and artefacts including the as-yet undeciphered *rongorongo* tablets which may be a Polynesian language. The large numbers of *moai* statues in what is today a bleak and inhospitably barren landscape have led to many theories about the origins of the society that created them. Thor Heyerdahl (1952) suggested that they were made by Peruvians, travelling from South America, on the basis of similarities in the stonework and his own *Kon-Tiki* voyage which replicated a journey from South America to Polynesia. Seventy per cent of the island is now included in a National Park (Figure 5.1), managed by the Chilean Forestry Department (CONAF), which received World Heritage designation as a cultural landscape in 1996. Easter Island is often referred to as the world's largest museum, and tourism to the island is almost exclusively motivated by an interest in the tangible remains of its prehistoric culture, although attempts are being made to make visitors aware of the islanders' Polynesian heritage.

Geography

Rapa Nui is a small island some 180 km² (16.628 ha) in extent with a subtropical climate and annual average temperature of 20.3°C. August is the coldest month (14.7–17°C) and February the warmest (23.8–27°C) and there is an annual rainfall of 152.9 mm falling mainly in July and August. Some 2891 people live on the island, speaking Rapa Nui and Spanish, but only 30 per cent of this population are native Rapa Nui, many being mainlanders brought in for roadbuilding projects. Although formerly heavily wooded, Rapa Nui has no indigenous trees but efforts are being made to reintroduce the native *toromiro* palm tree (*Sophora toromiro*) from cultivated seeds taken from the last living example. The *toromiro*, which formerly grew up to 3 m high in dense woodland, was probably cut down to facilitate moving the giant statues, but it may have trouble re-establishing itself in an environment now dominated by newly introduced exotic species and soils altered by fire. Rapa Nui landscapes are bleak, grassy and windswept and the island is circled by dramatic cliffs, 300 m high in places. There is no natural deepwater harbour so that ships must offload passengers and freight into small boats up to 1 km from shore. The islands highest point, Maunga Terevaka, is less than 500 m above sea level and most cultivated land is found in the vicinity of the only settlement, Hanga Roa, in the south-west (Figure 5.1)

Cultural history

Rapa Nui was colonized by Polynesians from the west (and ultimately from Asia) around AD 400. Heyerdahl's theory of South American influence now has few supporters since the Rapa Nui culture is so clearly Polynesian. The language is a Polynesian dialect related to Marquesan and isolated since around AD 400, the date by which the island had been settled by Polynesian farmers growing bananas, taro, sweet potato, sugarcane and paper mulberry. Radiocarbon dates associated with early human activity confirm these first settlements at between AD 400 and 700, and place the peak of statue construction at AD 1200–1500. By that time the population may have reached as high as 10 000, far exceeding the resource capacity of the small island's ecosystem. Scarce resources and destruction of lush palm forests both for agriculture and to transport the massive stone *moai* probably plunged a thriving and complex society into decline, culminating in civil war and cannibalism.

Around 1000 *moai* seem to have been made between around AD 700–1500, 200 of which once stood on coastal *ahu* platforms, facing inland and carved from volcanic tuffs with coral eyes and red topknots. Another 700–800, in varying stages of completion, were abandoned in the quarry or along the ancient roads between quarries and the coast. Most of the erected statues came from a single quarry (Ranu Raraku, Figure 5.1) and were transported as far as 8 km despite heights of up to 11 m and weights of up to 82 tons. Abandoned statues include some true giants up to 21 m tall weighing 270 tons. The perennial fascination of the island is the 'mystery' of who carved the statues and how they were moved, an issue made especially interesting by the barren, desolate nature of the island. Similar 'mysteries' are constructed around any megalithic building project from Stonehenge to the Pyramids, and seem to reflect a general public reluctance to accept sound archaeological evidence when fantasy and extra-terrestrial origins are more romantic. Modern archaeological experiments suggest that even the largest statue could have been completed by around twenty carvers within a year, and required only a few hundred people with wooden rollers and bark ropes to move into a standing position. Pollen analysis confirms the existence of subtropical forests on the island at the time of the initial colonization, but forest clearance was well under way by AD 800 and the final palm trees became extinct around 1400, about the same time as statue carving stopped. The destruction of the forest and accompanying soil erosion and over-exploitation of all resources including shellfish and seabirds turned Easter Island into a desert. Cannibalism became common, streams dried up and wood was no longer available for cooking fires. Local chaos replaced centralized government and by 1700 the population had crashed and rival clans had started to topple each other's statues. Some *moai* were seen upright by the first European visitors in 1773 but all had been torn down by the islanders themselves by 1864. Any *moai* standing today have been raised by archaeologists such as William Mulloy working at Ahu Akivi (Mulloy and Figueroa, 1978).

Further disasters were in store for the island as a result of European contact. A Peruvian slave raid in 1862 took away more than 1000 islanders, including the king, to work in the guano deposits of Peru's offshore islands. Less than 100 returned and many of them died of smallpox, leaving less than 100 islanders at the turn of the century. Between 1860 and 1888 the island was successively owned by a French sea captain and a Chilean–Scottish sheep-grazing operation until it was annexed by Chile in 1888. Rapa Nui came under Chilean military rule until the mid-1960s but now has local self-government, although many islanders are still dissatisfied with the Chilean presence. Complaints include neglect by the Chilean government, who clearly regard the island as of peripheral significance, poor health and education services, deficient transport and scarce farmland increasingly pressured by a rising population who are forbidden to utilize National Park land. Some militant Rapa Nui pressure groups feel that the island should be returned to their ownership and resent outside interference, including World Heritage designation. The islanders' Polynesian identity is still very strong, preserved in traditional wood carvings, *tapa* crafts, tattooing, music and dance.

Tourism on Rapa Nui

Visitor arrivals on Rapa Nui have been growing steadily at around 10 per cent per year but this is less than one might expect and slower than the growth rate for mainland Chile. Table 5.1 shows that in 1995 Rapa Nui received 10 161 visitors of whom 3181 were cruise passengers who came on just three large ships and remained on the island for only four to six hours.

This indicates slow but erratic growth, and SERNATUR estimates that the figures under-represent tourists on the island by about 20 per cent since they only refer to guests in official SERNATUR-registered accommodation. Still, the growth is slower than might have been expected given the intrinsic interest of the destination, a factor attributable almost entirely to limited flight capacity. There is really only one way to reach Rapa Nui and that is by the scheduled services of LanChile two or three times a week from Santiago, depending on season. The flight takes 5.5 hours from Santiago and there is the possibility of continuing on to Tahiti but most visitors take package tours involving a return flight from Santiago and the services of one of the many ground handlers based in Santiago or Hanga Roa, often with offices in both places. Despite persistent rumours over the last decade that LanChile is prepared to relinquish its monopoly over flights to Rapa Nui there is no evidence that this is the case. Rapa Nui does receive a few charter flights, including a first visit from Concorde which was scheduled for early in 1997. The arrival statistics also include the few business visitors to the island such as a large (100-person) delegation from NASA who visited in late 1996 in connection with the Space Shuttle landing programme.

Tourism on Rapa Nui is a seasonal business with low season between May and September (Table 5.2). High season lasts from October to the end of April with a peak in January and February, which is also the time that cruise ships arrive. This seasonality is governed by the weather which can be cold and rainy during the winter months.

Table 5.1 Tourist arrivals on Rapa Nui 1986–95

Year	Tourist arrivals
1995	10 161*
1994	7188
1993	7203
1992	5498
1991	6449
1990	4961
1989	5007
1988	4018
1987	4163
1986	3564

* Of which 3181 were cruise-ship passengers
Source: Sernatur

Table 5.2 Seasonality of visitor arrivals to
Rapa Nui during 1995

Month	Visitor arrivals
January	1453
February	1202
March	821
April	1034
May	545
June	484
July	605
August	756
September	467
October	957
November	938
December	899

Source: Sernatur

Despite the lack of precise information it seems that less than 10 per cent of visitors originate from Europe or North America. Most come from Chile or neighbouring South American countries with many Hawaiians, Australians, New Zealanders and Japanese. The latter are arriving in increasing numbers and are welcomed as being high spenders. The European market is dominated by the French (often combining Rapa Nui with French-speaking Tahiti), Italians and Germans with very few British.

Accommodation

All accommodation on the island is owned by Rapa Nui people and a law prevents potential development by foreign corporations. Most people take an inclusive package involving hotel and tours (a typical 5-day package would cost around US$500 in low season and include a hotel room with breakfast, one full- and two half-day tours plus transfers but excluding airfare). This price can be doubled in high season or for an independent traveller. Tour operators have worked out packages to match LanChile flights – it is even possible to get a 45-minute whirlwind tour if the flight is just a refuelling stop. There are ten hotels on Rapa Nui plus 28 *residenciales* (guest houses) and the possibility of staying in private homes. All accommodation is in Hanga Roa (Figure 5.1) and the top three hotels have a swimming pool, take credit cards and include conference facilities. All hotels and most *residenciales* offer meals, some of the latter have a bar and all have a TV room. Many organize tours and rent horses and jeeps. Extra accommodation is provided in private homes, making it difficult to calculate bedspace or occupancy, although SERNATUR estimate around 700 bedspaces. Many hotels and guest houses are actively refurbishing or adding new rooms and facilities.

One problem is the erratic nature of demand. During the summer season demand is relatively constant but in the winter a hotel may be full one day and empty the next, not to refill until the arrival of the next plane. Moreover, the large number of available bedspaces (approximately 700 for 10 000 visitors) indicates that occupancy rates must be low as well as erratic except in the larger hotels, which are usually pre-booked via mainland travel agencies. Demand is particularly heavy during the cultural Tapata Rapa Nui festival which takes place late January/early February. All hotel accommodation is fully booked, frequently at 100 per cent surcharge.

All supplies for tourism with the exception of fresh fruit, vegetables and eggs must be imported, including vehicles and building materials. These arrive by means of a cargo ship approximately five times a year but because of the lack of a deep-water harbour all cargo must be off-loaded into small boats. The same is true for cruise-ship passengers who must transfer to local boats. The need to import all materials makes it necessary to charge high prices. A typical top-range hotel room will cost US95–125 (more in peak season) with meals ranging from $20 for a packed lunch to $30 for dinner. Drinks are also expensive, as is car hire, and the range of in-house services is severely restricted when considering the high prices charged. Even the best hotels have no real room or laundry service and lack direct-dial telephones. There is one officially designated campsite in the north of the island near Anakena beach but *residenciales* often allow camping in their grounds. The island had no running water or electricity until 1987 but today's water supply is derived from steadily replenished underground sources and is reliable; the growing tourism industry is seen to present no problems.

Training and information provision

There is a surprising lack of information about Rapa Nui in Santiago, making planning a trip heavily reliant on good guidebooks and European tour operators. Booking a private trip involves negotiating with Spanish-speaking operators and

Spanish-language information leaflets and books. The CONAF and SERNATUR offices in Hanga Roa sell maps and information leaflets in different languages but much of the material in Santiago is available only in Spanish. No one on the island has received any formal tourism industry training yet the visitor management system is efficient and works well. The Rapa Nui say that they have learnt quickly by experience and the process is helped by a web of family connections and excellent language skills; most guides or hotel managers speak four or five languages fluently (Spanish, Rapa Nui, English, French and sometimes German).

Transport

The island is served by Mataveri Airport which has one of the South Pacific's most advanced electronic landing support systems and a 3.25 km runway recently upgraded at an investment of US$11.5 million (the largest investment on the island ever made by the government) which is now available as an emergency landing strip for the space shuttle. Should it wish to, Rapa Nui now has the capacity to cater for jumbo and even super-jumbo jets. LanChile now operates a daily flight from Santiago in high season, reduced to four flights a week during the winter. Costs are high; a round trip fare from Santiago exceeds US$800 although economies can be made using one of the LanChile airpasses if Easter Island is being combined with other Chilean destinations.

Many road improvement schemes are also being carried out, including paving the inner road to Anakena with work scheduled to start on the coast road during 1997. There is no public transport on Rapa Nui. Visitors must walk (the coastline is 40 miles around but many interesting areas are within a day trip of Hanga Roa), rent horses, motorbikes or jeeps or take a tour. One taxi has just started operating (April 1996) but passengers arriving at Mataveri Airport are almost compelled to take up an offer of accommodation if they have not pre-booked, as otherwise they will have no means of transport.

Visitor management

Visitor management is entirely in the hands of the Rapa Nui people themselves, working in partnership with CONAF, who run the National Park, and SERNATUR. Entrance fees of US$10 per person are charged by CONAF who return 60 per cent of these fees, an estimated $60 000 per year towards the management of the Park which includes all the archaeological sites and occupies 70 per cent of the island (Figure 5.1). Around 10 rangers are employed whose duties include generally watching the archaeological sites to prevent vandalism or erosion, answering visitor queries and giving directions. Few recent problems have been reported although twenty years ago graffiti, souvenir hunting and climbing over the monuments had a deleterious effect. Nothing of the kind is visible today. Park management is unobtrusive, livestock are grazed within the Park and managed by mounted herdsmen but no one is allowed to live within the Park boundary except CONAF rangers.

A few paths at heavily utilized or dangerous sites such as Orongo have been strengthened to resist erosion by the provision of steps and railings but there is little intrusive signage. Major archaeological sites are indicated from the road by small, non-intrusive signs and the only other evident visitor facilities are 'no-go' signs for dangerous areas such as the 1000 m sheer cliffs at Orongo or the Rano Kau crater and the provision of (carved basalt) litter bins. Roads around the island are dirt but in good condition and one may park anywhere. At the major sites a small car park is designated. During low season it is usual not to encounter other visitors at the majority of the sites which are located in a landscape bearing a strong resemblance to the Outer Hebrides. The most famous sites become crowded during peak season at peak hours since most guided tours leave Hanga Roa at the same time, but no visitor erosion is evident and the grassy tracks recover naturally during the rainy winter season. No visitor facilities or concessions are available within the Park, with the exception of toilets at Anakena beach and Orongo (Figure 5.1). The Park has no debris or litter but the type of tourism that can develop is realistically limited to motorized transport (with the exception of horse riding near Hanga Roa) as the distances are too great to walk and in the summer the island is very hot and completely devoid of shade or surface water.

An interesting visitor management problem is being posed by the arrival of cruise ships when suddenly more than ten per cent of the annual tourism arrivals can appear within an hour. This creates great pressure on food availability and all ground-handling agencies and most private cars are pressed into service to conduct the tourists on a trip round the island.

World Heritage designation

World Heritage designation was approved for Rapa Nui on 22 March 1996, the culmination of a process started by CONAF in 1981 which did not receive government support. The idea was reactivated in 1992 when the Chilean Foreign Affairs Ministry conducted a UNESCO mission around the island which ultimately resulted in the inclusion of the Rapa Nui National Park, but not the whole island, in the World Heritage Cultural Landscape category. Such a designation should not affect the way in which local people use the island if current management practices are continued, although the government of Chile is formally bound to maintain the park. In the event of a natural disaster such as the *tsunami* which overwhelmed Ahu Tongariki, toppling its 15 *moai*, world resources would help. The WHS designation has met with considerable opposition from some Rapa Nui people, including the current mayor, Petero Edmunds, on the grounds that it would restrict progress by prohibiting construction or works that modify the present environment. However, other groups of Rapa Nui have welcomed the designation for precisely that reason and intend to continue with existing management practices that restrict settlement to the Hanga Roa area outside the Park and minimize visitor facilities within the Park itself.

The World Monuments Fund, together with CONAF, has already produced an excellent explanatory map of the National Park which, however, omits the location of fragile lesser-known archaeological sites to afford them greater protection. Vandalism of the sites seems to have stopped but original archaeological artefacts such as obsidian tools are still being offered, although these may be surface finds rather than the product of looting. Most islanders feel that World Heritage designation is unlikely to have any great effect on tourism and is significant only because it will prevent any development within the National Park and allow access to potential conservation money from the World Monuments Fund.

At present no more than $122 000 per annum is spent on archaeological heritage (half of that derived from admission fees), only a fraction of the estimated $1 million required for statue stabilization and conservation. Many of the coastal *moai* and *ahu* exhibit extensive wind and saltwater erosion features in contrast to the fresher, sharper *moai* in the quarries. Ongoing restoration work continues with a broken statue at Ahu Tautira having been recently repaired and re-erected with the cost paid by Municipality of Hanga Roa and a crane donated by a Japanese company. The great *ahu* of Ahu Tongariki with its fifteen *moai* has now been completely restored and there are many archaeological projects being carried out on the island. Designating Orongo as a World Heritage Site In Danger assisted with the generation of funding to stabilize and protect the site.

The future

Various scenarios are possible for the future of Rapa Nui but some are less likely than others. It is possible, if unlikely, that the island will gain independence from Chile which would have disastrous repercussions for tourism. It is also possible, and more likely, that the LanChile monopoly will be broken with a marked increase in tourism. Other variables which contribute large numbers of visitors for short periods include possible increases in charter flights and cruise ships. Rapa Nui is an interesting case since its tourism combines an astronomical level of import dependency with almost total control by indigenous people. This does not mean that all tourism revenues stay on the island. Far from it – many Rapa Nui have friends and family in mainland Chile and the USA. Realistically it seems likely that tourism will continue to grow in a bumpy way entirely constrained (or not) by air capacity as the number of available bedspaces is more than adequate to meet demand and infinitely expandable into private homes. Natural disasters, including earthquakes and *tsunami*, cannot be predicted and the real question is that, barring marked policy changes, can the existing high quality of the visitor experience be maintained? Having said this it is sad to report that a serious fire in December 1996 burnt and damaged forty-six *moai*. The fire seems to have started in the interior of the Rano Raraku volcano and spread rapidly. The cause is uncertain and could be arson, accidental fire or related in some way to the volcanic rock. Fortunately, only minor damage occurred but the incident reinforced the views of the island's mayor that increased funding was required to protect the giant statues. It is significant that lack of funding prevented any of the Park's eight rangers from having a phone with which to communicate with the others. On the day of the fire the single ranger on duty had to walk twenty miles into Hanga Roa for help.

Today's visitor to Easter Island in low season may experience the cultural landscape almost devoid of fellow-tourists and intrusive signage or facilities in a way seldom seen in National Parks. Even in high season such an experience can be repeated by judicious choice of timing. Visitor facilities are totally confined to Hanga Roa with the exception of occasional small-scale attempts by local people to sell souvenirs at especially popular sites (largely ignored by officials). The archaeological heritage of Rapa Nui is no longer being affected by its visitors, but is being severely damaged by the effects of wind and weather. Can visitors be used to provide extra funding? Rapa Nui is an extremely expensive destination whose accommodation, at least, must be near an acceptable price ceiling. The high prices charged are acceptable only because the visitor experience cannot be repeated anywhere else. However, the very lack of visitor facilities which makes the experience dramatic and strangely spiritual also means that the National Park has no means of generating additional visitor revenue. Maps, postcards, food, drink and tee-shirts must all be purchased in Hanga Roa, contributing to Rapa Nui private enterprise but not to National Park funds. The strangeness and mystery of the island does not remain on cruise ship days and SERNATUR has, at present, no plans to limit visitation levels which it considers quite acceptable. It would be interesting to establish from visitors at what level they found the presence of other tourists irritating. Under normal conditions very low visitor numbers at individual sites could easily be maintained by cooperation between tour guides in Hanga Roa who could alter routes and departure times. At present almost all tours leave at either 10 a.m. or 3 p.m. and follow the same routes linking major sites. This means that on any one day at least half the tourists on the island will be lunching at Anakena and visiting the Ranu Raraku quarry in the late morning, whereas more creativity in route planning could ensure low visitor densities even with much greater numbers.

Realistically, tourism is the only development option open to the Rapa Nui but it has not led directly, as in many other Pacific islands, to economic dependence but the high import intensity of the industry controls its prospects (Hall and Page, 1996). Ironically, Chile is able to control the economy of Rapa Nui far more effectively through controlling tourism than it did in the pre-1960s dictatorship. At present, there is no possibility of resort development as laws prescribe what can be done and forbid external investment. Most Rapa Nui want appropriate and sensitive development to minimize tourism impact on a fragile ecosystem whose non-renewable heritage is its only real renewable resource. Demand is not being stimulated by marketing and is constrained by air transport supply.

The concept of a cultural landscape closely involves the spiritual and contemporary uses of a landscape with the management of its archaeological heritage. Part of the fascination of a trip to Easter Island is to marvel at the statues and speculate how they were made. Many visitors see Rapa Nui as a potential metaphor for the fate of the world, devastated by over-population and poor resource management. The price the original inhabitants paid for the way they chose to articulate their spiritual and political ideas was undoubtedly an island world which became a shadow of its fomer self (van Tilburg, 1994). However, it is essential to remember that the final downfall of Rapa Nui was actually encompassed by Europeans profiting from a weakened society. The archaeological heritage of the island is of deep and fundamental importance to its present inhabitants, enhancing their cultural pride and supporting a new generation who are experiencing a renaissance of interest in their Polynesian past (a phenomenon also observed on Hawaii). The history of Rapa Nui as a heritage tourism destination really starts with Thor Heyerdahl and the *Kon-Tiki* expedition, although many of the myths this work supported have been subsequently disproved. Some are more enduring and were used by the actor Kevin Costner in his recent film *Rapa Nui* which was a box office disaster. Local people say that this was no bad thing since the filming generated employment and cash even though the final product was so bad that it perpetrated old myths and distorted island aesthetics.

The *moai* of Easter Island are not only links to the past but also the kingpins of its future. Commercial proposals to restore various *moai* and *ahu* are frequently put to the Rapa Nui people but the scientific value of many of the projects is doubtful and Rapa Nui archaeologists and National Park staff are rightly cautious about acceptance. Determining the direction of Rapa Nui archaeology requires the cooperation of the whole scientific community. The *moai* are artefacts which have curiously transcended their time frame (van Tilburg, 1994) to enter into modern consciousness and their rising again has spiritual as well as symbolic value.

References

Bahn, P. and Flenley, J. (1992) *Easter Island, Earth Island*, London: Thames and Hudson

Heyerdahl, T. (1952) *American Indians in the Pacific: the theory behind the Kon-Tiki expedition*, London: Allen and Unwin

Hall, C. M. and Page, S. J. (1996) *Tourism in the Pacific: issues and cases*, London: International Thompson Business Press

Mulloy, W. and Figueroa, G. (1978) *The AKivi-Vai Teka Complex and its relationship to Easter Island architectural prehistory*, University of Hawaii at Manoa: Asian and Pacific Archaeology Series 8

SERNATUR (1996) *Tourism Manual – Chile*, Santiago: SERNATUR

van Tilburg, J. (1994) *Easter Island: archaeology, ecology and culture*, London: British Museum Press

6   Giza (Egypt)

The use of GIS in managing a World Heritage Site

Katie Evans and Lindsay Fielding

Man fears Time, yet Time fears the Pyramids (Arab proverb)

Keywords: Pyramids   Tourism   GIS   Heritage Masterplan

Location grid reference: 30° 01′ N   31° 13′ E

World Heritage List inclusion date: 1979

Summary

The Giza Plateau is experiencing environmental damage from tourism and the encroachment of Cairo. To this end, a Masterplan was commissioned by UNESCO to provide for the sustainable management of the site and to protect the remaining archaeology. The plan concentrated on the impacts created by tourists and the local tourism industry and proposed the removal of visitor amenities to the edge of the Plateau, in order to protect the monuments. This chapter reviews the problems identified at the site, the Masterplan itself and examines ways in which a Geographical Information System might be used to help achieve some of the management objectives.

Introduction

The Pyramids of Giza and the Sphinx are some of Egypt's most important archaeological monuments and they were built on what is known as the Giza Plateau (Figure 6.1). Noted in antiquity they are now the only remaining Wonder of the

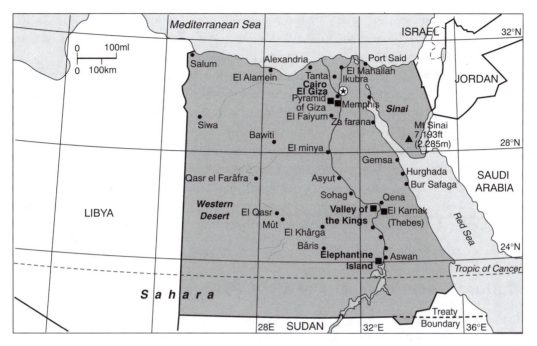

Figure 6.1 Location of Giza

Ancient World and are listed by UNESCO as forming a World Heritage Site. As with many World Heritage Sites, the Giza Plateau is a major tourist attraction and it is estimated that over 1.25 million international tourists visit the site each year (Mabbit, 1992). As well as the pressure from visitor numbers, the site also suffers from the problems posed by the encroachment of urban Cairo, which now extends to the south-eastern edge of the Plateau.

In the early 1990s, concerns were raised by UNESCO regarding the impacts caused by tourism and urbanization which had resulted in notable deterioration of the monuments. This deterioration occurred despite the efforts of the Egyptian Antiquities Organization (EAO) to improve the management of tourism at the site. It was in March 1992 that The Conservation Practice, a British based team of conservation architects, were commissioned by UNESCO to undertake preliminary work in the preparation of a Masterplan for the 'Giza Pyramid Plateau and its buffer zone'. The initial research undertaken by The Conservation Practice examined the state of the Plateau and its surrounding area and existing studies were reviewed and discussed with the Egyptian Antiquities Organization and other relevant authorities. The initial report prepared for UNESCO included a first outline of a management plan for the archaeological site and surrounding 'buffer zones'. This was followed throughout the early 1990s by progress reports reviewing the developments taking place at the Plateau.

The aim of the Masterplan is to permit the sustainable management of the World Heritage Site. It is intended to conserve the remaining archaeology and control further deterioration of the site, whether this is caused by the pressures of the tourism industry or by other, inappropriate developments and uses of the site. In order to support these aims and to monitor the implementation of the Masterplan the authors propose that a Geographical Information System (GIS) would be a useful management tool. This chapter outlines the pressures facing the Giza Plateau, considers the proposed Masterplan and suggests ways in which a Geographical Information System could support site management.

Cultural resources at the Giza Plateau

The Giza Plateau contains some of the most outstanding monuments from Pharaonic times; the scale and engineering accuracy of the Pyramids has fascinated visitors for thousands of years. These gigantic structures represent the epitome of pyramid building in ancient Egypt and the feats of the architects that designed them were not surpassed by succeeding generations.

The three granite and limestone Pyramids at the site were built at the height of the Fourth Dynasty of Pharaonic Egypt, that is from 2613 to 2498 BC. The Great Pyramid built for Pharaoh Khufu is 137 m high and the granite blocks used in its construction weigh between 3 and 15 tons. Not only is Khufu's the largest of the Pyramids, it is the only one that tourists can enter. If they do, a steep narrow walk takes them to the claustrophobic centre of the structure. The other smaller Pyramids were built for Khufu's son and grandson. These three Pyramids are the most striking features of the site and thousands of years of erosion have left them standing, apparently in isolation; this is misleading as they were originally part of a complex system of burial structures. The Pyramids would all have been linked to an individual mortuary temple, boat pits, and a long causeway that ended at the valley temple on the banks of the River Nile. The Nile used to flow to the south of the Plateau and was used to transport the Pharoah's body to its final resting place. The roles played by the different buildings in these burial complexes have been described by Roberts (1995) but are lost on the modern visitor to the Giza Plateau, as much of the archaeology has not survived or is not clearly identified.

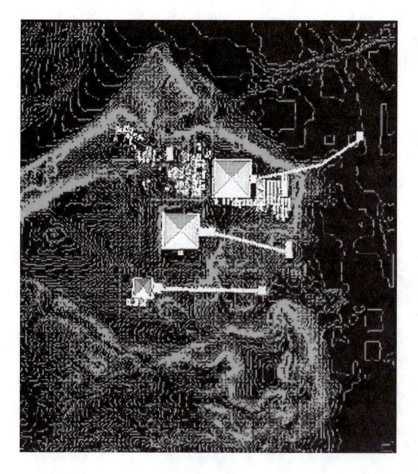

Figure 6.2 Digital map of Giza showing topology

What is not visible to the tourist on the ground is clearly identified in aerial images of the site, such as the digital map (Figure 6.2) and in satellite images (Figure 6.3). These aerial views identify the Pyramids and the relative location of the connecting structures that formed the original burial complex. The location of the causeways is clearly shown (Figure 6.2) ending at the valley temples, and the subsidiary pyramids and numerous smaller tombs are clear in both figures. To the visitor, however, these smaller unexplained structures appear to have no relevance and are not perceived to be of any historical importance. But these small structures are important as they reveal much about the social order that prevailed and contain the tombs of members of the Pharaoh's court, including pre-eminent figures such as the architects of the Pyramids.

The site also contains the Sphinx whose origins and functions have been the subject of recent discussion by Lehner (1992). It is thought that construction was

Figure 6.3 Soviet Satellite data showing the pyramids

started by Khufu's son and that the Sphinx was adapted by succeeding Pharaohs. The Sphinx stands at the lower, southern edge of the Plateau close to the original course of the Nile. With the Pyramids rising behind it, this forms one of the most dramatic views of the site.

The tourist experience

Observational studies have shown that the majority of visitors spend only 90 minutes at the site (Evans, 1995). There is very little encouragement for them to stay any longer as the site is devoid of any but the most basic of visitor facilities. Information about the site is virtually non-existent, maps and leaflets are not available and guidebooks have to be purchased in central Cairo or in the tourism-generating country. There is no interpretation on the site or even basic signage to indicate the location of various features. As a result, whether visitors gain any understanding of the significance and meaning of the Pyramids and remaining structures can depend upon the professionalism of their guide, or on whether they have brought information with them. As explained above, many of the smaller site features are not easily identified at ground level and without maps or information panels to locate them visitors are often unaware of their significance. This current lack of site and visitor flow management has contributed to many of the negative impacts resulting from tourism development as tourists fail to understand the results of their actions as they walk, ride or drive over the Plateau.

Impacts at the Giza Plateau

The focus for this study is cultural tourism and usage of the site and it is these impacts that will be discussed in detail. The impacts are mainly environmental and can be classified in relation to the behaviour of tourists, the provision of services for them, and the role of the local tourism industry. As already stated, the majority of visitors stay for an average of 90 minutes with two coach stops, one by the Great Pyramid, the other close to the Sphinx. During this time they spend an average of £E20 (£4 sterling) on entrance fees (Evans, 1995). It is unclear if the coach groups pay even this set amount or whether they receive a discounted rate. Whatever the situation, it is apparent that there is a lost opportunity to generate income for the conservation of the site via higher entrance fees or the provision of other services such as official guided tours.

Tourist behaviour

Much of the damage on-site is a result of the inappropriate behaviour of tourists which is exacerbated by the lack of visitor management and information provision. It could be argued that in many cases tourists are unaware of the fact that the type of behaviour outlined below constitutes a problem, as they do not fully understand the nature of the site. Problems include:

- Casual damage to sensitive areas of the site by visitors on foot, horseback and camel
- Climbing of monuments
- Exploring areas of sensitive archaeology
- Dropping of litter
- Removal of 'souvenir' pieces
- Graffiti on-site
- Urination against the limestone structures

The local tourism industry

With over 1.25 million foreign visitors per annum (Mabbit, 1992), and in a country suffering from severe unemployment it is not surprising that a substantial local tourism industry has developed to serve the needs of tourists. As in many developing countries, the industry is fragmented and largely unregulated. Local `travel agencies' sell daily coach tours that include the Giza Plateau and the Egyptian Museum in central Cairo. Private taxis offer tailor-made tours and on the site itself local residents offer camel and horse rides. Coaches and taxis park as close to the monuments as possible and tourists are allowed to ride camels and horses over the Plateau. Issues include:

- On-site parking, pollution and uncontrolled access from coaches, cars, taxis, trailbikes
- The growth of new settlements such as Nazlet el Semmane and Kafret el Gabal at the base of the plateau with subsequent sewage leakage onto the plateau
- Dumping of litter, sewage, horse and camel dung, plus the occasional dead camel on the site
- Unofficial 'guides' who may encourage inappropriate tourist behaviour, e.g. climbing monuments

Past developments

Although primarily seen in the West as a tourist attraction, the site is also popular as a local recreation area for the 16 million population of Cairo (Adley, 1995). It has also been used for the official residences of the government and the Egyptian Antiquities Offices. As such, a range of 'inappropriate developments' now exist, which include:

- Modern buildings
- Temporary structures
- Tar roads
- Defunct power cables
- Banks of lighting
- Street lights
- Litter bins
- Toilets
- Electricity substations
- Fencing/barbed wire barriers

These developments have been identified as unsympathetic to the aesthetic features of the site (Mabbit, 1992), and are seen to add to the overall problems of the plateau. The extent of the environmental impacts outlined above has resulted in an inevitable degradation of the tourist experience. Further the lack of effective management strategies has substantially reduced the potential for economic benefits from conservation, potentially resulting in a downward spiral as respect for the site diminishes further. This situation has been commented on by Fowler (1996), who raises concerns about the lack of any sense of spirit of place amid the apparent chaos.

The Masterplan for the Giza Plateau

The Masterplan was drawn up in response to the problems that were identified at the site and the proposals in it will change the nature of the tourism experience in a number of ways. Some of the strategies proposed restrict and control access to the monuments and limit the modern facilities within the site. By providing new facilities and better information on the edge of the site, the intention is to improve the visitors' experience of the monuments and provide further opportunities for income generation. The overall aims of the plan are:

1 To improve the visitors' experience
2 To reduce the impact of visitors on the site and monuments
3 To provide a framework for the conservation and further study of the archaeology

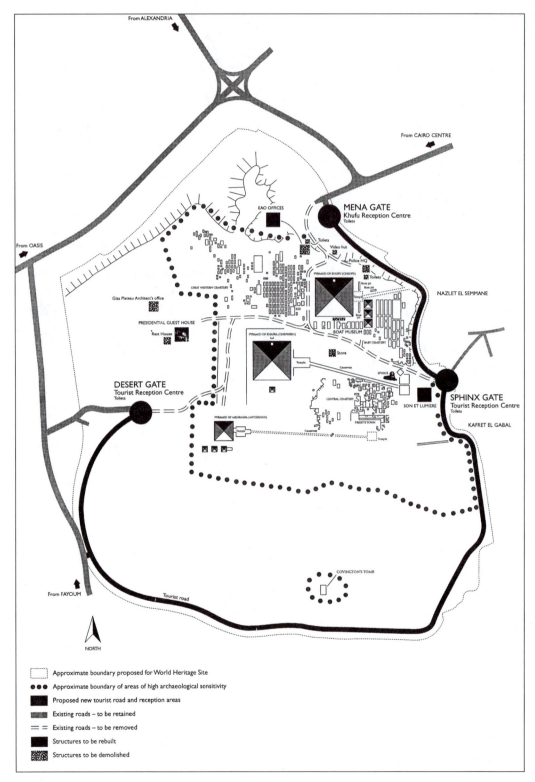

Figure 6.4 The Giza Plateau Masterplan

Figure 6.4 illustrates the proposals for management of the site and demonstrates the intention to control and spread the impact of tourists. It highlights the problems that currently exist, such as the tar road network extending throughout the areas of sensitive archaeology, and proposes the removal of these and other modern structures. Problems relating to tourist activity are addressed by the construction of three visitor centres at the Khufu Gate, the Sphinx Gate and the Desert Gate; these would be linked by a landscaped tourist ring road which would define the boundary of the site. Each visitor centre would be related to a key attraction of the Plateau and will provide a different experience and the opportunity for the organization of guided tours and the sale to tourists of guidebooks and other goods that are themed and appropriate to that particular feature. The plan follows current practice of locating tourist facilities at a reasonable distance from the main attraction, in order to protect the local environment, which should ensure that the sense of place is protected or possibly in this case recreated. The information is drawn from the original Masterplan prepared by Mabbit (1992), on behalf of The Conservation Practice.

Khufu Gate Centre

Located close to the Great Pyramid of Khufu but away from sensitive areas on the site, this centre will concentrate on the building of the Pyramids, the dynastic connection between the families and on the spiritual dimension of the monuments. It is recommended that the Sun Boat, and possibly the Night Boat, be relocated here as part of the story of the Pharoah's journeys with the Gods across his empire. The Boat Museum where the Sun Boat is currently exhibited is not clearly signposted and coach operators do not encourage visits. Only 10 per cent of tourists visiting the Plateau go to the boat museum and pay the £E10 entrance fee. This represents a significant loss of potential income for the site (Mabbit, 1992). Concerns have also been raised about the environmental conditions in the museum that have caused the exhibit to deteriorate. Both of these issues can be addressed with the planned development of a new centre that will include other facilities such as toilets and car parking away from areas of sensitive archaeology. If current visitor patterns continue this will be the main gateway for the majority of tourists and their first experience of the site.

The Sphinx Gate Centre

This centre would represent the Sphinx and its cults. The current *'son et lumière'* presentation will be integrated to become the core of the Sphinx Centre and the proposed removal of the 'son et lumière' building will leave an open space creating a new sightline which is vital for the appreciation of the Sphinx and Temple buildings. The plan proposes to limit the expansion of Kafret el Gabal and remove the locally owned animals kept in the vicinity.

The Desert Gate Centre

This reception centre will provide the tourist with the story of the discovery of the Pyramids and their treasures. As the name suggests, it would provide an interpretation of the Plateau in its original desert setting. This would be an area designated for tourists to ride camels and horses in the desert, with the Pyramids as a background, avoiding the damage to the Plateau that currently occurs. It is planned to keep any structures in this area below the 95 m contour in order to preserve the sightline to the Pyramids. Parking spaces for both cars and coaches will be provided, shaded by palm trees and lattice halls. Animal-holding areas will be established well away from the cafeteria, restaurant and food facilities. Where permanent shelter is required, it is recommended that tents and awnings are used which are more sympathetic to the setting of the desert.

Within the site

It is anticipated that the requirements of the vast majority of tourists would be fully satisfied by the experience of the major monuments, all of which are within walking distance of the three visitor centres. Pedestrian walkways will allow the more serious visitor to walk through the site at leisure. They will be designed to be negotiable by wheelchairs and the elderly, and built from materials which complement the site, to avoid unnecessary visual pollution. As the archaeology and preservation of the Plateau develops, these routes can be extended. The Masterplan does not favour electric cars or an urban transport system to carry visitors through the site as they would further damage the archaeology and detract from the atmosphere. A continuous bus shuttle service would operate between the three visitor centres, however, using the proposed ring road.

It is intended to clear the Plateau of unsightly new buildings and to provide new offices for the EAO in a courtyard around the existing store buildings. New structures will complement the architectural styles of the plateau and add to the improvement of the site. The recommendation of the Masterplan to provide a tourist ring road around the site (Figure 6.4) would rely in part on existing highways rather than provide totally dedicated tourist roads. The proposed Masterplan tackles the site problems by removing tourist amenities to the new visitor centres, away from areas of sensitive archaeology. Activities on the Plateau itself are restricted and access to the monuments controlled. These changes will necessitate some formalization of the local tourism industry and of the visitor experience itself, which should be improved. The resulting changes will present site managers with new challenges and it will be important to monitor these over time, so that the impact of the Masterplan can be assessed.

Tourism management plans are invariably constrained by the funding and manpower resources that were open to them at the time of definition. After the survey of resources and market forecasts, all further conclusions and planning are based upon these results. In a rapidly changing tourism environment, the data can be redundant even before the management plan has been implemented. Additionally, decision making can only take place using the available data and it may be very expensive or complex to manually integrate all data, so there is an inherent tendency to overlook data that cannot be easily taken into account at the comparison stage. There is an inertia against the updating of information from this comparison stage, and in order for new information to be taken into account, the whole process needs to be rerun. This is costly, and leads to time limits being attached to management directives and the five- and ten-year plans.

A GIS is a computer-based tool that can store, manipulate and analyse spatial data (Aronoff, 1989). Many different types of data are stored (such as locations of roads and areas of fragile archaeology), and can then be analysed to show (for example) the areas of road which are close to areas of fragile archaeology. Although this analysis could be done by hand, it would involve hours of overlaying and redrawing maps. More complex problems could take weeks. The value of a GIS is its ability to compare and reference thousands of different features.

Using a GIS to store and update information would allow the Giza Masterplan to address current problems as well as to monitor the effectiveness of directives. As the road network is being redefined to avoid areas of sensitive archaeology, the GIS could be used as a tool to analyse information about tourist flows and help answer questions such as 'what routes are tourists now following?' and 'has the traffic re-routing been successful?'. Areas that are at risk of becoming degraded can be identified using the GIS and possible solutions modelled, to decide which of several potentials might be the best. The use of technology is not intended to replace the traditional management plan but to enhance its applicability. This is achieved through the ability to integrate more up-to-date information, and monitoring changes on-site; thus introducing a feedback mechanism to enable the plan to adapt across a spatial and/or temporal arena.

In the case of Giza, a GIS could be used to contribute valuable information to the proposed management plan, and also to explore some of the historical aspects of the site, which could be useful for visitor interpretation, as this UNESCO World Heritage Site has a clear boundary and contains important structures that represent the cultural heritage of the Pharaonic era.

Benefits of a GIS for the management of Giza

A GIS could be used at several levels to aid the Giza project. First, it may be employed as a management tool to help analyse data produced by monitoring systems, for example analysis of visitor flows. This would enable site managers to review the management plan, and see whether visitors are utilizing the whole of the site or concentrating on certain areas. Steps could then be taken to implement visitor flow management to encourage a more even distribution across the site. Tourist usage of the new visitor centres could be monitored to establish the popularity of the different themes and facilities on offer. If current trends continue then the Khufu Centre would be the most visited, and analysis of the flows could identify times at which it was at, or exceeded, full capacity.

Second, and perhaps most importantly, the system could be used for decision support. This includes modelling potential developments and supporting changes to the management plan, In this context, it could be used to locate appropriate refreshment stands and litter bins in the most-utilized areas, or to keep them away from more sensitive regions. As more tombs on the site are opened, the system could be used to help monitor visitor numbers, and thereby identify times and places where numbers exceed safe limits and access restrictions should be enforced. This information could be linked back to the visitor centres informing tourists of any likely queues ahead.

The burial regions located around the Pyramids are not properly defined or signposted, and so are walked over. By identifying those areas of the site that are the most sensitive, using the GIS, a series of trails could be described that would avoid these areas, and alert visitors to their presence. This would assist in the future development of the Masterplan as more walkways are proposed. As well as being a control on visitor movements, this information could improve the visitors' experience of the site and provide a greater understanding of the Plateau as a whole, as they could take part in a guided or self-guided tour of a particular area.

Third, it may be used to provide a source of information for promotional activities. This may include map production, generation of statistics and material for site interpretation (which may include multimedia developments), and also with an interface to the Internet where, as well as marketing the Pyramids, information could be provided and bookings taken. Egypt's presence on the World Wide Web (WWW) is presently provided by the IDSC (1996a,b). The current absence of information on-site has contributed to problems such as negative tourism impacts due to a lack of understanding that tourists might have of the site. As a consequence, this impacts upon their potential enjoyment of the visit.

This tertiary level is viable if GIS is already used for monitoring and decision support because it links the technology already in use, and thus changes in information are widely disseminated throughout the networked services. If GIS is not taken up, then its use for promotional activities may seem a little software intensive, and not efficient. A dedicated multimedia system might be better.

Finally, the contribution that a GIS could make to this site as a whole is to support the overall improvement of the visitor experience that the management plan hopes to achieve. This should in turn result in an extended length of stay by tourists and allow the site to command a higher level of entrance fee. If tourists stay for longer, there will be more opportunity for them to spend money on the new services and souvenirs that will be available – contributing to revenue that could be used for conservation.

Data sources

To illustrate these points, some sample data have been collated that might be used as a basis for a Giza GIS. Figure 6.2 is a digital survey of the region, to which other data – such as the roads network, location of refreshment stands and zones of archaeological sensitivity – can then be linked. The idea is to create many 'layers' of information, each of which can then be analysed with respect to any other layer. Recently released Sovinfosputnik (Figure 6.3) data clearly show the burial sites located around the area and could be used as a means of identifying areas of 'sensitive' archaeology. All this information would then be stored in a database (Figure 6.5). Other 'applications' could use this information – for example, a multimedia presentation about the site could be placed at the main tourist centre. Using the data shown in Figure 6.2, the computer could build a

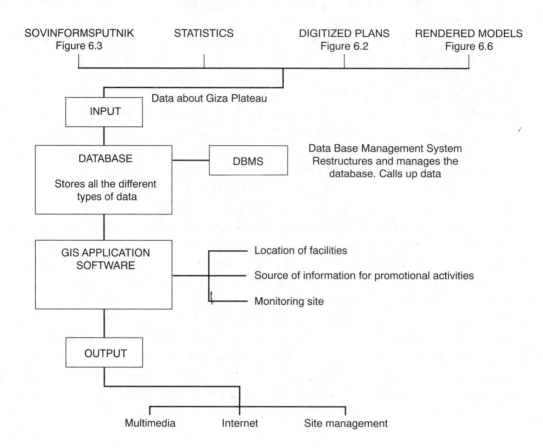

Figure 6.5 Information flow through a GIS

three-dimensional model. Figure 6.6 is a view of the site, generated from Figure 6.2. Working with three-dimensional imagery is one way of modelling what the site would have looked like in different time periods, or as a non-degenerative method of exploring it today, by 'flying' through and around the area.

However, there are some problems inherent with the use of a GIS. There is a temptation to believe that because the output produced by the GIS is of such good quality, the data is of similar standard; when in fact it may be very poor data displayed well. This issue of data quality develops because the database only has the accuracy of the poorest data, since other data may be analysed against this. Thus, a set of data with poor accuracy may propagate errors across the analyses

Figure 6.6 Rendered model of the Giza Plateau from the north-east

performed. One way of mitigating these effects is to attach a metadata file to each set of data. Metadata contains information about how and when the data was collected, and its expected accuracy.

Implementing a GIS changes the way in which management works and relies heavily upon an initial influx of time, money, people, equipment and data. In addition, there are the costs in time and labour of work-procedure redesign, education and training, and the use of specialist personnel, at least, in the short term. Although the initial start-up costs of a GIS system seem to be large in comparison with established manual methods (Figure 6.7), over a longer term it

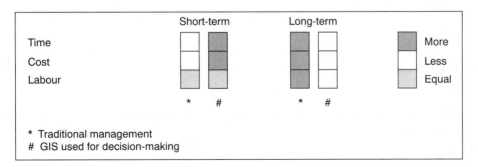

Figure 6.7 Comparisons with other forms of management

carries a number of benefits that traditional systems do not. Perhaps the greatest benefit is the ease by which information can be copied and transferred to other people, for different applications.

Conclusions

In summary, a GIS may allow the undertaking of a complex mapping task at Gizá, and save time and storage space. However, the initial costs may be high, learning the system and data input can be time consuming, and the organizational changes involved can lead to interdepartmental conflicts. Overall, these costs are outweighed by the benefits which include fast data retrieval and the ability to keep maps more up to date, as well as the ease of production of customized maps. The use of GIS is probably quicker than manual methods, but may not be cheaper – at least in the short term.

The integration of IT such as a GIS is not common in visitor management and instead tends to be restricted to scientific area surveys or municipal management. This is possibly due to a lack of understanding of the potentials of IT and where to begin, rather than a lack of understanding of the technology itself. The availability of data for Giza (in contrast to the majority of sites) is perhaps the main reason why this type of system could be successful, although how likely it is to be considered – in the foreseeable future – is unknown. A centralized body such as UNESCO would be the most likely candidate to commit to such a project, but would also require close collaboration from the Egyptian authorities. However, the overriding justification for the integration of IT is that it may help to more efficiently preserve some of the world's most ancient monuments for the benefit of future generations. In this context perhaps we should see benefits in terms of value, rather than cost.

References

Adley, E. (1995) 'Environmental issues in Egypt', Med-Campus Workshop, University of Alexandria, Egypt, 13–15 May 1995

Aronoff, S. (1989) *Geographic Information Systems: A Management Perspective*, Ottawa: WDL Publications

CIA (1994) *Egypt*. [Online] at http://www.odci.gov/cia/publications/nsolo/factbook/eg.htm

Evans, K. (1995) 'Pyramids, mosques and museums – resolving issues of resource management', *Urban Environment and Tourism International Conference*, South Bank University, 11–12 September 1995

Fowler, P. (1996) 'Heritage tourism, tourism heritage – towards a respectful relationship?' In Robinson, Evans and Callaghan (eds), *Tourism and Cultural Change*, Sunderland: BEP Ltd.

IDSC (1996a) *The Pyramids of Giza (Egypt's Tourism Net)*. [Online] at http://www.idsc.gov.eg/

IDSC (1996b) *Egypt's Tourism Statistics*. [Online] at http://www.idsc.gov.eg/tourism/min_sts.htm

Lehner, M. (1991) Computer rebuilds the ancient Sphinx. *National Geographic*, **4**, 179, 32–9

Lehner, M. (1992) *Excavations at Giza, 1988–1991: The Location and Importance of the Pyramid Settlement*. [Online] at http://www-oi.uchicago.edu/OI/PROJ/GIZ/NN_Fall92/NN_Fall92.html

Mabbit, R. (1992) *The Masterplan for the Giza Plateau*, The Conservation Practice/UNESCO

NASA (1995) *SIR-C/X-SAR Image of Giza, with blowup*. [Online] at http://www.jpl.nasa.gov/sircxsar/giza.html

Roberts, D. (1995) Egypt's Old Kingdom. *National Geographic*, **1**, 187, 68–9

Sanders, J. C. and Sanders, P. M. (1994) *Giza Plateau Computer Model*. [Online] at http://www-oi.uchicago.edu/OI/DEPT/COMP/GIZ/MODEL/Giza-Model.html

Sovinformsputnik (1996) *Pyramid.tif*. [Online] at http://www.spin-2.com/download.html

University of Chicago (1998) *Egypt: Archaeological Sites*. [Online] at http://www-oi.uchicago.edu/OI/DEPT/RA/ABZU/ABZU_REGINDX_EGYPT_ARCHSIT.HTML

University of Memphis (1996) *Giza*. [Online] at http://www.memphis.edu/egypt/giza.htm

Zajac, J. (1996) *The Great Pyramid: A Dreamland Report*. [Online] at http://www.europa.com/edge/pyramid.html

7 Hadrian's Wall (UK)

Managing the visitor experience at the Roman frontier

Sophie Turley

It is neither desirable nor possible to attempt to fossilise or homogenise the character of the land which has to earn its keep (Stevens, 1996, p. 3)

Keywords: Hadrian's Wall   multiple use   multiple ownership   visitor experience

Location grid reference: 55°N   2°E

World Heritage List inclusion date: 1987

Summary

In 1996, English Heritage published the *Hadrian's Wall Management Plan* in an attempt to provide a clear objective and vision for the future of the Hadrian's Wall Military Zone – the elaborate northernmost defence frontier of the Roman Empire. At 73 miles (117 km) in length the line of the Wall runs from coast to coast through the urban areas of Newcastle and Carlisle and the open countryside of Northumbria and Cumbria. Multiple use, ownership and responsibility render management of this World Heritage Site a complex task. There exists a network of sites – both paid-entry and free – where visitors can learn about and/or gain access to the Wall and its associated remains. Visits to paid-entry sites have, over the past twenty years, been in decline, with a corresponding increase in visits to free sites creating visitor management challenges. The most spectacular remains of the Wall and its fortification can be found in the central section, which, correspondingly, attracts the most visitors and has suffered most from visitor pressure. A cooperative and sustainable approach to visitor management is necessary for the future protection and enjoyment of the Wall. Visitor experience must thus be carefully managed in order to minimize harmful impacts at free sites, while maximizing enjoyment, understanding and appreciation of the resource through adequate and appropriate access and interpretation.

Introduction

There is no doubt that England's architectural heritage is a resource of great significance in the attraction of domestic and overseas visitors. It is estimated that in 1995, 67 million visits were made to historic properties, with over £200 million generated in revenue (BTA/ETB, 1996). Further, figures for 1995, a bumper year for inbound tourism, suggest that historic properties, over all attraction types, were the main beneficiaries of the 13 per cent increase in overseas visitors (Hanna, 1996). Heritage tourism is experiencing a period of growth, and with over two thousand years of architectural history, the UK has a comparative advantage over other countries.

In the UK there are currently sixteen World Heritage Sites of cultural or natural significance. Hadrian's Wall – the remains of the Roman Empire's north-western frontier – was, together with the city of Bath, one of two sites incorporating Roman remains awarded World Heritage status in 1987. Indeed, the Roman Wall has been described as the most important monument left behind by the Romans during their occupation of Britain, providing direct evidence of Roman military practice and the ways in which this interacted with the terrain and climate of Britain (English Heritage, 1996).

Hadrian's Wall has been attracting recreational visitors for more than four centuries (English Heritage, 1996). However, it is a tourism resource under pressure from visitors and the living and working landscape in which it is situated. The sheer size and complexity of the Roman remains, and its consequent multiple use and multiple ownership, render management of this World Heritage Site a perplexing task. Further, managing visitor experience of such a significant yet potentially under-appreciated site presents some fundamental difficulties.

Hadrian's Wall

The Romans, under the leadership of Claudius, invaded Britain in AD 43. Some thirty years later the Roman governor Agricola led the invasion of Scotland which he failed to conquer. Hadrian's Wall was built between AD 120 and 130 (Birley, 1977) under the orders of Hadrian, who visited Britain in AD 122, during his reign (AD 117–138) as emperor. A permanent and obvious frontier, ten feet thick, and stretching from sea to sea, was to be constructed to demarcate the extent of the Roman

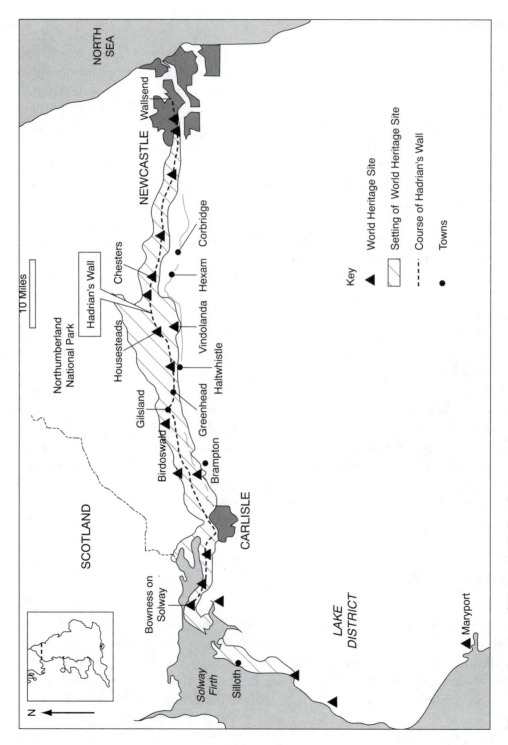

Figure 7.1 Location of Hadrian's Wall and associated remains

territory (Birley, 1976). Hadrian's Wall stretched 80 Roman miles or 73 modern miles (117 km), from Wallsend on the river Tyne at Newcastle to Bowness on the Solway Firth (Figure 7.1). It was built of stone in the west and turf in the east, and, including a six-feet parapet, reached twenty-one feet in height. Today, the Roman Wall is seen to be a symbol of both the power and the failure of the Roman Empire.

The term Hadrian's Wall is deemed very misleading (Turnbull, 1974), as, to the archaeologist, it fails to encapsulate the elaborate nature of this defence frontier which comprises a complex of military and related sites along the wall itself and in its vicinity. Along the length of Wall, castles were constructed every (Roman) mile, with two turrets placed between each pair of milecastles (Figure 7.2). In front of the north-facing wall, where the character of the land necessitated, a ditch was created. Forts were built along the wall, and where possible lay astride it. To the south of the wall a great earthwork, or vallum, stretching the whole length of the frontier, was constructed. The purpose of the vallum was to act as a perimeter fence, defining the rear of this military area (Birley, 1976).

Figure 7.2 Hadrian's Wall and milecastle 39 between Steel Rigg and Housesteads

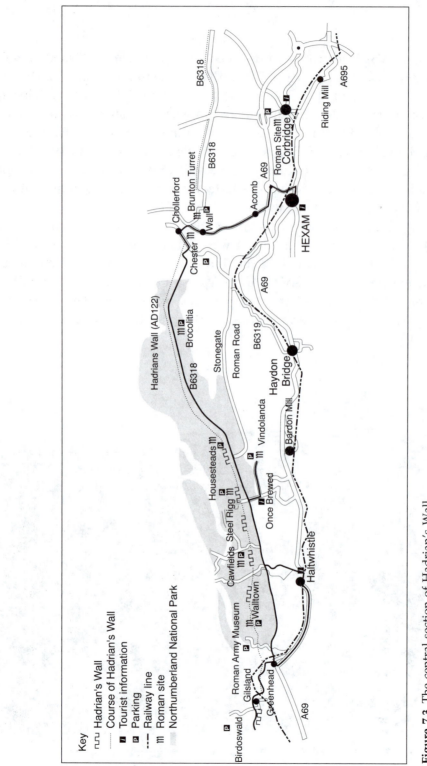

Figure 7.3 The central section of Hadrian's Wall

Behind the wall lay the forts, camps, roads and extensive civilian settlements, which supported the military presence. Indeed, it is the Hadrian's Wall Military Zone which has been recognized by UNESCO as being an historic and cultural phenomenon of international significance. However, the extent of the Military Zone was not mapped, rather it was loosely described (English Heritage, 1996). The *Hadrian's Wall Management Plan* defined new boundaries for the World Heritage Site in an attempt to preserve the material cultural heritage, as well as the physical setting of the remains. The following passage highlights the necessity for such an approach:

> In the central section, much of the Wall's impact derives from its craggy, upland setting. There, it is a combination of ancient remains and rugged terrain which is so evocative – archaeology and landscape blend together to form an harmonious whole. To preserve the Wall's stones themselves would be meaningless if we did not also try to protect their picturesque setting (English Heritage, 1996, p. 1).

At the western end of the wall the remains are less visible. It is the central section of the Military Zone which arguably contains the most impressive archaeological remains, including those excavated forts and settlements on the Wall, (e.g. Chesters, Housesteads and Birdoswald); and those positioned on the Stanegate – the Roman road running westwards to Carlisle (e.g. Vindolanda and Corbridge) (Figure 7.3). The central section, in open country, is also home to the most spectacular remains of the Wall itself, which in some places, survive to a height of ten feet (Breeze, 1989). To the east, in the urban areas of Tyneside, and to a lesser extent in Carlisle to the west, the remains of Hadrian's Wall exist alongside the modern roads, housing, retail and industrial developments of the twentieth century. This setting, of course, is not conducive to preservation nor admiration. The Military Zone is thus subject to multiple use in both urban and rural landscapes. In the central section of the Zone it is the necessary balance of agricultural concerns with conservation and access which must be achieved.

Ownership of the Wall and its setting

As English Heritage (1996) have emphasized, unlike many other World Heritage Sites, Hadrian's Wall and outlying areas do not form a self-contained archaeological zone. The sheer size of such a monument, lying serpent-like across the breadth of the country, in rural and urban landscapes, is problematic. Further, the complex of remains, characteristic of such a heavily defended frontier zone, renders management of the Hadrian's Wall Military Zone an unwieldy task.

Multiple owners, occupiers and bodies with powers and duties relating to the Military Zone exacerbate these physical complications. Hadrian's Wall Military Zone lies in a living and working landscape, which in the central section is dominated by agricultural activity. The site and its setting are owned and occupied by numerous private landowners and bodies including the National Trust, English Heritage and the Vindolanda Trust. Less than ten per cent of the Wall is managed purely for the purpose of conservation (English Heritage, 1996). In addition to landowners and those charged with the protection of the site, a large number of additional bodies and interested parties are 'stakeholders' in the future of Hadrian's Wall. Such bodies include the regional tourist boards of Northumbria and Cumbria, twelve local authorities, and regional offices of the Department of Culture, Media and Sport (formerly National Heritage) and the Department of Agriculture, Fisheries and Food. Further, the Countryside Commission are currently developing the Hadrian's Wall National Trail, a public footpath to run the length of the Wall; English Nature protect numerous Sites of Special Scientific Interest (SSSI) in the Zone; and 27 km of the Wall in the central sector falls within the Northumberland National Park. Interested parties also include representative bodies such as the National Farmers Union, the Country Landowners Association, and the Ramblers Association. This list is not exhaustive, but nevertheless it serves to illustrate the nature of multiple ownership and responsibility which render management of the site involved and complex.

Management and planning initiatives

English Heritage, the agency charged with securing the protection, public understanding and enjoyment of England's built heritage, has taken the lead in planning for the future of Hadrian's Wall. The aim of the *Hadrian's Wall Management Plan* published in 1996 is: 'to provide a clear objective and vision for the future of the World Heritage Site and a means for all those involved to achieve those objectives through consensus and partnership' (English Heritage, 1996, p. 5).

It was the designation of Hadrian's Wall as a World Heritage Site and the increasing emphasis on management plans by UNESCO which provided the impetus for production of the latest management plan (English Heritage, 1996). World Heritage status does not imply additional statutory controls in the UK, and the resulting management plan is not a statutory document. Rather, the plan is a consultative document, seeking to establish an overall vision for the future of the World Heritage Site, while seeking to gain the commitment of those involved in its eventual realization (English Heritage, 1996).

In light of the physical dispersal and consequent multiple ownership and multiple use of this fragile site and its setting, the *Management Plan* revolves around the need to balance four major factors (English Heritage, 1996):

1   Conservation of the archaeological sites and their characteristic landscape
2   The needs of agriculture and the living and working landscape of the Hadrian's Wall corridor
3   Managing public access and the experience of visitors – fostering enjoyment, understanding and appreciation of the site, whilst avoiding further damage to the archaeological remains and their setting, and minimizing conflict with other land uses
4   Maximizing the contribution made by the World Heritage Site to the regional and national economy; within which, of most significance, is the economic contribution of tourism development.

The plan of 1996 is not the first attempt to coordinate action for the future of Hadrian's Wall; rather it is the third in a series of major planning initiatives to take place since the 1970s. In 1976 there was the publication of an advisory report by the Dartington Amenity Research Trust (DART) prepared for the Countryside Commission (DART, 1976), which analysed problems and suggested solutions with regard to a lack of provision of visitor services and corresponding pressure along the Wall corridor. In order to implement the DART report, in 1977 in excess of thirty public and private organizations involved in managing the Wall and its visitors formed the Hadrian's Wall Consultative Committee (HWCC). The HWCC, though without direct powers of its own, prepared a strategy for Hadrian's Wall to guide the work of member organizations, providing a single policy framework (HWCC, 1984).

Though a number of the recommendations of these earlier planning initiatives have been implemented, it has been recognized that the translation of proposals into actions has been minimal (English Heritage, 1996). In learning from such past errors, increasing attention is being paid in the 1996 planning initiative to the coordination of activities proposed in the plan. Indeed, objectives set for 1996–2000 include the establishment of a Hadrian's Wall Management Plan Committee to act as a primary forum for issues concerning the management of the World Heritage Site; and the appointment of a small coordination unit to deliver the objectives of the plan, coordinate action on implementing recommendations, establish communications, and secure the commitment of those who have an interest in seeing the plan succeed.

In addition, there are other independent initiatives, operating within the context of the *Management Plan*, already under way, involving the establishment of new committees and partnerships. The Hadrian's Wall Tourism Partnership (HWTP), at the heart of which lie the tourist boards of Northumbria and Cumbria and their twelve local authority partners, was established in order to encourage more people to visit more of the wall in a sustainable manner (Andrew Duff, Northumbria Tourist Board, in ETB, 1995). The Partnership's vision for tourism in the area hence combines economic development with resource protection. However, in order to achieve these objectives, the visitor experience must be carefully managed – improving and developing the product in line with visitor expectations, while enforcing the environmental message (Northumbria Tourist Board, 1994). The resulting sustainable tourism marketing strategy, 'Hadrian's Wall and the Borderlands', follows the recommendations of a six-month study into the tourism prospects of the Hadrian's Wall corridor, conducted on behalf of the Partnership, chaired by the Northumbria Tourist Board. A project manager has subsequently been appointed to coordinate existing marketing activities and encourage developments in sustainable tourism in the Hadrian's Wall region.

A Trail Development Officer has been appointed by the Countryside Commission to coordinate the development and implementation of the Hadrian's Wall National Trail, due to open to walkers in summer 2001 at a cost of approximately £5.1 million (*Leisure Management*, 1997). The continuous long-distance footpath of approximately 80 miles will run close to, and at times separate from, the line of the wall. The initiative was originally proposed in the DART report of 1976, and was highlighted as a priority in the HWCC strategy document of 1984. Benefits of the initiative are thought to lie in its potential ability to:

- Disperse visitors along the length of the wall, and thus address the issues of congestion at honeypot sites
- Enable people to enjoy the remains on foot, rather than by car
- Provide improved access to, and link, the principal archaeological sites
- Improve interpretation and thus visitor appreciation of the World Heritage Site and its setting
- Secure a greater level of visitor management to the site as a whole while seeking to maximize economic benefit to the local community (Countryside Commission, 1992).

However, the National Trail has met a degree of opposition from farmers and archaeologists (Lean, 1993; Brown, 1995), on the grounds of ease of access leading to over-visiting and conflicts with agricultural concerns, plus the potential damage to archaeological sites and the surrounding landscape.

Visitors to Hadrian's Wall

Hadrian's Wall has been a visitor attraction since the 1700s, and its potential as a major tourism resource was realized earlier this century. It is estimated that at present approximately one and a half million people visit Hadrian's Wall each year (Goodwin, 1996). Within the Hadrian's Wall Military Zone there exists a plethora of sites where the visitor can learn about the Wall and the Roman occupation of Britain, and gain access to the Wall and associated remains. According to English Heritage (1996), these include at least ten forts or settlements which charge for entry, eight associated museums, and at least fourteen locations which are relatively accessible, where entry is free and remains of the Wall and its fortifications are visible.

The central section of the wall, in view of the impressive standard of archaeological remains and the inherently attractive setting of spectacular open countryside, have rendered it the most well known and thus the most heavily visited. Visitor activity is therefore dispersed unequally across the Military Zone. The central section of the Wall falls under the umbrella of the Northumbria Tourist Board, comprising the counties of Tyne & Wear (including the city of Newcastle), Cleveland, Durham and Northumberland. Table 7.1 summarizes visitor statistics for the region and for Northumberland, the county through which the central section of the Wall runs.

There are some 240 visitor attractions in Northumbria, including twenty-one historic properties receiving in excess of 30 000 visits (BTA/ETB, 1996). Visits to historic properties in Northumbria totalled 1.9 million in 1995, representing 3 per cent of visits to properties in England (Hanna, 1996). The Northumbria Tourist Board estimates that overseas visitors account for 12 per cent of all trips to the region and 30 per cent of all overnight stays, with key markets being Scandinavia, the USA, Germany, France and the Netherlands (BTA/ETB, 1995). According to Hanna (1996), overseas visitors accounted for 16 per cent of all visitors to historic properties in Northumbria in 1995; overseas visitor figures for sites with the Hadrian's Wall Military Zone are, as yet, not recorded.

Table 7.1 Visits to Northumbria and Northumberland in 1994 – volume and value

	Trips (million)	Nights (million)	Spending (£ million)	Day visits (million)	Spending (£ million)
Northumbria	3.54	15.00	486	38	312
Northumberland	0.83	3.30	6	–	–

Source: British Tourist Authority/English Tourist Board

The four most visited paid-entry sites, presenting structural remains, along the Hadrian's Wall corridor include (from west to east – Figure 7.3) Vindolanda fort, civilian settlement and museum; Housesteads (*Vercovicivm*) fort and museum; Chesters (*Cilvrnvm*) fort and museum; and Corbridge (*Corstopitvm*) Roman town and museum. All four sites can be found in the central section, and, with the exception of Vindolanda, are managed by English Heritage. Visitor figures for these sites in 1996 can be seen in Table 7.2.

Collective visits to the four main charging sites peaked in 1973, following a dramatic increase in visitors during the period 1965–73, when numbers at Chesters and Housesteads Roman forts increased by 118 per cent and 168 per cent, respectively (HWCC, 1984). However, over the last two decades, visits to the four main attractions along the wall have dropped by over 30 per cent. In 1973 the four main charging sites received 457 000 visitors, in 1996 HWTP reported 518 000 visits, but to eight main sites along the Wall; only 295 000 visits were recorded at the four sites open since 1973, a drop of 162 000 visits. Trends in visits to the four main sites since 1970 are illustrated in Figure 7.4. The peak

Table 7.2 Visitor figures to paid sites in the central section of the Wall 1996

Site	Visitors
Vindolanda	71 385
Housesteads	122 189
Chesters	77 809
Corbridge	23 188

Source: Hadrian's Wall Tourism Partnership

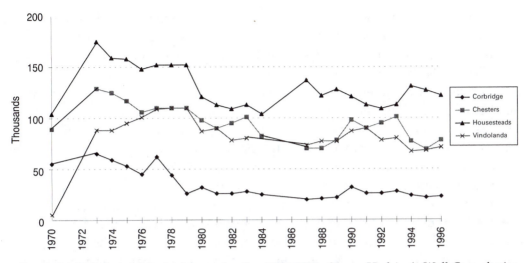

Figure 7.4 Trends in visits to four main sites 1970–1996. *Source:* Hadrian's Wall Consultative Committee, Hadrian's Wall Tourism Partnership

of visits in the early 1970s is evident, coupled with subsequent decline and a stabilization of visits since the early 1980s.

Reasons for this declining profile of visitation to these four sites are thought to be a function of increasing competition from other day-visitor activities and new attractions, including those within the Military Zone, such as the Roman Army Museum on the site of Carvoran Fort, which was opened in 1981 by the Vindolanda Trust and now receives over 54 000 visitors per year.

By contrast, anecdotal evidence suggests that numbers of visits to free sites and the use of public rights of way is increasing (English Heritage, 1996). However, formal figures are currently unavailable and until very recently, with the introduction of a number of stile counters by the Northumberland National Park, visitor figures for free sites have not been collected on a regular basis. Assuming anecdotal evidence is reliable, the situation is a serious one. Paid-entry sites appear currently under-visited, with other sites and stretches of the Wall suffering from excess pressure and a lack of visitor management, while failing to reap the economic benefits which visitors bring.

Managing access

Tourism and visitor access, as exemplified by the cases in this book, represent an opportunity for, yet also threaten, sites of cultural and natural significance. This is exactly the case at Hadrian's Wall. Tourism, and access to the site and its setting, lie at the heart of the *Management Plan* with opportunities to generate wealth for the region and its communities, and resources for conservation and landscape management for the World Heritage Site itself. Further, public access provides an occasion to foster an understanding and appreciation of the site, its setting and its cultural significance. Indeed, the guiding principles for management of the site to the year 2026, as highlighted in the *Management Plan*, emphasize the future significance of tourism as an economic provider, and the importance of the visitor experience in improving awareness and appreciation of the Wall and its associated remains.

However, visitors also prove to be a threat to the future of the site. Tourism has had a number of detrimental impacts in the area which are largely a result of over-visiting. Visitors bring litter and at times park cars insensitively. Indeed, their mere presence can be of annoyance to those living and working in the site and its setting. Inconsiderate visitors deviating from public footpaths and disturbing livestock can, and have, caused conflicts with farmers and landowners.

Disturbance and erosion of the archaeological remains is perhaps the most obvious impact of visitors, including the removal of stones and the erosion of visible and invisible remains. The Wall itself is physically unprotected and walking on the Wall is not prohibited, even at paid-entry sites. Figure 7.5 shows visitors walking on the Wall and on the remains of Housesteads fort. Some argue that walking on the Wall should not be prohibited. Andrew Selkirk, editor of *Current Archaeology*, states (in Brown, 1995) 'You should be able to walk on it, sit on it, get the feel of it, and imagine what it must have been like when it was new'.

Along some stretches, such as that west of Housesteads, the Wall has a turf top. As visitors have chosen to walk on the Wall, rather than on the footpath beside it, the turf has been worn away leaving the dry stone wall exposed to frost, which in places has caused the wall to collapse. Reseeding of the turf has taken place in some sections, (for example, east of Steel Rigg) in an attempt to manage this problem. It is the central section of the Wall and the series of 'honeypot' areas within this that visitor pressure is of most concern. The three-mile section between Housesteads and Steel Rigg is among that most badly affected, and in recent years pressure has been exacerbated by visitors seeking the filming location of a scene from the 1991 Kevin Costner film, *Robin Hood – Prince of Thieves*. Visitor pressure in these most sensitive areas has arguably exceeded the limits of acceptable change, with English Heritage (1996) highlighting the need to assess and manage these limits more effectively in the future. Of major concern is the condition of footpaths; the compaction of soil, reduction of moisture and resultant changing distributions of vegetation. When badly eroded, as illustrated in Figure 7.6,

Figure 7.5 Visitors to Housesteads Roman Fort

footpaths form unsightly scars on the landscape. Footpath maintenance and construction creates a permanent scarring of the landscape but, in encouraging visitors to keep to one path, is arguably less damaging than an ever-widening natural path. There is a fear that the National Trail will create further pressure on sensitive areas. Indeed, the Countryside Commission (1992), anticipate 20 000 visitors walking the length of the Wall annually, and a further 200 000–400 000 day visitors annually walking sections of the proposed trail, with pressure expected to be higher in the central section of the Wall.

The difficulty is thus highlighted. Visitors and public access are a necessity both economically and philanthropically, but managing this access is also a necessity if the Hadrian's Wall Military Zone is to provide visitors with satisfying experiences, and local people with economic benefits in years to come. Indeed, careful visitor management will be fundamental to the development of a symbiotic relationship between tourism and conservation of this fragile resource. What is necessary, as English Heritage (1996) and the HWTP have recognized, is a sustainable approach to tourism, i.e. that which:

Figure 7.6 Footpath erosion west of Housesteads

- Is managed in such a way as to protect the site and its setting from further damage, including managing access to safeguard sensitive locations, spreading visitor load, improving visitor education and raising awareness of the World Heritage status and its significance
- Minimizes conflict with other land users, including informing visitors about the problems caused by visitors to agricultural land
- Brings maximum economic and social benefits to the local communities, the region and nation, through effective marketing and the development of stronger links with local businesses and services.

Managing the visitor experience

The significance of visitors to the future of Hadrian's Wall is highlighted above. Ultimately, it will be the provision of a satisfactory visitor experience of the site and its setting which, in the long run, will facilitate the achievement of both economic and social objectives. The significance of visitor experience is recognized by English Heritage (1996), with enhancement of the quality of visitor experience, and improving visitors' enjoyment of the World Heritage Site stated as short-term objectives. Within the *Management Plan*, the importance of quality facilities; improved exhibitions, displays and provision for education; and the need for a more comprehensive information system along the Wall corridor are emphasized.

There are, it appears, some inherent complications associated with managing visitor experience of this World Heritage Site; most notably the sheer size and complexity of the resource, and the need for effective interpretation if visitors are to understand the site and have any appreciation of its significance.

In order to explore the nature of this visitor experience, the author visited the area as a participant observer. Over a period of three days in the summer of 1996, a series of field visits were made to paid-entry and free sites along and behind the Wall. Visits were restricted to the central, most popular, section – between and including the Roman Army Museum at Walltown, and Corbridge Roman town (Figure 7.3). The experience gained by the author, and reported on here, is thus only that of the rural setting.

The dispersal of sites which comprise the Military Zone is problematic with regard to presenting Hadrian's Wall as a World Heritage Site, as only the most serious and interested of visitors will be likely to make the effort to visit extensively or systematically. The typical visitor will thus fail to gain an appreciation of the extent and magnificence of the Site and its associated remains; rather, visitors will only get a snapshot of one fortification, settlement or stretch of Wall. To the average visitor, even the Wall itself, at times, cannot be easily distinguished from the proliferation of dry stone walls which are characteristic of farmland in upland Britain. The author overheard one American visitor at Housesteads claiming just that: 'Frankly, there are so many other walls around here.'

This statement perhaps is characteristic of a restricted experience of the Wall. Indeed, from Housesteads fort, though much thicker, visibility of Hadrian's Wall is not extensive. A walk either side into open country leads to a much more rewarding experience and greater appreciation of the Wall. It can be said that in visiting paid-entry sites only, the visitor is less likely to gain an appreciation of Hadrian's Wall and its setting than they are from a series of visits to free sites and short walks along public footpaths. Walkers of the proposed National Trail will thus experience the Wall far more effectively than the average visitor. Value for money from visits to paid-entry sites may thus be questioned, given the apparent similarity of the remains (to the average visitor) and the repetition of information obtainable at each. Anecdotal evidence from informal conversations with visitors indicates that visiting paid-entry sites is perceived as costly.

Free sites and public access are fundamental to enhancing visitor appreciation, but clearly there are implications for managing visitors to these sites. It is at free sites such as Cawfields, Walltown and Steel Rigg and along nearby rights of way that the temptation to walk the Wall as a Roman soldier may have done almost 2000 years ago is greatest. Enhancing visitor experience further, with the provision of appropriate interpretation, is also necessary. Among proposals pertaining to visitor experience, outlined by English Heritage (1996), is the sighting of a series of orientation centres, gateway sites and visitor information points. It is thought this network of information provision will educate visitors about sites in the area, methods of transportation, the significance of the World Heritage Site, and appropriate behaviour in view of potential impacts.

Interpretation can encourage those visitors who are to experience relatively little of the site to appreciate its vast size and archaeological value. Indeed, museums are present at all major paid-entry sites in the central section, which set construction of the Wall and its fortifications in its historical context. Roman Britain is a subject about which only a tiny fraction of the population will have any detailed knowledge. To the layperson there is a real danger of Roman remains resembling nothing more than neatly arranged piles of stones. To the archaeologist the stones in themselves are a source of knowledge, but to the average visitor such remains are meaningless without sufficient and effective interpretation. However, it is acknowledged that such interpretation must be sympathetic to the resource so as not to trivialize the cultural significance of the monuments or to create visual pollution.

Interpretation panels are the most common technique employed at sites along the Wall – both free and paid-entry. Generally these comprise an illustration of how the structure would have appeared in its heyday and are accompanied by a relatively brief description of its structure and function. Panels were translated into four languages – German, Italian, French and Japanese, though not in Dutch nor any of the Scandinavian languages, despite the fact such visitors represent 7 and 20 per cent of visitors to the region, respectively. At Vindolanda and Corbridge additional techniques of interpretation are employed. At the latter, panels are utilized and an audio tape and head set is included in the ticket price (though only available in English). This technique proved valuable in conjuring up an image of Roman Britain, combining music and sounds with general information about the Romans and Corbridge town. However, the content of the tape, and thus visitor flow, focuses around the interpretation panels, creating congestion at them. Further, social interaction, thought to be the focus of recreational visits to heritage sites (Silverman and Masberg, 1996), is restricted. At Vindolanda, there exists at the remains of the fort and civilian settlement little if no provision for interpretation. Visitors seem to pass through the excavations and instead head for the reconstructions of a Roman shop, temple and section of Hadrian's Wall. These provide the visitor with a tangible reminder of the past, with audiovisual presentations providing an insight into the Roman way of life.

Though all the main sites presenting remains within the central section have accompanying museums, they vary considerably. At Vindolanda, the ageing feel of the museum seems of secondary importance to the quality of the artefacts on display, and attempts to explain their relevance. The opposite is true at Chesters fort where the museum, which opened in 1903 has, quoting from the official English Heritage guidebook for the Wall, 'been little altered since that time'. It comprises the display of a vast array of finds, largely in the form of stonework, but also smaller artefacts housed in a series of glass cabinets. There is no interpretation of these relics, with the exception of single-line, sometimes single-word, comments. This museum has received positive reviews in recent years (Thomas, 1989; Knowles, 1996). If there is something for the visitor to gain from the experience of this museum it lies in its atmosphere; it is like stepping back in time – almost like a museum for museums. However, a review by *Holiday Which?* (1995, p.190) suggests that the museum at Chesters 'fails to do justice to the finds'. Indeed, visitors seemed to spend only moments in the museum, with lack of holding power likely to be a function of a lack of interpretation. Davis (1989) suggests that archaeological artefacts should be interpreted in ways that provide relevant information about ways of life, and not just about itemized curiosities. Museums at Housesteads, Corbridge and the Roman Army Museum do make this effort, though the latter is ageing. Museums at all sites failed to interpret information for overseas visitors.

There is no shortage of opportunities for informing visitors about the Wall, its construction and its historical and archaeological significance. Ultimately, it is adequate, appropriate and interesting interpretation of the Wall, its fortifications, and its setting which will provide visitors with the understanding and appreciation of the World Heritage Site which is necessary for its future preservation. Education through interpretation will play an important role in influencing the behaviour and thus impact of visitors which, in the long run, will enhance the experience of future visitors to the Roman Wall.

Conclusions

It is the past strengths of Hadrian's Wall as an elaborate and extensive defence frontier which now render management of this World Heritage Site a challenging task. In modern times, the line of Hadrian's Wall runs through urban and rural landscapes of northern England. The future preservation and appreciation of Hadrian's Wall is thus subject to pressure not only from the activities and impacts of visitors but also from its physical situation. The living and working landscape of which Hadrian's Wall is an integral part results in multiple use of the site and its setting, and thus the need to balance the demands of conservation and access, with the needs of landowners and users.

Public access is highlighted in the *Hadrian's Wall Management Plan* as being of fundamental importance to the future of the site. Indeed, despite the potentially negative physical impacts of visitors, Jocelyn Stevens, Chairman of English Heritage comments: 'We're going flat out to expand our numbers' (in Gilling, 1997, p. 15). Visitors not only bring economic benefits to the site, and local communities, but are also necessary if the public at large is to develop an understanding and appreciation for the physical remains and their cultural significance (Herrmann, 1989). Sustainable tourism is vital to the future preservation and appreciation of the Wall and its setting, maximizing economic opportunities and education while minimizing visitor pressure and preserving the resource.

In order to maximize economic benefits, a satisfactory visitor experience must be delivered. The need to improve visitor experience is emphasized in the *Hadrian's Wall Management Plan* and inherent difficulties have been observed by the present author with regard to managing this experience in the most popular central section of the Wall. The sheer size and dispersal of the Wall and associated remains, and the corresponding collection of free and paid-entry sites, make the visitor experience and management of this experience complex. Free sites and access via public rights of way provide visitors with an experience of the Wall which arguably is not equalled through visits only to paid-entry sites; though it is at free sites where most pressure is exerted, visitors can be less effectively managed, and direct economic benefits are not derived. The Hadrian's Wall National Trail will compound some of these difficulties though opportunities to provide meaningful and rewarding experiences of the Wall and its setting are clearly apparent, particularly if plans for a more comprehensive interpretation strategy are implemented. The need for interpretation of Hadrian's Wall and the forts and settlements which comprise the Military Zone is obvious. Remains of this nature are not easily comprehensible without the provision of adequate information in an interesting and appropriate format. The quality of information provision varies throughout the paid-entry sites of the central section, though, in general, there are inadequacies with regard to meeting the needs of overseas visitors.

The future of this World Heritage Site lies in the future cooperation of those owners, users and managers of the site and its setting. A sustainable future will be the result of careful and collaborative visitor management – minimizing impact while maximizing understanding, appreciation, and economic returns. However, in order to manage the future experience of visitors there is a need to explore further the expectations and experience of visitors to the Roman frontier. Moreover, there is a need to collect far more accurate information, on the number of visitors to free sites and the corresponding flow of visitors within the Wall corridor. Ultimately, if the visitor experience fails to meet expectations, visits to paid-entry sites and thus potential financial resources for preservation of this World Heritage Site and its setting may continue to decrease.

Acknowledgements

I am very grateful to Dr Christopher Young, Director of the Hadrian's Wall Co-ordination Unit for the supply of visitor figures and copies of the *Hadrian's Wall Management Plan*. My thanks also to friends and colleagues at the Centre for Tourism and Visitor Management for their research assistance and advice. Funding for fieldwork was provided under Research Enhancement Funding by the Nottingham Trent University.

References

Birley, A. (1976) *Hadrian's Wall – An Illustrated Guide*, London: HMSO

Birley, R. (1977) *Vindolanda – A Roman Frontier Post on Hadrian's Wall*, London: Thames & Hudson

Breeze, D. (1989) *Hadrian's Wall – A Souvenir Guide to the Roman Wall*, London: English Heritage

Brown, E. (1995) 'Outdoors – whose wall is it anyway? A national issue', *Daily Telegraph*, 11 November.

BTA/ETB (1995) *Regional Tourism Facts – Northumbria*, London: BTA/ETB Research Services

BTA/ETB (1996) *Sightseeing in the UK in 1995*, London: BTA/ETB Research Services

Countryside Commission (1992) *The Hadrian's Wall Path Proposed National Trail – Formal Consultation*, Manchester: Countryside Commission

Dartington Amenity Research Trust (DART) (1976) *Hadrian's Wall, A Strategy for Conservation and Visitor Services*, Countryside Commission, CC98

Davis, H. (1989) 'Is an archaeological site important to science or to the public, and is there a difference?' in Uzzell, D. (ed.), *Heritage Interpretation Vol. 1.- the Natural and Built Environment*, London: Belhaven Press

English Heritage (1996) *Hadrian's Wall – World Heritage Site Management Plan*, London: English Heritage

ETB (1995) *Annual Report 1995*, London: ETB

Goodwin, S. (1996) 'Hadrian's Wall repels the new marauders', *The Independent*, 10 July, p.3

Hanna, M. (1996) 'Sightseeing trends in 1995', *Insights*, November, London: BTA/ETB, pp. A91–99

Hadrian's Wall Consultative Committee (HWCC) (1984) *The Strategy for Hadrian's Wall*, Countryside Commission

Herrmann, J. (1989) 'World archaeology – the world's cultural heritage', in Cleere, H. (ed.), *Archaeological Heritage Management in the Modern World*, London: Unwin Hyman, pp. 30–37

Holiday Which? (1995) 'Northumbria', September 1995, pp. 188–191

Knowles, P. (1996) 'Hadrian's astonishing wall', *Today's Seniors – Travel*, on-line at http://novatech.on.ca.80/tstravel/augtrav3.html, 14 January, 1997

Lean, G. (1993) 'War flares over Wall walk – hikers set to go where Picts feared to tread', *Observer*, 1 August

Leisure Management (1997) Hadrian's Wall trail looks likely', **17**(3), p.20

Northumbria Tourist Board (1994) *Hadrian's Wall, Linking People, Linking Places – A Sustainable Tourism Marketing Strategy for Hadrian's Wall/Tyne Valley Corridor*, Summary Report, September

Silverman, L. and Masberg, B. (1996) 'History and more: a study of visitor perspectives on Heritage Sites', in Robinson, M., Evans, N. and Callaghan, P. (eds), *Managing Cultural Resources – Tourism and Culture: Towards the 21st Century Conference Proceedings*, Sunderland: Business Education Publishers/University of Northumbria at Newcastle, pp. 377–88

Stevens, J. (1996) in Goodwin, S., 'Hadrian's Wall repels the new marauders', *The Independent* 10 July, p. 3

Stevens, J. (1997) in Gilling, J., 'Sir Jocelyn Stevens', *Leisure Management – Attractions Management International*, March, pp.13–15

Thomas, D. (1989) *Telling a Different Story? a Study of the Presentation of Selected Historic Sites in the USA, Drawing Comparisons with Examples in Britain*, London: British Travel Education Trust

Turnbull, L. (1974) *The Archaeology of Hadrian's Wall – History Trails Book 1*, Newcastle: Harold Hill

8 Kakadu National Park (Australia)

A site of natural and heritage significance

Chris Ryan

The rock paintings of this region ... represent the world's longest continuing tradition of this art form... It is a record of encyclopaedic magnitude (Chaloupka, 1983, pp. 4–5).

Geese were there in millions, landing, taking off and just paddling around sticking their heads into the water. The din of their squawking was almost deafening (Cole, 1988, p. 257)

Keywords: Kakadu Northern Australia National Park Aboriginal Rock Art Tourism Management

Location grid reference: 14°S   133°E

World Heritage List inclusion date: 1992

Summary

The unique biosystem of Kakadu National Park is currently the subject of intense conservation efforts. It was established as a National Park in the Northern Territory, Australia, in three stages during 1979, 1984 and 1987. This phased introduction of the Kakadu as a National Park was in part due to the controversy which accompanied its inauguration as the interests of conservation, mining, Aboriginal land rights and tourist potential were reconciled. Subsequently, the Park obtained the status of a World Heritage Site for both natural and cultural values, consolidated nomination being accepted by the World Heritage Committee in December 1992.

The Kakadu National Park is an area which represents a cultural heritage in close association with a physical environment. Any cultural management of sites without reference to the physical environment would fail to reflect a culture which has close ties to the land. This case study first outlines the features of each of these components and then seeks to identify some of the specific management actions that have been undertaken to manage the Park and tourism within it. The Kakadu represents an attempt to permit people to retain a traditional lifestyle which has a value system very different from that of conventional Western patterns. The ability of Aborigines to share, learn and, where necessary, rediscover traditional values within a context of environmental conservation is perhaps one of the success stories of the present form of Park management.

Introduction

The Kakadu National Park was established as a National Park in the Northern Territory, Australia, in three stages (Figure 8.1). Stage one occurred in 1979, the second in 1984 and the third in 1987. Subsequently, the Park obtained the status of a World Heritage Site for both natural and cultural values, consolidated nomination being accepted by the World Heritage Committee in December 1992. The phased introduction of the Kakadu as a National Park was in part due to the controversy which accompanied its inauguration as the interests of conservation, mining, Aboriginal land rights and tourist potential were reconciled. This case study first outlines the features of each of these components and then seeks to identify some of the specific management actions that have been undertaken to manage the Park and tourism within it. Additionally, the physical features and climate of the Park are also mentioned, as it is these that give the Park much of its unique biosystem which is the subject of conservation efforts and which forms the basis of the bond between Aboriginal peoples and the land.

The physical environment

The first important physical determinant of the Park's ecosystem is the climate. Temperatures are high around the whole year, with daytime maximum mean temperatures varying within a small band from about 30°C to 37°C. In winter months (July and August), temperatures can fall to below 20°C at night, but are generally above 20°C. Europeans divide the year into two seasons, the dry, which lasts from about April to October, and the wet season from October to March. During this latter season, particularly in January to late February, humidity can be in the high 80s, while at other times of the year relative humidity is less than 40 per cent. The mean annual rainfall in Jabiru is 1460 mm, the great majority of which falls in 3 months.

   The result of such heavy rainfall in short periods is widespread flooding of the riverine floodplains, when vast areas can be covered by several metres of water for three or more months. Yet by the time the next rainy season arrives, the plains will have been baked dry with a parched and cracked soil. Thus, in a well-known tourist area like the Yellow Waters, the car parks, well-defined river valleys and drainage patterns of the dry season will have been swamped by the rising waters. Hence, while in the dry season visitors leave for boat trips from near the car park,

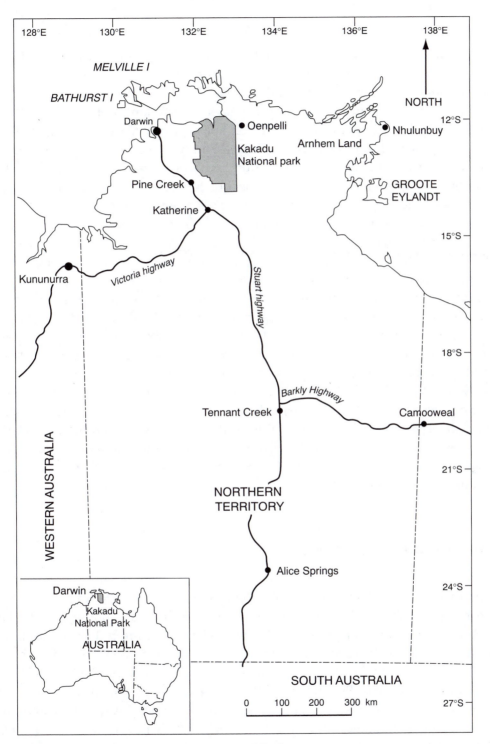

Figure 8.1 The location of Kakadu National Park

in the wet season embarkation occurs from higher ground near the hotel and camping grounds. Therefore each year decisions have to be made as to when dry-season itineraries can be safely undertaken.

However, as Kakadu covers approximately 20 000 km², not all of the Park is characterized by floodplains. The landscape features have a geological record extending over 2000 million years (Russell-Smith, *et al.*, 1995, p. 103). In the east, sandstone escarpments rise several hundred metres above the plain, and form spectacular waterfalls, especially at the Jim Jim Falls. The Park has a complex drainage system with several large rivers and countless numbers of streams and springs. Many of these provide swimming pools for visitors.

However, of more importance is the habitat provided for wildlife. Over one third of Australia's bird species can be found in the Park (approximately 280 in number), and more than 50 different fish, over 120 reptiles and amphibians, over 55 types of mammals, 1500 types of butterflies and moths, 100 species of termites (various CSIRO reports), and 300 species of ants while Brennan (1991) lists 1682 different botanical species. Visitors to the Park are able to see egrets, sea eagles, ibis, heron, cockatoos, kingfishers and storks to mention but a few commonly seen birds. For many visitors the prime focus of a visit is an opportunity to see the saltwater crocodiles. During the dry season, as the channels dry up, the chance of seeing these is very high in areas like the Yellow Waters, but in the wet season they disperse over a wider area. Braithwaite *et al.* (1996) record high correlations between visitor satisfaction with trips on the Yellow Waters and numbers of crocodiles seen. The crocodile is the largest native reptile, but other large animals include feral water buffalo.

Aboriginal settlement

Speculation exists that human habitation of the area may date from over 100 000 years ago. Roberts *et al.* (1990, 1993) note results from optically stimulated luminescence dating of the site at Nauwalabila which imply human occupation of the site between 53 000 and 60 000 years ago. Carbon dating at various sites in the Park show human occupation being established between 20 000 and 25 000 years ago (ANPWS, 1991). Keen (1980) estimated that prior to European settlement the area between the Adelaide and East Alligator Rivers supported about 2000 Aboriginal peoples, but by 1980 the number of people who could claim a traditional connection with that area now covered by the northern part of the Park was approximately eighty. The main cause of population decline was illness contracted from the Europeans against which Aboriginal peoples had no immunity. Additionally inter-Aboriginal conflict, which intensified after the disruption of Aboriginal society that accompanied the arrival of the Europeans, may also have played a role (Levitus, 1982). Today two main groups of Aboriginal peoples exist within and around the Park, these being the Jawoyn people in the south and the Mayali in the north, but boundaries are blurred, and the two groups share many sites of cultural significance. Also, each grouping is further divided into clans, for example the Mirarr Gundjeyhmi of the Jabiru-Mudginberri area. The total number of Aborigines currently living in the Park (1996) is thought to be about 300.

One of the major cultural components of the Park are the rock paintings. Over 5000 separate locations have been recorded, and it is thought that possibly the same number have yet to be itemized. Kakadu is therefore one of the most important collections of rock art in the world. The paintings fill a number of purposes. They are a repository of traditional knowledge, a source of teaching, a manifestation of the spiritual made physical, a link between the Dreamtime and the present by which artists and people could reconfirm the links with ancestors and beyond into a time when spirits walked the earth. Some illustrate everyday life, such as a hunt, others represent the abstract. Today, some are a tourist attraction. A number of researchers have catalogued and categorized the paintings, and Chaloupka suggests a classification of the Pre-Estuarine Period (over 8000 years ago), The Estuarine Period (from 8000 to 1500 years ago), The Freshwater Period (from 1500 to 300 years ago), and lastly the Contact Period from about AD 1600. This distinction is based upon the style of art, pigments being used, and themes being explored. Climatic change can be noted, with animals being represented that are no longer found in the region.

The rock art and the Park's natural features mean that for native peoples Kakadu is a living entity. Kakadu continues to possess a living presence of ancestral forms and powers. Literally, magic places exist, and some are sacred and associated with various taboos. Two particularly important Creator figures associated with the Park are the Rainbow Serpent and Bula. The former is a powerful spirit known through much of Aboriginal Australia, and is associated with deep waterholes where the Snake rested. Bula is a more local figure confined to the Jawoyn country of the southern part of the Park.

The relationship with land creates a cultural bond which is both metaphysical and practical. For example, Aborigines have a detailed understanding of the medicinal value of plants. A list of plants used by the Gundjeyhmi people of central Kakadu for pain relief, as antiseptics, bandages, for the relief of eyesores and other medical needs is provided by Aboriginal Communities of the Northern Territory (1993). Additionally, plants provide the basis for mosquito repellents, fish poisons, glue, sandpaper and snack foods as well as more substantial meals. Dyes are extracted for not only rock painting but also bark painting. While, as noted, Europeans generally describe the climate as having two seasons, Aboriginal peoples of the region discern six. These are the cold weather season (*Wurrgeng*, June and July), hot dry weather (*Gurrung*, August and September), Pre-Monsoon storm season (*Gumumeleng*, October to early December), Monsoon period (*Gudjewg*, January to late March), Knock 'em down storm season (*Bang-Gerreng*, late March to April) and the cooler but still humid season (*Yegge*, May and early June). This relationship or kinship with the land has formed the basis of Aboriginal land claims since 1977, and has resulted in the present management systems outlined below.

Mining

Mining first occurred outside the boundaries of the Park. The Northern Territory, like other places in the world, experienced its gold rush in the nineteenth century. Not only were Europeans seeking their fortune but also large numbers of Chinese and remnants of these old gold camps and mining exist in the area between Pine Creek and the Adelaide River. A second revival of mining interest occurred in the 1930s, and while not particularly profitable, stable communities were established in places like Yimalkba, and Aborigines could also be found living and working in these communities.

The discovery of uranium in the 1950s caused a new phase in mining, and some mines were established at Rum Jungle, but closed in 1964. However, in the 1970s significant uranium deposits were found elsewhere at Ranger, Jabiluka and Koogarra. (Figure 8.2 shows the location of these mineral leases in the north-east of the Park.) It was these discoveries that acted as a catalyst for establishing a framework within which the interests of Aborigines, conservation and mineral exploitation could be encompassed. The essentials of this structure was that title to much of the Park was invested in Aboriginal peoples under the 1976 Aboriginal Land Rights (Northern Territory) Act, while the means of establishing land rights over as yet undesignated areas were also established. However, the township of Jabiru was also established within the Park on a lease held by the Jabiru Town Development Agency on land not granted as Aboriginal land. It was designated as a 'mining town' and initially

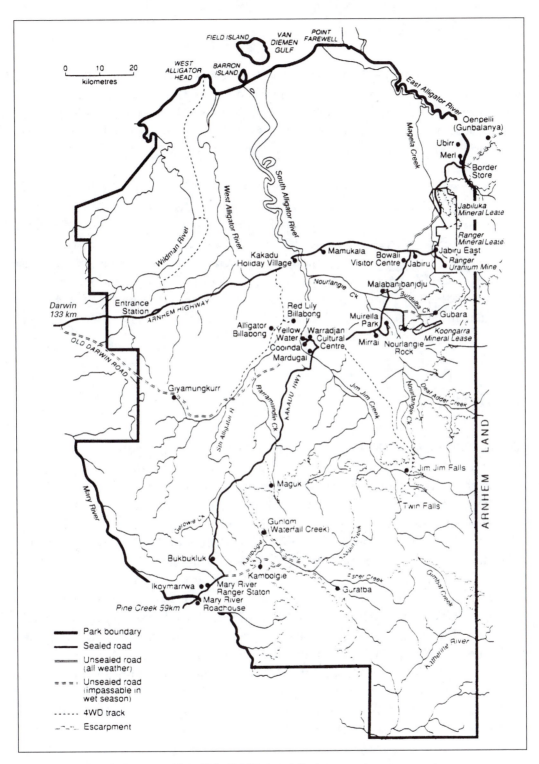

Figure 8.2 Main locations within Kakadu National Park

under the first management plan of the Park tourism development was explicitly denied to the area. However, in the period since the 1980s, subsequent plans have permitted tourism and the town includes major hotel and camping ground accommodation that services the Park. Additionally commercial services have developed which serve other communities in Arnhem Land east of the Park's boundaries.

This arrangement sprang from the conclusions reached by Justice Fox who was appointed Commissioner heading an inquiry into the region in 1976. A major conclusion reached by the inquiry was the need to establish a National Park, but one over which Aboriginal peoples had ownership. Consequently this happened, and in 1978 an agreement was established whereby the Aboriginal peoples lease the Park to the Director of National Parks and Wildlife. The lease has subsequently been amended, and indeed is subject to continuous monitoring, but the primary management system has been retained. This is described below after the impact of tourism is briefly outlined.

Tourism

The establishment of Kakadu as a National Park and the subsequent applications for World Heritage Park status brought the Park to the attention of more people than ever before. The number of visitors to the Park for the period 1982 to 1993 is shown in Table 8.1. The slight decline in numbers in the latter part of the period considered relates to pricing and access policies. Knapman and Stoeckl (1994, p. 605) found that demand for recreation at Kakadu was 'highly price-inelastic in the relevant price range and for small price increases. Indeed, entry fees have to rise to almost A$100 before demand becomes elastic.' However, the findings are subject to a caveat as to the type of visitors to National Parks. These 'tend to be better paid, better educated and more likely to be employed in white-collar jobs than the 'average' Australian' (Knapman and Stoeckl, 1994, p. 607). The imposition of charges has had some impact on repeat visits by local people, and this partly explains the figures. None the less, the conclusion that increased charges increase revenue has been generally sustained, while the charge also partly mitigates against one-day visits from Darwin, which type of visit some local operators feel is detrimental to the environment. The average length of stay to Kakadu is generally about 3 to 4 days – the one-day trips are often by light plane from Darwin. In 1996 a special

Table 8.1 Visitors to Kakadu National Park

Year	Numbers of visitors to Kakadu (000s)
1982	45.8
1983	57.8
1984	75.2
1985	101.6
1986	131.0
1987	195.0
1988	220.0
1989	230.0
1990	238.0
1991	210.0
1992	205.0
1993	220.0

Source: Australia National Conservation Agency

'Territorean pass' was introduced where, for A$60, residents of the Northern Territory are able to purchase a ticket permitting entry to the Park for as many times as they wish within a 12-month period.

A major destination within the Kakadu is the Yellow Waters region. Here the core product is a wildlife experience, the opportunity to go bird watching and a scenic boat trip. Although it varies over the year, approximately 75 per cent of visitors to the Kakadu visit the Yellow Waters. In a detailed study of tourist satisfaction with the actual boat trip, Brathwaite *et al.* (1996, p. 211) identified four major factors which influenced satisfaction. These were:

- Biodiversity (measured by the number and importance rating of species able to be seen)
- Climatic comfort (measured by a Relative Stress Index), which could be adversely affected by high humidity
- Vastness – the sense of enormity and spaciousness derived from being with a few people in a large open wilderness region. This was found to be especially prevalent during the wet season
- Personal space – defined as being the number of other people in the boat, and the number of boats on the water.

This list indicates not only the sources of satisfaction but also dissatisfaction. High humidity, the intrusion of noise from other people and boats, a scarcity of animals and birds and, at the height of the dry season, more obstructed views in the channels would create less satisfactory visits, especially if visitor expectations are high. For example, tourists who had viewed the 'jumping' crocodiles on the Adelaide River could be disappointed if few crocodiles were spotted on their boat trip. At certain times of the year it is quite possible that few birds and animals might be seen, and another factor is that much of the wildlife in the area is nocturnal.

This list of potential sources of satisfaction/dissatisfaction also implies a number of management issues. While visitors would ideally like smaller boats, this in turn means a higher number of boats on the river with potentially more disruptive effects. These issues are examined in more detail below.

Aboriginal involvement in tourism is significant, although not always direct. First, the Gagudju Association, which is Aboriginal, owns the most famous hotel in the area, the Gagudju Crocodile Hotel in Jabiru, which is built in the shape of a crocodile. The association also owns the Yellow Water boat tours referred to above and the Gagudju Lodge Cooinda Hotel-Motel plus camping grounds. The association also manages on behalf of its members about ten settlements and outstations where its members live. There are three main Aboriginal associations in the Park. The second, the Djabulukgu Association, owns and operates the Marrawuddi Gallery at the Bowali Visitor Centre and the East Alligator River Cruise. The third is the Jawoyn Association, who also have commercial interests. Thus, the Aborigines obtain economic benefits from tourism, but much of the money is ploughed back into the sustaining of the Park and the traditional lifestyle. However, educational programmes are also carried out, and today about 40 per cent of the seventy-five officers of the Australian National Conservation Agency's staff working at Kakadu are Aboriginal people.

Management

The management structure

The Park is administered by a Board of Management which was established in 1989. The personnel who comprise the board are ten Aboriginal nominees of the traditional owners, and four others, who are the Director of National Parks and Wildlife, the regional Australian Nature Conservation Agency (ANCA) executive, an ecologist, and someone with tourism expertise. The Board has a responsibility for overall planning for the Park, and four five years plans have been created in 1981, 1986, 1991 and 1997. This last plan was delayed because of the high number of submissions made about the plan. Two other factors complicate the issue. The first is that the 1997 plan seeks to increasingly place at the forefront of management the fact that the Park is Aboriginally owned, and that tourists are visiting not only a natural heritage site but one of cultural importance. From one perspective this is little more than an evolutionary process commenced at the outset of the first five-year plan, but in 1997 and in the political atmosphere created by the Howard Government's policies which seek to emasculate the Wik Decision, which recognized Aborginal land rights over land held subjected to pastoral leases, such policies unfortunately are perceived as being 'political'. Second, mining interests are seeking to develop the Ranger uranium mine – a wish which is attracting opposition from conservation groups and, in early 1997, a mixed and confused reaction from Aboriginal representatives.

The day-to-day management of the Park is undertaken by officers who are employees of the Commonwealth's ANCA, and, as already noted, a significant proportion of these are drawn from the traditional owners. They are supported by a considerable research effort which covers the physical and cultural components of the land and the impacts of increasing visitor numbers. The Plans are comprehensive, and among issues considered are roads, the establishment and maintenance of out-stations (which, as noted, are the basis of Aboriginal settlements) as well as the location and design of information centres, licence arrangements for local tour operators, maintenance work on channels subject to erosion effects, research into insects, mammals, birds and flora and rock paintings. All research has to obtain an express permission of the Aboriginal people, can only proceed after consultation, and only within the terms of a permit.

Tourism management issues

A number of management issues arising from tourism can be identified. Among these are the following.

The location of tourist accommodation and capacity of accommodation

It has been noted that Jabiru was originally deemed to be a mining town, and initially tourism development was curtailed, partly because it existed separately from the Park under a different leasing arrangement as described above. However, as it has grown and established an infrastructure of shops, garages, etc. it was pertinent to concentrate much of the accommodation there on. It permits a control of tourist routes, and is consistent with a zoning policy that basically has four areas (as shown in Figure 8.3). These are (1) where built accommodation is permitted, (2) where camping is permitted, (3) where entry is allowed, but no overnight stays, and (4) no tourist entry is permitted at all. These last areas are open only to officers of the ANCA, permission may be required from traditional owners, or at least consultation, and the reasons for such controls are environmental, cultural and the safety of visitors.

As noted, the use of pricing mechanisms for entry to the Park is limited because of inelastic price demand. Whether the same is true for the length of stay in the Park may be more debatable. It can be hypothesized that visitors are comparatively price inelastic in the sense that high total prices may need to be charged before elasticity exceeds one, and visitor numbers are adversely affected, but within the total budget, visitors will trade off expenditure with length of stay. Hence, the measure of elasticity is not a price/number of visitors relationship but one of price/number of days stayed. From a conservation perspective a relationship of sustaining revenue combined with shorter visits might appear attractive, but certain impacts would still occur. Impact due to car trips would remain the same in that the number of trips remain a constant, while accommodation maintenance still continues even if occupancy levels fall. Thus, say, a 15 per cent decline in visitor days does not translate into a 15 per cent decline in impacts. Additionally, it is questionable whether revenue would remain a constant. Although expenditure on accommodation might do so, the revenue gained in retail sales which include souvenirs (which notably feature the work of Aboriginal artists) would probably decline as visitors would concentrate upon core activities.

Erosion effects

Cullen and Taylor (1988), in their study of the Yellow Waters, used a threefold categorization of erosion effects. This was:

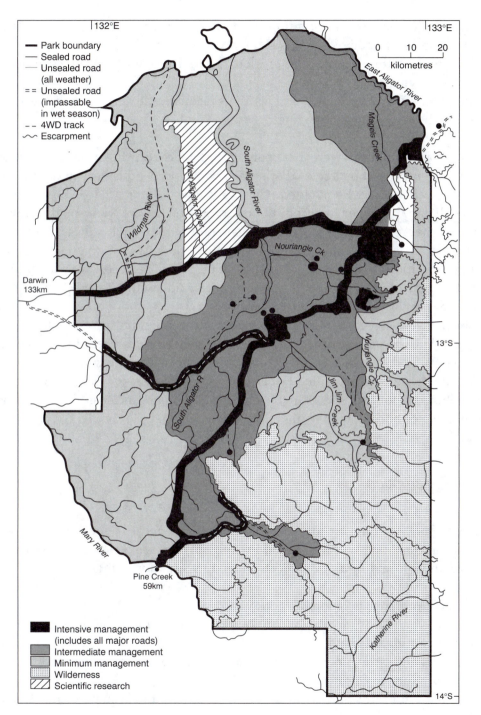

Figure 8.3 Management zones within the Park

1 Cliffing – severe erosion leading to the development of escarpments of up to 60 cm in height above a debris slope down to water level
2 Tree undercutting – moderate erosion, where the soil around trees is washed away, leaving exposed roots
3 Pugging – slight erosion, which is the systematic turning over of the topsoil through trampling and grazing.

Their recommendations were that boats should not exceed 10 km/h, which should be strictly enforced, boats should approach banks perpendicularly and cruising in shallow areas should be avoided. Generally it was found that if boats did not exceed 10 km/h at over 5 m from the bank, erosion effects were small. While the boats of the Yellow Waters operation generally comply with these regulations, visitors report several small craft ignoring the guidelines. Visitors become aware of the regulations because of comments made by guides. However, it should be noted that the guidelines emerged from studies made with a 14 m boat, and larger boats are now being introduced to the rivers.

Given that the area is subject to flooding, the question arises as to whether negative impacts are enduring. Evidence collected by researchers like Braithwaite *et al.* (1996) and Cullen and Taylor (1988) indicate that undercutting consistently exposed tree roots in areas like Fisherman's Alley. However, not all problems can be attributed to tourism. For example, damage in the same area has also been caused by feral water buffalo as they trample soil when coming to the river to drink.

Wildlife disruption

The general literature on tourism-wildlife impacts records several examples of adverse affects upon wildlife caused by tourism (e.g. see Shackley, 1996). Disruption of animals and birds can be categorized as situations where:

• Human presence is ignored
• Animals and birds move away but quickly regroup in the original location and assume original behaviour
• Animals and birds move away, resume original behaviour in new location, and slowly return to original location
• Animals and birds stay away from original area, but resume original behaviour

- Animals and birds move away from original area, seek to assume original behaviour, but some adaptation to the new area occurs because it is not so optimal as the original location
- Animals and birds move away, and significant changes to hunting and breeding occurs due to factors like increased competition between species in the new area due to over-crowding, or the new area is significantly less optimal to support the species.

Braithwaite *et al.* (1996) studied the effects of tourist boat trips on 196 biological entities or species observed over one year in the Yellow Waters. The category 'highly disturbed' was used when birds left an area during the presence of the boat. Thus, species like Sulphur-crested Cockatoos, Red-winged parrots, Bar-shouldered doves and Shining Flycatchers were highly disturbed. However, because the researchers were located on the boats, regrouping behaviour could not be observed. None the less, the research does indicate warnings about what may occur if the frequency of boat trips is increased.

Cultural site management

The Management Plans call for the systematic recording of all rock art sites and the interpretation of Aboriginal prehistory and rock art for visitors in full consultation with the traditional owners. Like similar sites elsewhere in Australia, the rockfaces are subject to damage from a number of natural causes, which include water washing over the area, birds and wasps nesting on the sites, the growth of vegetation and lichen, dust, dirt and faeces from animals, termite nests, and also pollution and impacts due to human intervention. Therefore the sites are protected in many ways, including the use of silicone driplines to divert water from the art, the removal of encroaching vegetation and nests, etc. A continuing project is research into the nature of the pigments used and assessments of whether restoration is desirable and feasible.

Since one of the major purposes of the Park is the explanation of Aboriginal culture, it is possible for visitors to see some rock art *in situ*. Most visitors obtain their initial information about Aboriginal culture from a visit to the Bowali Visitor Information at Park Headquarters. In 1995 the Warradjan Aboriginal Cultural Centre was opened near Cooinda. Here the traditional owners present their culture in a form which is acceptable to them. A visitor guide is produced and over 100 activities per week exist. Guided walks and talks are a popular feature of the programme. Guides and educational packs are produced for different client groups, including schools and tour operators. Additionally, private sector business enterprises exist in the Park and about 175 companies are licensed to undertake some form of commercial activity in the Kakadu. However, visits to rock art sites are controlled through guided walks, the building of observation platforms and wooden walkways.

A register of sacred sites is also maintained by the Park staff, but generally these are not made known to the public. If there is a risk of sites being visited two subsequent phases in the management plan may become operational. First, boundaries may be defined and access denied under the 1975 National Parks and Wildlife Conservation Act. Second, if there are very high risks of visitation which may include a danger of vandalism, a site will be formally described and signposted on the premise that care is more likely to occur under the public gaze. Such a step would only be taken after the fullest consultation with the Aboriginal people concerned.

Fire management

As the majority of visits to the Kakadu take place in the cool season from May to July, many comment on the amount of burning that takes place. Their concern arises in part from the damage done by forest fires out of control in Southern Australia, but the tropical savanna fires are generally of much lower intensity. Burning has been long used by Aborigines, while careful burning can actually constrain the damage that can be caused by out-of-control camp fires that are lit by visitors. From a conservation view the different habitats caused by burnt and unburnt areas help to sustain a diversity of flora and fauna.

Within Aboriginal culture fire was used as a means of managing food resources. Burning grasses encouraged regrowth, and thus fresh green shoots. While these might have directly provided foodstuffs for human consumption, a major reason was that it provided food for target animals who foraged on the growth. Such animals, like kangaroos and wallabies, could then be more easily hunted. Russell-Smith (1994) provides a review of changing fire management policies in the Park in the period since 1980 as attempts have been made to emulate older practices. The historical evidence implies that burning was widespread, and today as much as a third of the Park's land area may be burnt through natural causes and controlled burning. The subject is under continued monitoring, and in the early 1990s the regime changed to more early dry season burning as evidence suggested that monsoon rainforest and cypress pine communities were being adversely affected by late dry-season burns.

Conclusions

The Kakadu National Park is an area which represents a cultural heritage in close association with a physical environment. Any cultural management of sites without reference to the physical environment would fail to reflect a culture which has close ties to the land. Smith (1996, p. 287) has argued that the tourism of indigenous peoples has four interrelated elements, 'which are, the geographic setting (habitat), the ethnographic traditions (heritage), the effects of acculturation (history) and the marketable handicrafts'. The Kakadu represents such a case. It also represents an attempt to permit people to retain a traditional lifestyle which has a value system very different from that of conventional Western patterns. While the Park has created job opportunities for Aboriginal people, either as wardens or as artists, the Western concept of individual employment is not consistent with the social fabric of Aboriginal communities able to sustain themselves directly from the land in a cooperative manner. The ability of Aborigines to share, learn and, where necessary, rediscover traditional values within a context of environmental conservation is perhaps one of the success stories of the present form of Park management.

References

Aboriginal Communities of the Northern Territory (1993) *Traditional Aboriginal Medicines in the Northern Territory*, Darwin: Conservation Commission of the Northern Territory of Australia

ANPWS (1991) *Kakadu National Park Plan of Management*, Canberra: Australian National Parks and Wildlife Service

Braithwaite, D., Reynolds, P. and Pongracz, G. (1996) *Wildlife Tourism at Yellow Waters, Darwin*, Australia: CSIRO and Northern Territory University

Brennan, K. (1991) *Checklist of Vascular Plants of the Alligator Rivers Region, Northern Territory*, Supervising Scientist for the Alligator Rivers Region, Open File record no. 2, Jabiru

Chaloupka, G. (1983) 'Kakadu rock art: its cultural, historic and prehistoric significance', in Gillespie, D. (ed.), *The Rock Art Sites of Kakadu National Park: Some Preliminary*

Research Findings for their Conservation and Management, ANPWS Special Publication No 10, Canberra, 1–33

Cole, T. (1988) *Hell, West and Crooked*, Sydney: Collins

Cullen, P. and Taylor, G. (1988) Report on Bank Erosion: Yellow Waters Billabong, Kakadu National Park, Unpublished Report to Australian National Parks and Wildlife Service, Canberra

Keen, I. (1980) The Alligator Rivers Stage II Land Claim, Unpublished Report to the Northern Land Council, Darwin

Knapman, B., and Stoeckl, N. (1994) 'Recreation user fees: an empirical investigation', in Cheyne, J. and Ryan, C. (eds), *Proceedings of Tourism Down Under – a tourism research conference*, 6–9 December, Massey University, 601–11

Levitus, R. (1982) *Everybody Bin All Day Work*, A report to ANPWS on the Social History of the Alligator Rivers Region of the Northern Territory 1869–1973, Australian Institute of Aboriginal Studies, Canberra

Roberts, R. G., Jones, R. and Smith, M. A. (1990) 'Early dating at Malakunanja II, a reply to Bowlder', *Australian Archaeology*, **31**, 94–7

Roberts, R. G., Jones, R. and Smith, M. A. (1993) 'Optical dating at Deaf Adder Gorge, Northern Territory, indicates human occupation between 53,000 and 60 000 years ago', *Australian Archaeology*, **37**, 58–9

Russell-Smith, J. (1994) 'Fire management in Kakadu National Park: an overview, in McDonald, K. R. and Batt, D. (eds), *Workshop Proceedings on Fire Management on Conservation Reserves in Tropical Australia*, Queensland Department Environment and Heritage, Brisbane, 89–94

Russell-Smith, J., Needham, S., and Brock, J. (1995) 'The physical environment' in Press, T., Lea, D., Webb, A and Graham, A. (eds), *Kakadu, Natural and Cultural Heritage and Management*, Darwin, Australian Nature Conservation Agency, North Australia Research Unit, The Australian National University

Shackley, M. (1996) *Wildlife Tourism*, London: International Thompson Business Press

Smith, V. (1996) 'Indigenous tourism: the four Hs', in Butler, R. and Hinch, T. (eds), *Tourism and Indigenous Peoples*, London: International Thomson Press, pp.283–307

9 Lalibela (Ethiopia)

A religious town in rock

Sheena Carlisle

Very well hewn churches excavated from the rock, the likes of which cannot be found anywhere else in the world....I weary of writing more about these buildings because it seems to me that I shall not be believed if I write more (Francis Alvarez, Member of the Portuguese Mission and the first European to visit Lalibela between 1521 and 1525)

Keywords: historic route   Lalibela   Ethiopia   rock-hewn churches

Location grid reference: 12°39N'   39°2'E

World Heritage List inclusion date: 1978

Summary

The town of Lalibela with its eleven ancient rock-hewn churches in the Northern Highlands of Ethiopia is largely unknown to Western Europe. Visitor numbers have only recently increased, owing to a renewed development of tourism in Ethiopia following years of civil war. As a major tourist destination on the Northern Historic Route it is struggling to absorb this new influx of visitors. The neglected church buildings and their surroundings are now under increasing pressure with urgent need for comprehensive restoration and an EC-funded preservation project is now at the research stage. The religious and community life of Lalibela is equally vulnerable: the churches form an important centre within the Ethiopian Orthodox Church where daily devotional worship and study continues much as it has done for many centuries.

Visitor management and tourism policy require urgent attention in order to enhance the quality of the tourist experience, protect the churches' structure, contents and function and bring real benefits to the local community.

Introduction

Lalibela

Since the end of the civil war in 1991, Ethiopia's new government has been keen to promote tourism as a means of increasing economic diversity, foreign exchange earnings and employment, and diversify the market towards new investments and developments. Ethiopian tourism is primarily culture and heritage driven with Lalibela as one of the most popular destinations on the Historic Route combining the six significant political and religious towns (Axum, Lalibela, Gondar, Bahar Dar, Addis Ababa and Harar), which over the centuries have had a direct influence in the development, culture, traditions and politics of Ethiopia (Figure 9.1).

Lalibela and its rock-hewn churches can be described as a living museum where deeply traditional forms of Christian faith have continued uninterrupted for centuries. Vitally, this is a living site where sensitivity to the host community is required. The churches are in daily use for prayer, liturgy and study, all of which tourists are permitted to witness.

The World Heritage Site of Lalibela consists of eleven rock-hewn churches which are divided into three groups (Figure 9.2). The first group consists of six churches which lie one behind the other north of the river Jordan. This group includes The Selassie Chapel or Chapel of Trinity and the Tomb of Adam. The second group of four churches and sanctuaries lie south of the river. The third group consists of only one church, Bet Giorgis, which is in the symmetrical shape of a cross. It lies away from the first and second group towards the south-west of the town on a sloping rock terrace. To see the roofs and layout of all three groups one has to stand either on the surrounding trenches or high up on a hill. Otherwise, the churches are invisible as they sink into the undulating landscape. All the churches are linked by a maze of subterranean tunnels and alleys which enter into the trench where the church stands (Figure 9.2).

There are three basic types of rock church found in Ethiopia: first, *built-up cave churches*, which are built inside a natural cave; second, *rock-hewn churches* are cut inwards from a steep cliff face, sometimes using and widening an existing natural cave; third, *rock-hewn monolithic churches* which imitate a built-up structure cut in one piece from the rock and separated from it all around by a trench. The World Heritage Site is only a small niche of rock-hewn churches and there are hundreds throughout the Tigrayan region whose history and archaeology are still being documented. However, Lalibela is unique in its layout, number of churches and style.

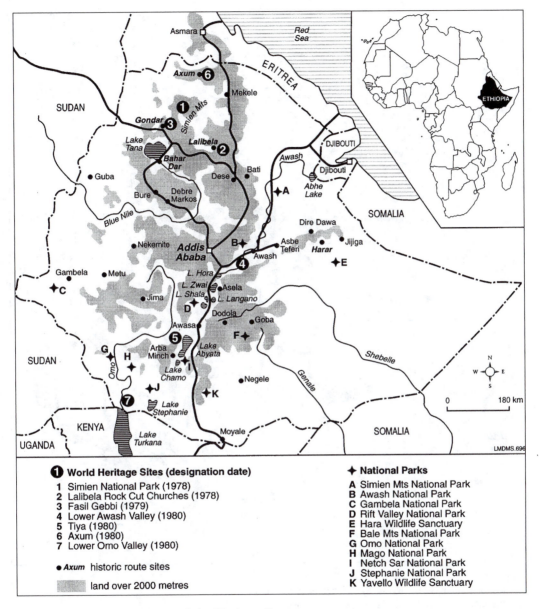

Figure 9.1 Map of Ethiopia and the Heritage Route

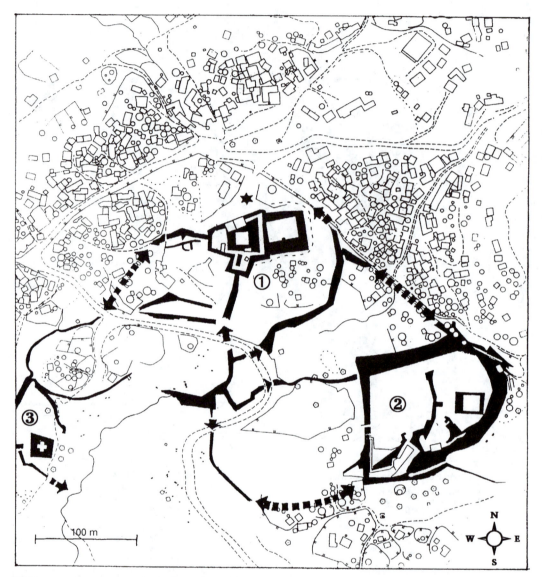

Key
1 Medhane Alem, Mariam, Maskal, Debre Sina-Golghota
2 Emanuel, Abba Libanos, Merkurios, Gabriel-Rufael
3 Beta Ghiorgis

Figure 9.2 Plan of Lalibela and the church area. Black areas are deep trenches between all churches. The broken lines with arrows indicate possible original connections which are now covered by soil. The boundary of the church and historic area is not defined. The present main entrance to the church area is indicated by a star. *Source:* Finnida, 1995

Church groups

First group of six
Bet Medhane Alem (House of the Redeemer of the World)
Bet Maryam (The House of Mary)
Bet Maskal (The House of the Cross)
Bet Danaghel (The House of the Virgins or Martyrs)
Bet Debre Sina (The House of Mount Sinai)
Bet Golota (The House of Golgotha)

Second group of four
Bet Emanuel (The House of Emanuel)
Bet Mercurios (The House of Mercurios)
Bet Abba Libanos (The House of Abba Libanos)
Bet Gabriel-Rufa'el (The House of Gabrile and Raphael or the House of the Archangels)

Third group of one
Bet Giorgis (The House of George)

Location

Lalibela is situated within the rural Bugna Woreda District in the Northern Wollo Administrative Zone of Ethiopia. (Figure 9.1). By road Lalibela is 650 km from Addis Ababa via Dessie and lies on a high plateau at an altitude of 2600–2800 m. The Bugna Woreda consists of thirty-two rural *kebeles* (local administration units) and two urban *kebeles* in the market town of Lalibela. The population of Lalibela is approximately 10 000 (Van ter Beek, 1995), a dramatic increase since the 1960s when Lalibela was a small farming village of traditional round *Lasta*-style houses, with a population of about 1000. This change is due to a variety of factors including tourism but is also related to population movements associated with the civil war, drought and famine. Subsistence farming predominates throughout the area although many citizens still rely on food relief supplies. For nearly 200 years there has been a food deficit in the Northern Wollo Region due to too much or too little rain, frosts, soil erosion, human and cattle disease, civil war and over population. The market is often poorly stocked and variety of food stuff is limited.

History of Lalibela

Fattovich (1990) suggests that in pre-Christian times trade contacts between the lowlands along the northern Ethiopian-Sudanese border and South Arabia occurred in the late third early second millennia BC. It was during this pre-Christian period that Ethiopia had strong connections with the Sabean Culture of Saudi Arabia and North Africa. There was a monopoly on the incense trade between the southern Arabian states and the Ethiopian Axumite Kingdom. Bidder (1958) notes how at this time they assisted each other in the face of aggression and commercial competition from Romans, Greeks and Persians.

The transition from an ancient form of religion to Christianity originated in AD 328. The advent of the official religion came about through considerable political upheaval. 'Though the Ethiopian Church began in an ascetic way and was dependent on the Mother Church of the Copts in Alexandria, it became world famous at the time of the Crusades and a refuge to many Christians of Arabia, of the Orient and Egypt who were fleeing from Islam' (Bidder, 1958, p. 10). A Christian Kingdom was born and it continued the unbroken line of Solomonic Rulers. This is recognized by Gilkes:

> The centre of the Church's spiritual control over the imperial power is in the coronation ceremony. The ceremony is a religious and liturgical one that can be carried out only by the Abuna. It is the sanctification of the individual as a descendent of the dynasty of Menelik Ist, eldest son of King Solomon by the Queen of Sheba, and thus of the royal lines of Israel and the House of David. Above all it is the investment of the Emperor with a religious aura (Gilkes, 1975, p. 53).

The close communication between Ethiopia, the Holy Land and the Egyptian Empire is evident in the skilled design and workmanship of the churches. It is also reputed to symbolize the Holy City of Jerusalem in its orientation and religious significance. Simultaneously, a marked influence is evident in the style of craftsmanship from the Ethiopian Axumite Empire (2000 BC to AD 1000) especially in the decoration of the windows, the banding on external stone features and the wooden beams within the churches.

There is no known written documentation relating to the origin of the World Heritage Site which to an extent is shrouded in myth and legend. However, the churches are generally believed to date from the Zagwe Dynasty (AD 1150–1270), during the reign of King Lalibela, whose name means 'He who commands the bees'. The Zagwe kings had their capital at Adafa just outside Lalibela, then the centre of religious and political life in the Kingdom of Abyssinia. It is not known when King Lalibela ruled, although there is proof that he ruled for forty years. According to Tamrat;

> the references to King Lalibela in the history of the patriarchs belong to AD 1205 and 1210 and contain no mention of the rock churches. It is likely that they were not built as yet. Tradition has it took twenty-four years....' (Tamrat, 1972, p. 59).

Many of King Lalibela's courtiers were drawn from the same district and held high ecclesiastical and administrative positions and it is asserted that during his reign he commissioned the construction of the Lalibela churches.

Uncertainty over the exact dating of the churches presents an intriguing question that can only be answered through archaeological and geological research and detailed analysis of the different paintings, relics and antiquities inside the churches.

The Ethiopian Orthodox Church (EOC) in Lalibela

The EOC owns the church site in Lalibela. However, the precise boundaries of its territory are not known which has created problems over land ownership and housing developments in close proximity. Traditionally the churches of Lalibela are named Debre Roha, Roha being the old name for the town. The Debre Roha Council is responsible for the day-to-day running of the churches and comprises six representatives of the laity, six of the clergy and two of the Sunday School. The Civil Administration Council intervenes in the life of Debre Roha only on questions of public order, important sanitary issues and on the legality of works of construction on the churches.

Throughout history the EOC has had considerable control over land ownership where it has had a legitimate authority, independent of imperial power and operating on both religious and feudal systems. This encouraged strong hereditary and hierarchical elements within the church. 'The land was often organized around particular churches and the major obligation laid on the land is the provision and support of a priest and of the church services' (Gilkes, 1975, p. 58). This fact has had a direct influence on housing in Lalibela where those who work within the church have priority. Significantly, there are a total of 560 priests and deacons in Lalibela, excluding monks and nuns and young people who are training to be part of the clergy. Over half the population is directly linked with the church through family connections within the church.

Tourism development in Lalibela

Period 1 (1957–74)

In 1957 the Ethiopian Imperial government first recognized tourism as an economic feasibility in their first Five-Year Development Plan (Sisay, 1992). During the late 1960s international tourism arrivals had begun to increase (Table 9.1) through the promotional activities of the new Ethiopian Tourist Office in Addis Ababa, established in 1961. Tourism policy mainly focused on publicity campaigns and the development of tourist infrastructure. Tourism development priority zones were allocated with the principal focus being the promotion and development of the Historic Route linking Axum, Gondar, Lalibela and Bahar Dar in the north.

Prior to 1966 Lalibela had only been host to the occasional explorer/adventurer or researcher on an expedition to the north. There are recordings of very early explorers dating back to the sixteenth century. 'Francis Alvarez, a member of the Portuguese Mission and the first European to visit Lalibela between 1521 and 1525, was full of admiration for the churches' (Giday, 1992, p. 87). Lalibela first began tourism officially when the Seven Olives Hotel was opened in 1966, providing facilities for international visitors. The hotel, owned by the imperial

Table 9.1 Foreign visitor arrivals in Ethiopia 1962–73, including business

Year	Arrivals
1962	19 215
1963	19 836
1964	25 649
1965	25 412
1966	33 696
1967	29 401
1968	42 114
1969	46 418
1970	53 187
1971	64 542
1972	63 940
1973	73 662

Source: Ethiopian Tourism Commission, Statistical Section

government, was run by Princess Ruth, granddaughter of Haile Selassie I. At that time a runway was also completed for the Ethiopian Airline domestic flights which flew from Addis Ababa via Gondar, Bahar Dar and Axum.

Period 2 (1974–91)

The transition from Haile Selassie's centralist and feudalist regime to an Afro-Marxist state under Mengistu Mariam in 1974 meant that tourism facilities were nationalized and most hotels were split into regional chains located all over Ethiopia. Under the Mengistu regime the National Tour Operator (NTO) had a monopoly. Thus tourists who wanted to travel with assistance around the historical route used the NTO. During this time tourist numbers were low due to political instability and inter-factional fighting (Table 9.2).

Despite political unrest there was still interest from the West in Ethiopia's rich cultural heritage and on 8 September 1978 Lalibela was registered on the UNESCO World Heritage List. Gondar, Axum, the Simien Mountains and the Valley of the Omo River also were recognized as World Heritage Sites. It was hoped that in doing so resources could be mobilized to enhance and preserve the Ethiopian heritage.

Table 9.2 Number of visitors to the Historic Route using the NTO 1984–93

Year	Tourists
1984	1816
1985	737
1986	878
1987	1253
1988	904
1989	453
1990	22
1991	194
1992	558
1993	830

Source: NTO in ETC Statistics Document 1994

Period 3 (tourism after the Civil War)

During the 1980s many of the international visitors to Ethiopia were either aid workers or business tourists. After the collapse of the Mengistu regime in 1991 and the upheaval of the change from socialist state to democratic republic tourism was back on the agenda and the popularity of the Historic Route began to increase once more. However, it was not until 1992/3 that tourist arrivals became significant in numbers and encouraged a national focus for tourism development including further tourist facilities, planning and policy development (Table 9.3).

Table 9.3 International arrivals to Ethiopia 1982–1993, including visiting friends and relatives and business/conference tourism

Year	Arrival
1982	60 624
1983	64 240
1984	59 551
1985	61 459
1986	58 529
1987	73 144
1988	76 450
1989	76 844
1990	79 346
1991	81 581
1992	83 213
1993	93 072

Source: ETC Statistical Department

Van ter Beek (1995) estimates that visitor numbers for Lalibela during the year 1995 were approximately 10 000. However, at present there is no satisfactory system for data collection as this total number includes both domestic and international visitors as well as pilgrims. Each year thousands of pilgrims come to Lalibela for religious festivals, particularly Timkat in January, Easter and Epiphany.

Visitor management

Accommodation, transport and visitor facilities

The total number of hotel rooms in Lalibela is 208; sixty-four at the Roha Hotel, twenty-eight at the Seven Olives, (which between them receive 70 per cent of all visitors), twenty-six at the new Lal hotel and ninety distributed between the ten private hotels. As the Seven Olives needs maintenance and repair the Roha is usually the first choice for many travel agencies as it offers a higher international standard, though the prices are the same. In line with the new free market policy in Ethiopia the present government wants to reduce its tourism assets and pass them to private investors. Both the Roha Hotel and the Seven Olives are up for sale.

The Lal Hotel, completed in April 1996, is a private Ethiopian investment providing an efficient, good-quality service for visitors. With its own twenty-four-hour generator, water pump and water storage tank holding 4000 litres, it does not face the operating problems of the older government hotels. The staff are well trained in hospitality for Western tourists and it will inevitably bring a new competitive outlook to Lalibela's tourist facilities.

Due to Lalibela's remote position, access has been restricted until very recently but a new all-weather road is due for completion in 1997. It runs from Alem Ketema in the Shewa Region to Sokota, 100 km north of Lalibela (Figure 9.1). A bus service operates between Dessie and Lalibela. Lalibela Airport, which opened in 1966, is currently being improved and expanded to cater for fifty-seater planes instead of the present seventeen-seaters, with all-year-round operation. Until this development, the airport had to be closed during the rainy season from June to September, which resulted in very seasonal tourism. The airport is thirty minutes drive from the town over dusty and bumpy roads. Lalibela is linked by Ethiopian Airlines to the surrounding destinations on the Northern Historic route. Long delays and shortage of planes for busy times are common problems that often leave tourists frustrated and disappointed.

Electricity supply can be erratic although the town has one main generator which supplies electricity from 6 p.m. to midnight. Some establishments have their own 24-hour electricity from private generators, notably the Lal Hotel, the Roha Hotel and external NGOs which are operating in the area. There are federal plans to connect Lalibela to a hydro power network. However, Lalibela is not expected to receive 24-hour electricity for another four years.

Considering the influx of tourism and NGO workers, telecommunications are relatively poor and minimal. The Roha Hotel, NTO, Ethiopian Airlines and SNV have radio contact otherwise there is one public radiophone which operates for a few hours a day. There are plans to develop a local telephone network and a post office, but this is in the early stages of development. There are no banking facilities in Lalibela, which creates problems for tourists who need to change money. There are seven privately owned souvenir shops, one at the Roha and six in the town. Three are owned by the Ashetan Hotel Manager including the one at the Roha and the others are owned by the guides. Few souvenirs are made in the area, although locals are now selling their jewellery to the shops and prices are often very high with tourists preferring cheaper products in Addis Ababa. Entertainment facilities are minimal other than local *tej* (honey wine) bars and there is little to encourage the package tourist outside the hotel.

Water supply is also insufficient for the general public and tourists, due to population increase, bad construction and poor management. It is hoped that in the future the Water Supply and Sewage Authority (WSSA) will implement a water supply project which would be based on groundwater near the new airport. The Roha Hotel has many problems with water supply as it is situated just outside the town on a hill. Although they have a well it tends to dry up very quickly, and water is often only available at set times in the early morning and early evening.

Tourist profiles

Tourist profiles in Lalibela were analysed by Van ter Beek (1995) who recorded that 40 per cent were luxury group tourists travelling on a package tour, mostly middle-aged or retired and staying at government hotels; 25 per cent fell into the low budget/backpacking group staying in private hotels and using local transport; 25 per cent of luxury tourists were individual tourists using private tour operator services on arrival in Ethiopia, staying at a variety of government and private hotels. Typically an Historic Route package tour tourist will stay just one night in Lalibela leaving one day to tour the churches.

Tourism policy and planning

There is no current tourism policy for Lalibela which is the responsibility of Region Three's Regional Bureau of Culture, Tourism and Information (RBCTI), based in

Bahar Dar. Due to a lack of manpower and financial assistance, the Bureau's capacity to bring about control and organization is very limited. Planning activities are mostly confined to the promotion and licensing of new tourism infrastructure. However, some progress is apparent with the construction of a Lalibela Tourist Office (LTO) funded by the RBCTI's promotion budget in 1995. Shortage of funding from the government for equipment and furnishing has delayed its opening although it is hoped to be completed in 1997. The LTO will provide vitally needed visitor information in the form of brochures, maps, fully trained guides and possibly walkmans with a recorded guide of the churches. This should also incorporate on-site visitor information including signs to orientate the visitor. The staff at the office will be responsible for tourist data collection in Lalibela together with developing a better relationship with the Local (*Woreda*) Administration Council. At the time of fieldwork no one within the Administration Council had a position connected with the development of tourism in Lalibela.

Policy and control is also required in relation to the role of the EOC and tourism in Lalibela. Members of the church strongly emphasize their reliance on tourism receipts to pay for priests' salaries, festivals, upkeep of the churches and other religious activities within the community. Nevertheless, no records are available on church expenditure in Lalibela or church earnings from tourism (such as entrance fees, photographs, video use and film crews). A breakdown of church expenditure and revenue would greatly help an analysis to assess the dependency on tourism. The entrance fee has fluctuated over the last five years between 50 Birr (£5) and 300 Birr (£30). However, at the time of research the cost was 100 Birr (£10) per person. Ethiopian Nationals do not pay an entrance fee. Within the church compound many priests, nuns and monks ask for money for photographs or to show ancient relics, crosses, manuscripts and robes. The Chief Bishop of Lalibela says this is not allowed and should be reported whenever it occurs this, however, rarely happens.

Tax gained from tourism revenue is also an issue needing attention. The churches are not required to pay taxes to the Woreda Administration. Local hotels and restaurants officially pay up to 35 per cent in tax but as the financial department of the Council does not have information on these revenues the enterprises tend to pay very little to the Council. The income of the guides, mule riders and the few craftsmen is generally considered insignificant and tends to be outside the control of the Woreda Administration. Government hotels, Ethiopian Airlines and the National Tour Operator pay taxes to the federal and regional authorities. Therefore tourism in Lalibela has a high level of economic leakage, greatly reducing benefits to the local community.

Conservation and restoration of the church site

Early research and restoration

Two Italians, Monti della Corte in the 1930s and Bianchi-Barriviera in the 1950s, carried out the first architectural and historical analysis of the churches. A German woman, Imgard Bidder, also undertook comprehensive research in an expedition sponsored by Haile Selassie I in the 1950s to discover further information on the dating of the churches and the artefacts they contain.

Over the years there have been a variety of attempts to restore and conserve the ancient buildings and this remains an urgent priority. Repairs between the years 1920 and 1968 were focused on the rebuilding of roofs and consolidation and partial reconstruction of cornices, pillars, renovation of facades and filling of cracks and fissures. In 1954 Bet Medhane Alem had a heavy cement cover poured between the crosses on the roof. Also in this year Bet Emanuel's pillars, cornices and outer walls were coated with a bituminous layer and later with a wash of red paint. One of the largest projects was led by Italian Architect Sandro Angelini between 1966 and 1968. Funded by the International Fund for Monuments Mission, comprehensive restoration of previous restoration took place as well as consolidation of structures. At the same time UNESCO also commissioned Angelini to carry out detailed proposals for the development of tourism on the historic route. The document was entitled *Proposals for the Development of Sites and Monuments in Ethiopia*, (Angelini and Mougin, 1968) and was hoped to bring about further awareness of the fragility of the monuments on the Historical Route as well as improve the tourism infrastructure. No further preservation work was carried out until 1986 when Bet Mariam's roof was reported to be leaking and for the first time scaffolding and a tin roof were erected.

Degradation of the churches

There are four types of degradation of the churches which are apparent to the visitor. These are cracks in the rock, granular disintegration, scaling and erosion. The degradation process involves a variety of contributing factors including the heterogeneity of the rock, people walking on and around the church area, rain water, the encroachment of residential land use and the formation of nitrates in the rock.

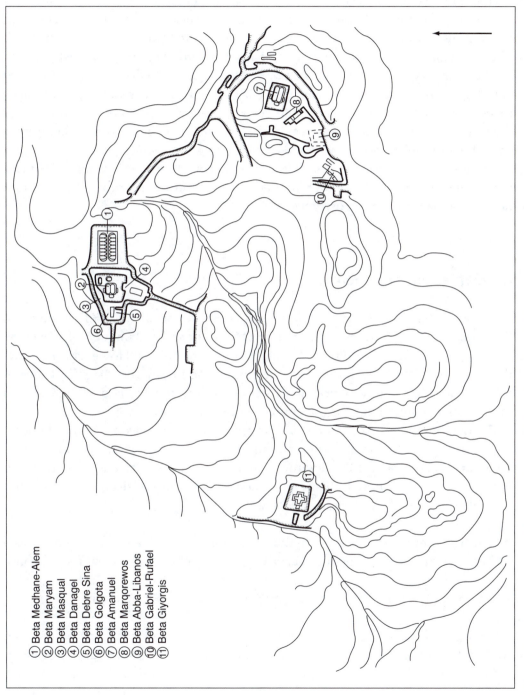

① Beta Medhane-Alem
② Beta Maryam
③ Beta Masqual
④ Beta Danagel
⑤ Beta Debre Sina
⑥ Beta Golgota
⑦ Beta Amanuel
⑧ Beta Marqorewos
⑨ Beta Abba-Libanos
⑩ Beta Gabriel-Rufael
⑪ Beta Giyorgis

Figure 9.3 The church site at Lalibela. *Source:* UNESCO and EC, 1994

The contents of churches are also suffering degradation and there are few means of providing safe and secure storage for ancient artefacts. The care and maintenance of artefacts within the church is officially under the responsibility of the Ministry of Culture, Tourism and Information (MCTI) (previously known as the Ministry of Culture and Sports Affairs until 1995). There is frequent handling of handcrosses, ancient manuscripts, prayer sticks, drums, umbrellas, robes and carpets by priests and tourists, children and local people, which over the years has caused excessive wear and tear. Natural causes such as the humidity of the buildings, the hydrology of the churches, the passing of time, dust and wind, insects and sunlight also have an effect on the deterioration of articles within the church. Flash photography is also contributing to colour deterioration of facades, paintings and costumes.

Conservation management

The responsibility of the preservation and conservation of the WHS is given to the Ministry of Culture and Information (MCI) under Proclamation No. 36/1989 which provides for the Study and Protection of Antiquities. However, until now the management of cultural heritage in Ethiopia has been very poor and uncontrolled. The MCI is now working closely alongside the EC and UNESCO in a major preservation project of the churches, discussed later.

The deterioration of the churches is an issue of much concern among the local population, tourists, the government and international agencies. In Addis Ababa there are concerns about the environmental carrying capacity and overcrowding of the church site, although it is impossible to set a limit for visitor numbers until a number of facts are determined. These include:

- The actual number of visitors to the site (statistics which are yet to be recorded)
- The specific nature of the tourist activity, where they go and what they do once at the site
- The fragility of the environment relating to the number of visitors.

There are no restrictions on the areas where citizens, pilgrims and tourists can walk in the church site. It is even permitted to walk on the surrounding walls of the monolithic churches and on top of tunnels. Heavy walking boots contribute to erosion of the rock as well as everyday wear and tear of the rock through constant treading. Safety of individuals is not taken into consideration and there are many steep rocky and slippery steps to negotiate. To implement conservation management, working within Lalibela's environmental and human carrying capacity, would require a number of changes to the running of the church sites. First, fragile areas may have to be closed off either temporarily or permanently, while archaeological research takes place. Second, the times at which visitors are allowed access to the site would need to be controlled. The theft and selling of priceless artefacts has also increased since the end of the civil war which has led officials to recognize the need for a detailed inventory of all movable heritage within the church site.

Another problem that has arisen recently is that of sanitation in the village compounds situated within the close vicinity of the church site. Deterioration of the church walls is resulting from urine seeping into the ground from nearby households, causing nitrates to dissolve the rock. Finnida (a Finnish non-governmental organization working in the area on town planning and local community development) is keen to rectify this problem and there is also discussion of resettlement of families living within the church area. It is a sensitive issue as there are no determined boundaries of the church site.

The future of the churches

In 1992 the Ministry of Culture and Sports Affairs (MCSA) and the Centre for Research and Conservation of Cultural Heritage (CRCCH) applied to the European Community (EC) for a preservation project for Lalibela. The first steps were taken in February 1994 when UNESCO carried out a preliminary feasibility study of the churches and their condition. This project was financed by the Seventh European Development Fund (EDF). It was followed up in November 1994 by a team of archaeological experts from a university in Spain. In April 1996, the EC was developing a project to investigate methods of protecting and preserving the churches without destroying their visual beauty. All four of the monolithic churches are now covered by a tin roof and scaffolding, except Bet Giorgis. Tourists often complain of the ugliness of these structures which restrict the display of the external features. Many of the scaffolded structures are leaking and their usefulness is in question. In 1994 Bet Maskal received the second tin roof cover in Lalibela, followed by Abba Libanos and Bet Medhane Alem in 1995.

Social issues

Tourism has brought a variety of social impacts to the local community and it has affected some groups more than others. Five per cent of the population is estimated to be directly dependent on tourism via part- or full-time jobs in guiding, hotel work and taxi driving (Van ter Beek, 1995). This is a very small percentage and shows how tourism is benefiting only a small minority. The rest of the population work in agriculture, shops, teaching, road building or are employed by NGOs in administration and clerical work.

Children

For children the presence of Western tourists provides great interest and entertainment and many are receptive and approach tourists with 'unofficial' guiding services. Western styles of clothes and music are becoming fashionable and drinking at the *tej* bars, socializing with tourists, is becoming increasingly commonplace. During fieldwork it was evident that a core group of child guides (between the ages of 10 and 18 years old) existed. The children approach mainly tourists who are travelling independently without a guide or itinerary. A financial arrangement is developed whereby the tourist is guided around the historic site, the market, restaurants, mountain walks, and mule rides. This is an opportunity for children to improve their English which is taught both at primary and secondary schools. It is also hoped that a contact in the Western world can provide money for further education and also to have Western goods sent to children and their families. The money received from the tourists for guiding also contributes to the children's family households for food and living costs. However, there is unease within the community because the earnings of child guides are often more than those of a trained professional. In one or two days a child may earn the equivalent of a week's salary for a schoolteacher or doctor. The average salary of a teacher or doctor is 250–300 Birr (£25–30) per month. It is often assumed that any tourist who is travelling independently needs a guide, although visitors should be able to choose. There are approximately thirty official adult guides in Lalibela who have received some training in guiding and are registered with the Guides Association authorized by the Woreda Administration. There are also thirty-eight official shoekeepers at the churches who insist that shoes could be stolen otherwise.

Begging

A large group of beggars tends to congregate at the main entrance of the first group of churches. Tourists often complain of this 'unsightly' group, feeling intimidated if approached for money. However, begging is commonplace and generally accepted and it is not only tourists who are approached for money. Nevertheless, there is increasing frustration and anger from tourists towards beggars and pestering children.

Gender issues

Due to the civil war men between the ages of 20 and 40 years are significantly under-represented in the local population and thus there are many one-parent families who live on the poverty line. Resettled families who were moved from the area during the famine and civil war and have now returned to Lalibela are also among the poorest (Finnida, 1995, p. 2). Due to the many responsibilities expected of females in the household (cooking, cleaning, looking after children and carrying wood) the tourism business in Lalibela is dominated by the male population. Hotel managers, guides, drivers, airport staff, porters and cleaning staff are commonly male. It is mainly women, however, who run the *tej* bars, tea houses and local eating houses. Finnida recognizes women as an underprivileged group in society and new projects are being developed specifically for this target group.

Future plans for Lalibela

In 1995 the Ministry of Foreign Affairs of Finland, under the name Finnida, begun a town-planning programme for Lalibela. It has its local headquarters in Lalibela and has a very practical participatory community approach to the development of Lalibela. Finnida is playing a crucial role, pioneering wide-ranging initiatives including the linking of community development with tourism. In June 1993 the Ethiopian Government through the MCI presented to various donors a request for assistance to a conservation project for the Lalibela churches including environmental rehabilitation and community assistance components for the Lalibela town (Finnida, 1995, p. 2). With the support and funding from the RBCTI and the Federal government of Ethiopia, Finnida took on the role as a significant component of the project. Their influence on tourism will have a direct effect on the future of tourism planning. The primary aim of the project is 'to improve the living conditions for the inhabitants of Lalibela ... based upon the overall objective, three project purposes have been defined: (a) to preserve the historic values (b) to promote sustainable use of the environment and (c) to achieve sustainable livelihood.' (Finnida, 1995, p. 1). Finnida hopes to improve the historic values of Lalibela via heritage management, control of the site, an organized maintenance team for the churches, an awareness of current cultural values, together with a connection with the past history of Lalibela using the valuable resource of the community's pride over the churches. Finnida also recognizes the need to upgrade the World Heritage Site with attention to drainage problems, deforestation, soil erosion and undefined land use.

As the churches are currently the sole attraction for visitors in Lalibela other potential tourism resources could be developed, such as churches outside Lalibela, trekking in the surrounding mountains, honey production and demonstration of building traditions. Another possibility is a museum which could generate income locally and give the community some potential to present and interpret its rich cultural and historical heritage.

Conclusions

With its astonishing heritage, Lalibela is viewed as a major key to the successful growth of Ethiopian tourism. Along with the other towns on the Historic Route it is included in the itinerary of the majority of international tourists, whose numbers are increasing each year. The current expansion of Lalibela Airport clearly indicates the scale of projected tourist increase. While the necessary tourist infrastructure and services to meet this demand are only yet partially in place, there remain a number of outstanding management problems.

To the visitor the visual impact of the churches is often spoiled through the visible decay of the rock, the obvious deterioration of the artefacts inside the churches, the scaffolding and tin roofs which hide them and the apparent lack of rectifying improvements. A programme of comprehensive structural preservation has been initiated, funded by the EC, although it will be some time before work begins. Meanwhile there is a need to control where visitors may walk in order to reduce further deterioration and for visitors' safety. Being a living and working site, there is a clear need to preserve the sanctuary function of the churches by allocating times when tourists may have access and reserving areas for uninterrupted prayer and study.

Since the Ethiopian Orthodox Church is so closely connected with the management and ownership of the church site it is important that a forum for discussion is set up whereby key interest groups in Lalibela and the external government bodies who oversee tourism can integrate goals and aims which can assure the stability of the EOC and its religious practices in Lalibela. The sensitivity of a religious organization such as the EOC and its power and influence in government will evidently influence the future of the churches in Lalibela. Tourism should operate on a sensitive basis in an environment where religion is at the forefront of a society's cohesion.

The development of an appropriate tourism policy for Lalibela will therefore require the collaboration of the RBCTI in Bahar Dar (currently under-resourced), the Woreda Administration Council, the EOC in Lalibela and the Ethiopian Tourism Commission in Addis Ababa. It is likely that Lalibela can learn from the experiences of similar historical destinations particularly the nearby World Heritage Site of Axum. A major step towards formulating tourism policy would be an accurate survey of visitor numbers and environmental carrying capacity of the site. Data on church revenues from tourism would inform the apparent question of internal accountability within the Lalibela EOC.

The new Lalibela Tourist Office will provide much-needed visitor information as well as the opportunity to develop and implement further visitor management policy. The quality of visitor experience could be much improved, first by the provision of on-site interpretation including information signs and maps and the availability of printed information including advice on codes of conduct. In the town there is also a shortage of shops, entertainments, banking and telecommunication facilities for the tourist. In the case of package tourists there is almost no opportunity for genuine interaction with the community as during their short stay they are shuttled between airport, hotel and churches.

Considering the high level of poverty in Lalibela, tourism policy must address the needs of the community in relation to the growth of tourism. In this area the locally based NGO, Finnida, is playing a leading role. A high level of economic leakage and low level of employment in Lalibela's tourist sector (5 per cent) provides considerable scope locally for exploitation of further potential tourism resources such as the development of handicrafts.

References

Angelini, L. and Mougin S. (1968) Proposals for the Development of Sites and Monuments in Ethiopia as a contribution to the growth of tourism, unpublished document commissioned by UNESCO

Bidder, I. (1958) *The Monolithic Churches of Lalibela*, Cologne: M. duMont Schauberg

Briggs, P. (1995) 'Whispers and legends: Ethiopia', in *Wanderlust Magazine*, Issue 9, April/May, 9–13

Ethiopian Tourist Trading Corporation (1986) *Lalibela* Addis, Ababa: Ethiopian Tourism Commission

Ethiopian Tourism Commission. (1994) *Tourism Statistics*, Statistics Section of the Planning Service, December 1994, Addis Ababa

Fattovich, R. (1990) 'Remarks on the pre-Aksumite period in Northern Ethiopia', *Journal of Ethiopian Studies*, **xxiii**, 1–33, Institute of Ethiopian Studies, Addis Ababa University

Finnida (1995) Environmental Rehabilitation and Upgrading of Historic Sites in Lalibela. Project Document 1994–1997, 2nd Draft November 1995, unpublished paper by The Republic of Finland Ministry for Foreign Affairs and the Ministry of the Environment, Finland in collaboration with The Ministry of Planning and Economic Development in Ethiopia

Giday, B. (1992) *Ethiopian Civilisation*, Addis Ababa Press: Addis Ababa

Gilkes, P. (1975) *The Dying Lion: Feudalism and Modernisation in Ethiopia*, London: Friedmann Press

Hancock, G. (1994) *The Beauty of Historic Ethiopia*, Nairobi: Camerapix Publishers International

Sisay, A. (1992) *Development of Tourism in Ethiopia*, Addis Ababa: Ethiopian Tourism Commission Publication

Tamrat, T. (1972) *Church and State in Ethiopia*, Oxford: Oxford University Press

UNESCO and the EC (1995) *The Preservation of Rock Hewn Churches in Lalibela*, study funded by the European Commission Directorate General for Development, 7th European Development Fund

Van ter Beek, M. (1995) Tourism Development in Lalibela, unpublished document for SNV (Stichting Nederlandse Vrijwilligers), Netherlands Development Organization in association with the Bugna Integrated Rural Development Programme

10 Thebes (Luxor, Egypt)

Traffic and visitor flow management in the West Bank Necropolis

Jenny Rivers

I seemed to be alone in the midst of all that is most sacred in the world...
and it caused me to forget entirely the trifles and follies of life
(Belzoni, G. 1817)

Keywords: Thebes   West Bank   Luxor   Egypt   tourism   Valley of the Kings   Valley of the Queens

Location grid reference: 25°41'N   32°39'E

World Heritage List inclusion date: 1979

Summary

The Luxor area contains the stunning remains of the Ancient City of Thebes, the seat of Pharaonic power in Egypt during the sixteenth to eleventh centuries BC. The river Nile separates the temples in Luxor from the Necropolis area on the West Bank. The logistics of visiting the antiquities sites required a six-stage return journey entailing a ferry crossing, whereas after completion of the new Luxor bridge in late 1997 a two-way round trip by bus will be possible. Most guided group visits are organized at similar times to meet tour and Nile Cruise itineraries, thereby creating congestion at peak times. Drop-off points have been sited, where possible, at a distance from the monuments to reduce the risk of vibration from traffic, but at the tombs the volume of visitors increase damaging humidity and vibration levels. Although restrictions are imposed at two of the tombs visitor flow management is not applied at other areas.

   Luxor is once again becoming a major heritage tourism destination following periods of fluctuating demand with every sign that numbers will continue to increase. The risk of damage to the sites and the tourist experience becomes ever greater if a coordinated response by the authorities and tourist operators to address visitor management issues is not forthcoming.

Introduction

Luxor (Arabic: *al Uqsur*, 'The City of Palaces') is a small town in the province of Qena in Upper Egypt which stands at the heart of the Ancient City of Thebes on the East Bank of the River Nile. Thebes was never the actual capital of Egypt but remained the seat of power and the religious centre from 2100 to 750 BC, during the nation's greatest period of international influence known as the New Kingdom (eighteenth to twentieth Dynasties, 1570–1070 BC). The magnificent structures of temples and tombs reflect the importance of Thebes and that of its priesthood and succession of rulers. With the end of Pharaonic dynasties the city fell into decline and became a small undistinguished provincial village, until its treasures were rediscovered by Napoleon Bonaparte's expedition survey in 1798 (Clayton, 1982). Subsequent explorations and discoveries by numerous Egyptologists and archaeologists generated great public interest in the area and when Howard Carter discovered the tomb and treasures of Tutankhamun in 1922 the news thrilled the world and firmly established Luxor on the tourist map (Carter, 1972).

Tourism first developed during the early 1900s when Thomas Cook facilitated travel to the area with his line of Nile steamers which gave access to the temples and archaeological sites along the Nile corridor (Figure 10.1). The importance, scale and variety of the Theban monuments set in dramatic and attractive locations are factors which combine with the subsequent growth in heritage tourism to make Luxor a popular international tourist destination attracting approximately two million international visitors in 1996 (Lamy, personal communication). Government intervention has been crucial to tourism development, (Witt *et al.*, 1995) particularly since 1974 when President Anwar Sadat introduced liberal economic reforms recognizing the pivotal role of tourism in the economic development of the country. Successive government administrations have continued to encourage investment and facilitate tourism development with various measures including financial incentives, freeing the exchange rate market, privatization programmes, deregulating air traffic and diversification to attract new markets. Sustained growth in tourism, interrupted by periods of political unrest in the Middle East area, the Gulf War and terrorist activities in Egypt, resumed in 1995 following a successful promotional and overseas marketing campaign costing an estimated US$80 million. Success, however, has brought uncontrolled growth in many areas and there are now indications that urgent attention needs to be given to the management of tourism and application of control procedures to minimize the impacts of

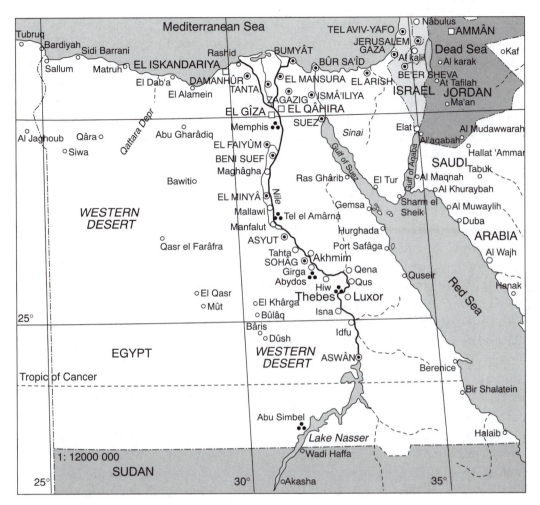

Figure 10.1 Location of Thebes/Luxor in Egypt

tourism on the environment, antiquities sites and the quality of visitor experience.

In Luxor, tourism has changed from a largely independent and small group market with a reasonably steady year-round flow of visitors to include many large groups on packaged tours organized by international tour operators. Tourist accommodation is mostly situated in the environs of Luxor and in the floating hotels moored along the riverside, which concentrates Thebes tourism on the East Bank of the river. Local traffic, taxis, horse-drawn carriages (*caleshes*) and tour buses all compete for road use to collect, deposit and distribute people variously between antiquities sites and other destinations. As people and vehicles must cross the river Nile by ferry to visit the West Bank the flux of people and traffic increases considerably at areas of embarkation and disembarkation. Ground handling is dominated by Egyptian travel agencies who plan and arrange all the tours, group travel and transportation independently, or on contract to incoming tour operators. Excursions to antiquities sites are timed to fit in with regular tour itineraries with little variation in routine or timetables throughout most of the year, irrespective of seasonal variations in opening hours, climatic conditions or volume of visitors. Visitor flows to the antiquities sites are largely determined by the similar schedules of group tours causing peak days such as Thursdays at Karnak and Luxor temples and Fridays at the Valley of the Kings when up to 3000 visitors may arrive on one day. The numbers of vehicles required to convey all these people to and from departure points and a lack of a counterflow of traffic gives some indication of the queues and congestion that occur, of both traffic and people. These conditions can prevail at all Theban sites but problems are exacerbated at the Necropolis, where there are frequently too many people for the small area of the tombs. It is here that the impacts of visitors are most pronounced and where the capacity of the tombs is frequently exceeded to potentially dangerous limits. The ancient monuments are under severe pressure from a variety of sources, not least from the volume of visitors which has led to some restrictions at certain sites but there is little evidence of a coordinated strategy to manage tourism either within Luxor or at the World Heritage Site of Thebes.

This case study examines the visitor management issues of traffic and visitor flows, and their relationship with aspects of visitor impacts, within the context of tourist visits to the archaeological sites of Thebes, in particular to the Necropolis of the Valley of the Kings. During the winter of 1996, while based in Luxor, the author made a number of field visits to the Theban sites to research these issues by means of observation and structured interviews with a cross-section of people involved in tourist activity in the area.

The World Heritage Site of Thebes

Concern to protect Egypt's ancient sites and control the export of antiquities led to the foundation in 1858 of the Egyptian Antiquities Service by the French archaeologist August Mariette (Aldred, 1984). The Ministry of Culture now confers responsibility for the management and preservation of antiquities sites and the Egyptian Museums in Cairo and Luxor to the Supreme Council of Antiquities. Organization for the archaeological sites is completely separate from that of tourism, and despite the fact that the department is directly involved (at the sharp end), there is little apparent integration of the Ministerial departments of Culture and Tourism to address the important issues of visitor management. The Supreme Council of Antiquities must balance the demands of ever-increasing numbers of visitors with the needs of continuous exploration and conservation, and do so with limited resources. Budgets for tourism administration have increased considerably in recent years but revenue from tourism is not used to support any improvements or conservation projects (Soghyar, personal communication). Nevertheless, one of a number of recent policy objectives for tourism development recognizes the need to increase coordination between the authorities involved in the tourism industry (Egyptian State Tourist Office, 1994). What is questionable is whether the government acknowledges the crucial role of the departments within the Ministry of Culture in the Egyptian tourism industry.

The Theban sites

The site of Ancient Thebes spans both sides of the river with the great temple complex of Karnak and Luxor Temple located on the East Bank, and the Mortuary Temples and vast Necropolis of the Pharaohs, Queens and Nobles on the West Bank in the 'Valley of the Dead'. All the Theban monuments are under constant threat from rising water levels and saline intrusion, continual archeological activity and the level of tourism they attract. In the area of the tombs, however, such threats are intensified by the physical features of the area, where the unstable limestone rock is greatly affected by moisture and vibration; and by natural hazards such as the earthquake in 1992 and periodic heavy rains. The paths and walls built around the groups of tombs also contribute to the risk of flood damage as they create conduits for the torrents of water, and despite records of previous floods, no damage-limitation measures had previously been put in place. However, following recent flood damage to one of the restored tombs, pressure from conservationists brought government action and engineers are now developing a system to deflect flood flow in conjunction with a 'flood' project, established by the Egyptian Antiquities Unit (a US-funded research centre), as part of their 'Centre for New Effort'.

The extensive **Karnak Temple** complex is located within the environs of Luxor (Figure 10.2). It was built over a period of 2000 years beginning in the Eleventh Dynasty around 2000 BC, dedicated principally to the imperial god Amun Re, who with his consort Mut and their offspring Khonsu comprised the Theban Triad. A number of structures are contained within the site but the Great Temple of Amun covering an area of 6000 m² dominates with its immense Hypostyle Hall (102 by 53 m) containing 134 sandstone columns. Carved inscriptions of hiero-glyphic texts and scenes of the gods and pharaohs cover the walls and pillars, some still showing the original, brilliant paintwork. Karnak is now the venue for a 'son et lumière' performance, with a weekly schedule of nightly shows presented in English, Arabic, French, Italian, Spanish, German and, since 1995, in Japanese. Close by at the edge of the river is the smaller **Luxor Temple**, built during the same era and similarly dedicated. It records the history of Thebes from Pharaonic through Ptolemaic, Roman to early Arab periods. This site also clearly shows the stratigraphic changes through the ages as the Mosque of Abul-Haggag, built in 1077 at ground level, now stands near the top of the excavated columns.

Across the river from Luxor lies the Theban Necropolis with its hundreds of decorated rock-cut tombs, royal funerary temples and workers village of Deir el-Medina (Figure 10.2). The main sites in the area include the following.

The Valley of the Kings, known in antiquity as 'The Place of Justification', contains the tombs of the pharaohs sunk deep into the limestone rock in an attempt to foil gravediggers. Of the sixty-two tombs discovered, many are merely undecorated shafts with small chambers, others were abandoned because of unstable rock formations and nearly half are unfinished. Decoration in the remainder varies in style, but the themes of religious rituals from the Book of the Dead are consistent. Inscriptions and paintings, some in vivid colours, embellish the architecture and impressive engineering of the tombs, and these are the ones of most interest to tourists. Tombs are periodically closed to visitors for protec-tion, study or restoration, such as those of Horemheb, Seti I and Rameses VI. The tomb of Rameses VI, reopened in 1996, shows Roman graffiti on its walls which testify that some of the tombs were open in antiquity. The famous tomb of Tutankhamun, the only one discovered largely intact, contains the body of the pharaoh lying within his sarcophagus. Despite the charge of an additional fee and its small size, the tomb is very popular and in 1996 attracted approximately 284 000 visitors (Table 10.1). The **Valley of the Queens**, known as 'The Place of Beauty', contains nearly eighty tombs of queens and high officials of which many are unnamed, small and with brightly coloured paintings. The most impressive decorated tomb is undoubtedly that of Queen Nefertari (the favourite wife of

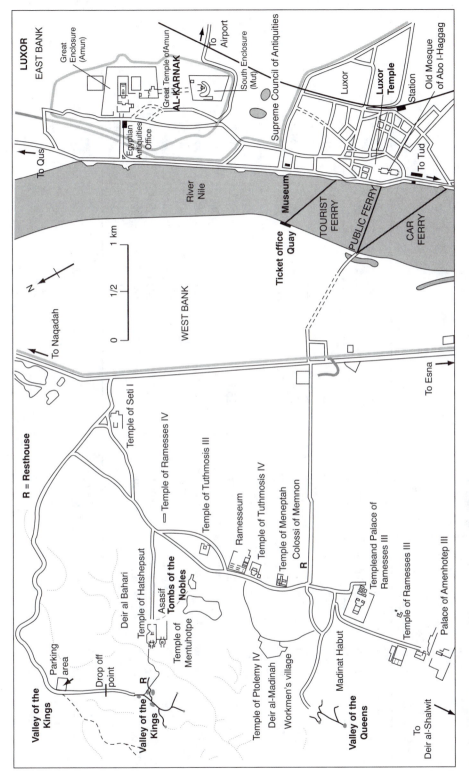

Figure 10.2 Plan of the Luxor area showing the Thebes sites

Table 10.1 Visits to antiquities sites in 1996

Luxor Temple	Karnak Temple	Valley of the Kings	Tomb of Tutankhamun	Valley of the Queens	Tomb of Nefertari	Deir El Bahri	Month
82 079	82 323	318 517	n.a.	25 429	5514	39 525	Jan
87 126	97 159	499 691	14 900	23 838	5221	49 975	Feb
107 550	118 541	693 448	39 500	27 622	5619	56 765	March
95 865	106 465	856 771	30 100	34 953	4571	20 285	April
61 739	68 844	110 560	19 600	22 515	2084	23 040	May
37 300	41 201	74 994	13 100	12 222	1297	23 024	June
45 953	50 469	89 237	15 900	15 142	1154	28 741	July
60 221	68 178	120 772	39 100	17 835	1970	28 292	August
72 200	70 040	138 569	26 619	20 698	2219	28 354	Sept.
81 600	94 121	101 124	26 000	25 467	4197	40 249	Oct.
73 704	84 996	89 642	29 100	21 523	4712	18 897	Nov.
80 000	84 000	300 000	30 000	24 000	5000	35 000	Dec (est.)
885 337	966 337	3393 325	283 919	271 244	43 558	392 147	6 235 867
2 426	2 647	9 297	848	743	119	1 074	Daily average

Note: Total and daily average figures are based on estimated numbers for December.
Source: Supreme Council of Antiquities, Luxor, 1996

Rameses II), discovered in 1904 by the Italian archaeologist, Ernesto Shiaparelli, and opened for the first time in 1995 following extensive restoration by the J. Paul Getty Conservation Institute. At the **Tombs of the Nobles** eleven of the 350 listed tombs are open to visitors, although hundreds of others are known to exist and remain to be discovered, excavated and restored. Another major attraction is **Deir el Bahri**, named 'Northern Monastery' after the Coptic Monastery that once stood in one of the monuments. The remains of three temples include the famous Mortuary Temple of Queen Hatshepsut who ruled in her own right as pharaoh (1478–1437 BC). It is reputedly one of the most remarkable structures in Egypt, set into a natural bay in the Theban hills with the cliffs as a backdrop, the temple rising in three imposing terraces: providing an impressive setting for a series of performances in October 1997 of Verdi's opera *Aida* to commemorate the seventy-fifth anniversary of the discovery of Tutankhamun's tomb. Among the remaining sites is **Deir el Medina**, 'The Monastery of the Town', the artisan's village; home to the skilled craftsmen who excavated and decorated the tombs of the Valley of the Kings, where archaeological excavations have revealed a uniquely clear picture of the duties and private lives of the villagers.

Most of the group tours visit only four of these sites with the Valley of the Kings as the main attraction, whereas independent travellers may make several visits to the West Bank during their stay in Luxor. Average stay varies between one to two hours at the Valley of the Kings and 30 minutes at the Valley of the Queens. Entry to the Valley of the Kings includes three tickets per visit for any of the tombs, except those of Tutankhamun and Nefertari, for which separate tickets (and an additional charge) are required. This allocation should be taken into account when assessing visitor numbers to the antiquities sites, as figures in Table 10.1 show the total number of tickets sold. Another attraction associated with the antiquities sites is the Luxor Museum of Ancient Egyptian Art which was opened in 1977. It displays a number of Theban artefacts in an open, modern setting very different from the crowded Cairo Museum, attracting over 200 000 visitors in 1996.

Tourism in Luxor

Tourist demand for Upper Egypt was especially affected by the renewed terrorist attacks in 1993, when Luxor was described as 'resembling a ghost town' (Lamy, personal communication). Recovery was slow and even by 1994 hotel occupancy was only 20–30 per cent of capacity (International Tourism Reports, 1996). The situation has since improved with an estimated 2 million tourists to Luxor in 1996 and occupancy rates at about 60–90 per cent during Christmas and New Year. Seasonality poses fewer problems although the 'premium' season reaches a peak at Easter (International Tourism Reports, 1996). Official figures specifically for Luxor are not provided by the Ministry of Tourism, but numbers and seasonal fluctuations can be gauged from visits to the antiquities sites shown in Table 10.1. Hotel capacity in Luxor is supplemented by about 400 non-categorized hotels and apartments, a few of which are on the West Bank (Lamy, personal communication). Floating hotels provide 63 per cent of the total bed spaces in categorized accommodation (Table 10.2); as numbers are expected to rise to 300 by the year 2000 there will be considerable pressure on facilities and services (Ahmed, personal communication). At any given time there may be from thirty to eighty floating hotels docked at Luxor, with five to seven vessels stacked alongside each other against the jetty; during peak times groups of eleven vessels have been seen. Guests must negotiate their way through all the vessels, and considering the potential numbers, the situation is fraught with risk. The pleasant Nile Cruise experience is also greatly diminished by the close proximity of so many large boats and the diesel fumes they produce (Figure 10.3).

Traffic management

Since the mid-1980s investment in the aviation infrastructure has substantially increased the terminal capacity at Luxor Airport improving access via international

Table 10.2 Accommodation in categorized and floating hotels

Hotels	1996			1997 estimated		
	Rooms/cabins	Beds		Hotels	Rooms/cabins	Beds
37	3788	7619		45	5788	11 691
Floating hotels						
209	10 450	20 933		231	11 649	23 136
Total						
246	14 238	28 552		276	17 437	34 827

Figures for floating hotels based on 50 cabins per vessel
Source: Ministry of Tourism – Luxor 1996 (estimated numbers for 1997)

Figure 10.3 Floating Hotels docked at Luxor

and domestic flights. Removal of restrictions on scheduled services competing with Egypt Air and charter flights has undoubtedly increased competition and traffic levels. Mainline railway links between Cairo, Luxor and Aswan offering direct services with air-conditioned carriages and sleeper cars are used mainly by independent travellers, business and long-stay visitors. However, terrorist attacks have affected the use of the rail services, especially to Aswan. To protect tourists the security forces impose restrictions on in and outbound travel by road beyond the environs of Luxor and the Thebes sites, requiring tourist transport to join escorted convoys which pass through a number of army checkpoints along the routes.

Improvements to the tourist infrastructure include the construction of a new road to the Valley of the Kings in 1995 and a bridge 4 km south of Luxor, linking the East and West Banks of the Nile is due for completion in late 1997. Most roads giving access to the monuments on the East and West Bank are in reasonable condition, but fallen boulders and rocks on the road to the Valley of the Kings cause obstructions to traffic and indicate a lack of maintenance. Responsibility for roads and traffic management rests with the City Council, and as in many countries, budget allocation from the government is considered insufficient to meet demand. Limited integration and resources weaken management and frustrate forward planning of improvements, although cooperation between the City Council and Government has reportedly become more effective in the last few years (Hafiz, personal communication).

Local transport is either by taxi or *calesh*. There are bicycles for hire and local mini-bus services operate, but a good knowledge of Arabic is required to cope with their erratic arrangements. Group travel is arranged by the Egyptian travel agencies with modern air-conditioned coaches of a much higher standard than those used for the local population. To cross the river visitors may use a traditional sailboat (*felucca*) or either the tourist or local public ferry that leave from separate quays on the corniche. River crossings by public passenger and vehicle ferry services were operated by private operators until five years ago when a dedicated tourist service was introduced. Misr Travel (a government-owned company) manage the landing stages and the ferry service, which includes six vessels with a total capacity of 1200 (four of 250 each and two of 100). They are well equipped and apparently maintained, and provide a frequent service with a crossing time of about ten to fifteen minutes, although delays are commonplace. It is a great improvement on the local ferry services which operate old, rusty vessels that are often dangerously overcrowded. This disparity in standards is not reflected in the pricing differential for tourists who pay £E2.50 – only £E1.50 (20p) per person more than the locals. All forms of transport are licensed, but the condition of many of the vehicles raises questions as to maintenance requirements, levels of inspection and standards of safety, although the tourist coaches and ferry boats do seem to be an exception. Good riverside facilities are an essential part of the tourist infrastructure in Luxor. The 3 km corniche and promenade is managed by a private company who received an initial government loan of £E2.7 million, with a further £E7 million to complete improvements to quayside facilities and berths for floating hotels, including on-line servicing of power and sewage. Unfortunately, the poor condition of the docking areas in December 1996 suggests that it is unlikely to finish on schedule during 1997 (Figure 10.4). Regardless, some travel agents and operators are developing their own quays along the banks of the river to the south of the town towards the new bridge.

Visiting Thebes

Located within the town, Karnak and Luxor are within walking distance of each other and easily accessible by taxi or *calesh*, although the greater majority of

Figure 10.4 The corniche at Luxor

visitors travel by coach as part of guided group tours. Traffic and visitor flow problems do occur within the town and at the temples with the volume of vehicles and visitors, but it is the combination of factors pertaining to the West Bank, and in particular the tombs of the Necropolis, that have the most impact.

Travel to West Bank antiquities sites

On the West Bank distances both from the ferry quay and between the antiquities sites are too great to walk and transport is necessary. Independent travellers may opt to join an organized guided tour or make their own arrangements, either in Luxor or on arrival at the West Bank. Operations to convey tourists to the antiquities sites are not coordinated or organized to meet any entry requirements of the Supreme Council of Antiquities and, for most of the year, guided tours to the Necropolis areas operate during the morning to avoid the hottest time of day. In the height of the summer the sites are closed in the afternoon, but during the rest of the year they remain open until dusk and visits could be phased throughout the day to relieve congestion and ease pressure on the sites. Nevertheless, only a few operators take the opportunity to adapt their schedules by including afternoon visits during peak periods or on Fridays, the busiest day for West Bank tours (Atiff, personal communication). Tour buses leave Luxor at about the same time, picking up from hotels and floating hotels along the corniche about 6 a.m. (7–7.30 a.m. in winter) and return to pick up from the ferry about 12.30 to 1.30 p.m. The arrival of several tours at the ferry quays creates traffic congestion along the corniche and the lack of ferry capacity for such large numbers of visitors causes inevitable delays. At the West Bank all visitors disembarking from the ferries must locate their guides and find their waiting transport, which creates chaos at peak times as hundreds of visitors, guides, taxi drivers and tourist police converge in the limited space between vehicles. On a quiet day in December a count of the waiting vehicles parked at the West Bank ferry point revealed thirty-three travel agencies operating forty-eight coaches, forty-eight mini-buses and twenty-seven taxis, all with engines running; on a Friday in the premium season there would be many more. Capacity in the parking area is inadequate for the numbers of vehicles (Figure 10.5), consequently taxis and mini-buses fill any available space and buses line both sides of the exit roads. Traffic control by the police, largely ignored by the drivers, is wholly inadequate and disorganized and the ensuing mêlée, as the traffic starts to leave, results in gridlock until vehicles at the head of the queue start to depart. A few agencies have negotiated the use of rough ground about two hundred yards along the exit road to provide them with exclusive parking, although passengers must walk the distance and safety is compromised as vehicles depart. Once away from the ferry point traffic disperses along good access roads to one of the main sites shown on the plan (Figure 10.2).

About 8 km from the ferry quay the 4-km access road to the Valley of the Kings follows the same route as the ancient path and actual funeral cortege of the pharaohs. At the approach to the valley there is a large parking area with capacity for approximately 100–150 coaches and a rest-house providing refreshments, souvenirs and toilet facilities. It is managed by a private company Atlanta Restaurant Co., and is the only part of the government-built complex of facilities that is in use, although a number of souvenir stalls are located near to the ticket entrance. Coaches are permitted to drive to a drop-off point on arrival but must return to the parking area immediately, leaving visitors to walk the remaining distance to the entrance and on their return to the rest-house, a distance of approximately 800 m (Figure 10.6). Drop-off points for buses were moved back some distance from the entrance because of concerns about vibrations from vehicles causing damage to the tombs' structure.

Figure 10.5 Car park at the West Bank Ferry Quay

At the smaller site of the Valley of the Queens there is parking capacity for about twenty-five or thirty coaches with a row of small shop units, many of which are unused. Traders hassle visitors who no longer pass the shop units on their way to and from the site entrance, since changes in parking arrangements require drivers to reverse into parking spaces directly in front of the shops, thereby impeding access. Facilities for visitors are limited in quantity, quality and, for those travelling with a group, opportunity. In addition to the rest-house at the Valley of the Kings there are toilet facilities in portacabins at various locations but often visitors, anxious to keep up with their group, either miss them or are reluctant to stop. A rest-house opposite the tombs of Rameses VI and Tutankhamun provides shade and seating on fourteen wooden benches and the low walls, and another smaller shelter opposite the tomb of Seti I. However, there is no shade or seating at the tomb entrances and queues mean that visitors frequently have to wait for some time in full sun.

On-site interpretation at all the temples and tombs is confined to an occasional board containing a brief description and plan in Arabic and English (with the

Figure 10.6 Drop-off point at the Valley of the Kings

exception of the tombs of Tutankhamun and Nefertari). There is no established protocol or guidance for visitors regarding behaviour at the antiquities sites. Information on protection of the sites is not included in tourist leaflets, on display boards or tickets, and as few tour operators inform their clients, visitors rely mostly on their own guidebooks for information or their tour guides, who play a major role in visitor management at the antiquities sites (Johnson, personal communication). Guides qualify in Egyptology and tourism and must speak at least one foreign language to obtain a compulsory licence; many also specialize with a Masters degree. In the absence of visitor interpretation, the guides are an essential source of information and explanation of Egyptian history and the inscriptions. They are also a potential educative resource to influence visitor behaviour when visiting ancient monuments. Unfortunately, however, many guides fail to remind visitors not to touch inscriptions or mention conservation needs and indeed can even contribute to the problems of visitor impacts, which are particularly significant at the tombs.

Visitor flow

Volume of visitors at one time, in groups that do not disperse, cause congestion at the Thebes antiquities sites and increase impacts in the confined area of the tombs; on occasion guided tours of up to fifty in a group were observed. The flow and volume of visitors at the sites are affected considerably by the transitory nature of the Nile Cruise. Because the residential tourist is, in effect, en route, tourist demand fluctuates during the cycle of the cruises' itineraries.

The lack of tourist accommodation on the West Bank is also a factor in creating excursionist problems of 'day-trip' visitors who arrive en masse from the East Bank (Glasson *et al.*, 1995). The size of the tombs, as visitor attractions, is obviously a major constraint to capacity levels and the numbers of visitors that can be safely accommodated at a time, both for the tombs and for the people themselves. The problems of excursionism are lessened somewhat at the sites in Luxor as their central location means that visitors have greater access and may visit more freely. Tours are also more frequent throughout the day which helps to regulate visitor flow.

Tour guides often disregard licence conditions, and do not seem to freely observe restrictions on entry and commentary within the tombs. At a few tombs, such as Tutankhamun (which is very small) and Nefertari, the guardians of the tombs (*ghafirs*) strictly impose the ruling and prevent guides accompanying their groups, but this is not the case generally. Some *ghafirs* collecting tickets at tomb entrances were seen regulating the numbers of groups, but it appeared to be an *ad-hoc* arrangement at the discretion of the person on duty, consequently the volume of visitors increases as groups cluster together, causing obstruction and interrupting the flow. Most guides follow a routine, observing etiquette to wait their turn, which often results in a whirlwind tour, and as guides also compete to make themselves heard commentaries are difficult to understand and very noisy. In all locations this detracts from the visitor experience, but in the tombs such noise levels and clusters of people have more serious impacts.

Visitor impacts

Overall, visitor numbers to the tombs are not considered a problem by the Supreme Council of Antiquities but conservationists are convinced that the volume of visitors is a major threat to the tombs as groups of people increase humidity and vibration levels and escalate the rate of deterioration; clearly they were not designed to be entered on a regular basis. If the flow of people is not regulated the volume increases and this is thought to have been a contributory factor when a roof collapsed in the tomb of Seti I, fortunately closed at the time (Johnson, personal communication). Results of a study on the recently restored Nefertari tomb by the J. Paul Getty Conservation Institute showed that 125 people staying in the tomb for an hour would produce the equivalent of 3 gallons of water poured onto the walls. It was concern about visitor impacts on the tomb which led to the decision to impose a limit of 150 visitors per day (International Tourism Reports, 1996), and various measures were tried by the Department of Antiquities to manage these restrictions. Entry is by a special ticket costing £E 100 which are currently issued directly to individual visitors at the ferry quay ticket office to prevent abuse by third-party purchasers. To minimize impacts to the tombs solar-powered air-conditioning is installed and only small groups are allowed in the tomb for 16 minutes at a time, a rule strictly applied by the *ghafirs*. Despite concern, the reported requirement for visitors to wear masks and shoe-coverings has not been imposed, and as the average daily figures in March 1996 of 181 show the daily limit of visitors has been regularly exceeded (Table 10.1).

Addressing the problems

A number of visitor management measures, listed below, have already been implemented in Luxor and the West Bank. Although they indicate an understanding on the part of the authorities of the factors required for tourism development and of visitor expectations, they are not part of an overall strategy (Page, 1994).

Visitor management and visitor facilities include:

- Provision of promenade and seating areas along the 3 km corniche in Luxor
- Visitor centre on corniche – not in use, cafeteria and gallery proposed
- Shaded seating areas at ferry points
- Toilet facilities at the West Bank parking area and at some attractions
- Pedestrianized area and seating at Karnak
- Pathways at attractions
- Rest-houses/cafeteria at the Valley of the Kings
- Tourist shop units at key attractions on the West Bank – some not in use
- Two visitor information boards in Luxor – one damaged
- Ministry of Tourism Information Office – no displays, must request information
- Tourist Police for safety and assistance

- Tourist ferry service and quays
- Fleet of modern tourist coaches
- Corniche and parking areas
- Bus and car parks at all sites – no land to build parking at Luxor Temple
- Access roads at all sites
- Tourist and traffic police – traffic system limited to directing traffic when congested
- Drop-off points at antiquities sites
- Electric shuttle bus at the Valley of the Kings – operated only a few months

There are two specific issues related to the management of visitor flows;

- Restricted entrance to the tomb of Nefertari
- A plan to create 'gateway visitor centre' in Luxor – not implemented

The new bridge is seen as the solution to most of the traffic management problems. It is estimated that the journey from Luxor to the West Bank sites will take approximately 30–45 minutes, although a spokesman for Misr Travel suggested that most operators will continue to use the ferry rather than make the extra journey, seeming to disregard the delays that already occur. Whatever the outcome, the bridge will undoubtedly ease congestion at the corniche and ferry points, but it will have the likely effect of transferring congestion to the antiquities sites and does not address the wider issues of pollution from diesel fumes, visitor flow or the impact on antiquities sites.

The implementation of traffic and visitor flow plans is often in response to an isolated problem rather than as part of the overall concept of visitor management. One such scheme was the introduction in 1995 of an electric bus shuttle service at the Valley of the Kings. Vehicles were required to stop at the rest-house car park, rather than the drop-off point, where passengers had to disembark and take the shuttle service to the entrance. It was doomed to failure and lasted about six months, not least because of a lack of spare parts and maintenance skills to effect repairs. Peaked arrival patterns also meant that the number of people requiring transfer to the entrance was far more than the capacity of the shuttle, so visitors and their guides had to either wait or walk (Hall, 1991). Another initiative by the Ministry of Tourism in Luxor, cognisant of the problems relating to the West Bank, also ended in failure: A plan was proposed to develop the visitor centre on the corniche as a gateway centre to provide information on the area's attractions for waiting visitors, thereby staggering the visitor flow to the West Bank. Both of these initiatives met with strong resistance from travel agents and guides who considered them unworkable, and according to those interviewed, such schemes and the concept of traffic and visitor flow management on the West Bank are dismissed as inconsequential, even though some acknowledge that impacts may be damaging. There seems to be little support for the application of procedures to regulate the flow of visitors at the antiquities sites, and yet their cooperation is vital for ideas to come forward and for changes to be made.

Indicators that pressure on the antiquities sites has reached levels beyond sustainable limits also point to issues of environmental effects and opposite enhancement of visitor experiences which merit concern. The necessary skills and resources exist within partnerships between government and the private sector, to look beyond the development issues declared by Mahmoud El Beltagui, the Minister of Tourism, towards those of visitor management (Goeldner and Gartner, 1995). Workable solutions are feasible if a clear set of guiding principles and planned steps are adopted. An evaluation of the extent of visitor impacts would require coordinating the quantitative data with more qualitative environmental and attitudinal data (Glasson *et al.*, 1995). Existing data currently used by the Ministry of Tourism for economic evaluation should be applied to assessing the long-term impacts of tourist activity. Recent cabinet resolutions by the Egyptian government (Egyptian State Tourist Office, 1996a,b) need to be backed up with local support and resources to implement visitor management strategies designed not only to maintain the economic benefits of tourism but also to minimize environmental impacts, protect the historic monuments and enhance the tourist experience (Glasson *et al.*, 1995). Neglect could lead to irreversible damage to the inscriptions and structure of the monuments, with potentially disastrous consequences, as the roof collapse in the tomb of Seti I demonstrated. Environmental degradation, traffic and visitor congestion could exceed tolerance levels and result in a downturn in tourism, an outcome which the government and the tourism industry has the power to prevent. Despite the temporary reduction in visitor arrivals resulting from the 1997 terrorist attack, tourism to Luxor is still likely to increase significantly over the next decade.

Acknowledgements

The author is most grateful for the kind assistance and support provided by a host of people during the field work for this chapter and particular thanks go to the following individuals and organizations. Professor M. Shackley, CTVM

(Nottingham Trent University), Paul Maltby (HPB Travel), Atiff Nassif (Abercrombie and Kent, Luxor), Oosama Abdul Hafiz and Mr. Lamy (Ministry of Tourism – Luxor), Dr Mohammed Soghyar (Director, Supreme Council of Antiquities, Luxor), Fati Yaseen (Official at the Valley of the Kings), Dr Ray Johnson (Assistant Director, Chicago House, Luxor), Mohammed Abdou (Supreme Council of Antiquities, Luxor), Said Abdul (Misr Travel), Natalie Roman (Egyptian State Tourist Office, London), and Samir Ahmed whose contacts and friendship were invaluable. Finally to Colin, my partner, friend and mentor, a special thank you.

Fieldwork funding was provided under Research Enhancement Funding by Nottingham Trent University and figures were drawn by Linda Dawes, International Studies (Nottingham Trent University).

References

Aldred, C. (1984) *The Egyptians*, London: Thames & Hudson

Carter, H. (1972) *Tomb of Tutankamen*, London: Barrie and Jenkins

Clayton, P. A. (1982) *The Rediscovery of Ancient Egypt, Artists and Travellers in the 19th Century*, London: Thames and Hudson Ltd.

Cockerell, N. (1996) 'Egypt', *International Tourism Reports No. 2*, London: Travel and Tourism Intelligence

Egyptian State Tourist Office (1994) *Tourist Development Programme*, London: Egyptian State Tourist Office

Egyptian State Tourist Office, (1996a) New Cabinet Resolutions to Boost The *Tourist Movement in Egypt*, London: Egyptian State Tourist Office

Egyptian State Tourist Office (1996b) *Press Release*, London: Egyptian State Tourist Office

Glasson, J. *et al.* (1995) *Towards Visitor Impact Management: Visitor Impacts, Carrying Capacity and Management Responses in Europe's Historic Towns and Cities*, Aldershot: Avebury

Goeldner, C. R. and Gartner, W. C. (eds) (1995) 'International academy for the study of tourism', Conference Report, *Journal of Travel Research*, **34**, No. 2, 62

Hall, R. W. (1991) *Queueing Methods: for services and manufacturing*, Englewood Cliffs, NJ: Prentice-Hall

Mathieson, A. and Wall, G. (1982) *Tourism: Economic, Physical and Social Impacts*, London and New York: Longman

Page, S. (1994) *Transport for Tourism*, London and New York: Routledge

Seekings, J. (1991) 'Egypt', *International Tourism Reports No. 1*, London and New York: Economist Intelligence Unit

Seton-Williams, V. and Stocks, P. (1983) *Blue Guide: Egypt*, London: Ernest Benn

Witt, S. F., Brooke, M. Z. and Buckley, P. J. (1995) *The Management of International Tourism*, London and New York: Routledge

11 Ninstints (Canada)

A deserted Haida village in Gwaii Hanaas National Park Reserve (Queen Charlotte Islands)

Myra Shackley

The totem poles told the people of the completeness of their culture, the continuing lineages of the great families, their closeness to the magic world of myth and legend (Bill Reid, contemporary Haida master carver)

Keywords: Haida   Gwaii Hanaas   Anthony Island   Queen Charlotte Islands   Native American   British Columbia   Canada

Location grid reference: 133°E   54°N

World Heritage List inclusion date: 1981

Summary

The village of Ninstints in Gwaii Hanaas (Queen Charlotte Islands) contains the most significant collection of thirty-two carved mortuary and totem poles produced by the Haida Native American people. The village was abandoned towards the end of the nineteenth century as a result of a dramatic population decline resulting from smallpox caught by the Haida from white fur traders and whalers. The Haida, who had once dominated western British Columbia, were a powerful trading nation with a sophisticated cultural and artistic tradition and a resource base of salmon fishing and hunting. Their descendants, who still live in Gwaii Hanaas, feel Ninstints to be their most significant sacred site, to be sensitively managed primarily for conservation purposes and for use in education and cultural-awareness programmes. Ninstints, arguably the most remote tourist attraction in North America, is located on Skungwai (Anthony) Island accessible only by sea kayak or boat with helicopter or floatplane landings forbidden.

Haida Watchmen guard the site, limiting visitor numbers and acting as interpreters. Many Haida opposed the inclusion of Ninstints on the World Heritage list in 1981 and no on-site marker will be found, but the designation was central to the development of the current management plan whereby Ninstints and other Haida sites are included in Gwaii Hanaas National Park Reserve and co-managed by the Haida Nation and Parks Canada.

Introduction

The abandoned Haida village of Ninstints lies 10 km from Rose Harbour on Skung-wai (Red Cod Island, or Anthony Island), the southernmost of the Queen Charlotte Islands off the coast of British Columbia, Canada (Figure 11.1). Although it was once a large and flourishing village of the coastal Haida Native Americans, now all that is left are the collapsed remains of log houses and an extraordinary collection of intricately carved but heavily weathered totem poles. The inaccessible site is gaining increasing numbers of visitors each year partly as a result of the rise in interest of sea kayaking (the easiest way to reach the island) but mainly as part of a wider resurgence of interest in Canada's indigenous peoples. Ninstints is one of a series of Haida sites whose remarkable carvings and spectacular locations have the ability to generate a powerful spirit of place, and it is this ability, combined with the stories underlying the abandonment of the sites, powerfully told by the Haida Watchmen who act as guide/interpreters, which are bringing increasing numbers of visitors. The totem poles of Ninstints are gradually being eroded by wind and weather (though not by visitors) but the site acts as a focus for the resurgence of interest in ancient Haida culture both by contemporary Haida and outsiders. World Heritage designation, achieved in 1981, has probably had little effect on visitor numbers but was instrumental in helping the development of the current site management plan.

The Queen Charlotte islands (Haida Gwaii) lie 100 km from the mainland of the Canadian Province of British Columbia, of which the islands form a part, separated by the Hecate Strait. They have a mild, wet climate with an average mean temperature of 8°C (46°F) and total population of 5500 people of whom approximately 3400 live in or around Queen Charlotte City and Masset. There are more than 130 islands, with 1600 km of coastline, which may be reached by plane directly from Vancouver (some 770 km south) or by ferry from Prince Rupert (Figure 11.1) which takes around 6 hours. The Gwaii Hanaas Reserve forms about 15 per cent of the island mass and is home not only to significant Native American cultural sites but also to an extraordinary fauna and flora including eleven species of whale, bald eagles and Canada's only confirmed nesting site for horned puffins. Pockets of the islands missed the glaciation which covered the rest of British Columbia, resulting in an isolated flora and fauna very different from that of the Canadian mainland. Weather in the Queen Charlotte islands is comparatively dry and sunny from mid-May to mid-September making tourism a highly seasonal activity. The rainy season begins again in August but thick sea fog can strike at any time. For most water-borne activities June and July are the only reasonable months. The west coast of the Queen Charlottes has treble the 128 cm of annual rainfall received by the east,

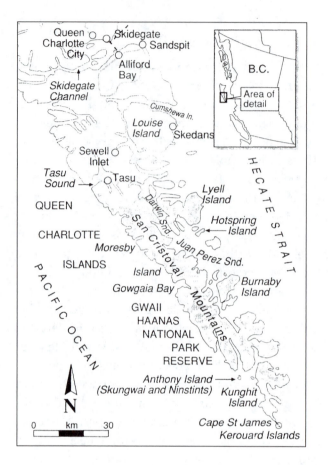

Figure 11.1 Location of Anthony Island

and is whipped by winds that can reach 200 km/h.

Some 5500 people live in the Queen Charlottes, most near Sandspit, supported by an economy dependent upon tourism and logging. Many are Native American, descendants of the island's original Haida inhabitants. Since the creation of the Park Reserve where no logging is allowed many residents have experienced a drop in income, but there has been a consequent expansion in the tourism industry. Most of the tour companies in the Queen Charlottes are owned and run by local people, many of them Haida and many also ex loggers. The Haida have been here for nearly 10 000 years, and when the Queen Charlottes were 'discovered' by a Spanish sea captain, Juan Perez, in 1774 more than 7000 Haida lived on the islands. They were a remarkable people, speaking a language unrelated to any other, possessing a rich artistic tradition and supporting themselves by fishing and trading activities up and down the Inside Passage, from Puget Sound in Washington State to Skagway in southern Alaska. Haida used cedar dugout canoes up to 23 m long and capable of carrying more than 2 tonnes of freight to raid villages and trade slaves. However, in the nineteenth century smallpox, caught from white men, reduced the Haida population by at least 70 per cent and by the turn of the century the remaining Haida had abandoned the southern islands, including Skungwai (Anthony Island) to settle on Graham Island.

Their ancient abandoned villages with their extraordinary totem poles and the remains of huge ceremonial houses embellished with carved and painted clan emblems constitute the major cultural tourism attraction of the Queen Charlotte Islands today, although visitors also come for the unique fauna and flora and great natural beauty. Contemporary Haida have managed a renaissance of their traditional arts and crafts whose distinctive flowing lines and stylized, almost abstract, animal patterns have translated well into painting, carving and metalwork representing many of the Haida traditional legends.

Many of the Haida sites are located on the complex of islands and islets which form a 90 km long archipelago set aside by the Canadian government in 1987 as the Gwaii Hanaas National Park Reserve and Haida Heritage Site. Before (and occasionally since) its designation Gwaii Hanaas has been the location of some epic battles between environmentalists (dominated by Haida and their colleagues opposed to intensive logging) and logging companies. This resulted in a victory for the Haida who today co-manage the Reserve with Parks Canada.

The Reserve is dominated by great forests of pine, hemlock and spruce. Very strong local community groups including the Haida Nation and ISCI (Islands Community Stability Initiative) with elected representatives from every community on Haida Gwaii aim to increase their demands for more protection from uncontrolled logging, despite the economic hardship that accrues. Many Haida see sustainable forestry as essential to protect and utilize the forests and pass on land to their grandchildren, a vital element in cultural conservation and connected with the Native American belief that people belong to the land, rather than the other way round.

Tourism in the Queen Charlotte Islands

Patterns of tourism demand

Nearly 3000 tourists visited the Queen Charlottes during 1995, a 10 per cent increase over the previous year. Most (84 per cent) came on some kind of tour and, on average, they stayed 4.25 nights (Table 11.1). The vast majority of visitors to Gwaii Hanaas are Canadian and US domestic tourists, most of whom arrive by ferry and many of whom use RVs (recreational vehicles or camper vans). The islands present a safe and friendly environment where everyone knows each other, as well as the opportunity to experience Haida culture. Fishing charter operators and lodge owners have reported a drop in sales during 1996 related to the high cost of taking an RV on the ferry. In the course of an average summer 7600 people come to the information centre at Sandspit. During 1995 nearly 1000 day-visits were also made to the Queen Charlottes, and more than 7000 people visited Haida cultural sites. The number of independent travellers has dropped slightly over the last three years, with a steady increase in packaged tours.

Within Gwaii Hanaas the biggest increase has been in the number of people going on day-trips to K'una (Skedans) which is outside the protected area and relatively near to Queen Charlotte City. Around 1500 visitors a year arrive at the Skedans Haida site but many less to the island of South Moresby and the much smaller islands of Lyell, Burnaby, Kunghit and Skungwai (Anthony Island) to the south. It seems probable that Ninstints never receives more 750 visitors per year.

The fastest-growing tourism activity on the islands is undoubtedly sea kayaking, although the west coast, with rocky bluffs and heavy surf, is dangerous as there are few haulouts for kayakers. Visitors not wishing to make the trip south to the Reserve can take land-based tours which use small buses, often including the Haida sites of Skedans and Koona, with its standing totem poles and longhouse depression, together with some time in Skidegate and Masset to watch

Table 11.1 Visitors to the Queen Charlotte Islands

	1992	1993	1994	1995
Independent travellers	652	566	493	417
Tour travellers	1370	1484	2324	2400
Total	2022	2050	2817	2817
User-nights	18 811	12 150	13 722	12 000*
Day-users	264	369	966	904
Information office visits	1630	1309	1395	3558
Watchmen camp visits	7455	7651	6600	7749†

*Corresponds to bed-nights but includes camping.
†Watchman camps are located at abandoned village sites. This therefore corresponds to visits made to Haida cultural sites.
Source: Tourism Association of British Columbia

contemporary carvers making totem poles and sample traditional Haida foods. However, it is worth noting that the Haida do not carve totem poles as tourist attractions but rather to preserve and transmit their elaborate techniques, mythology and culture, and to use them in cultural interpretation and teaching.

Tourism in Gwaii Hanaas National Park Reserve

No roads or shore facilities exist with the Reserve so visitors must arrange their own travel by boat, floatplane or helicopter. In order to visit the abandoned Haida villages it is necessary to make arrangements with the Haida Gwaii Watchmen office in Skidegate (Figure 11.1). In 1974 Haida communities, alarmed at the high levels of clearcut logging in the Queen Charlottes, started an Islands Protection Committee and began to pressure logging companies which had been granted licences, over the next decade. Although federal officials talked of resolving the long-running Haida land issues in South Moresby by creating a park they still issued logging licences, creating a tense situation which came to a head in 1985 when thirty Haida successfully blockaded a road to the logging areas. The blockade was maintained by Haida in traditional blankets and battle paint, generating valuable publicity, with the resulting court battles gaining national attention. In 1986 the government announced a moratorium on logging in South Moresby and in 1990 representatives of the Haida nation finally signed an agreement with the Canadian federal government to share the planning, management and operation of the new Park Reserve.

The abandoned Haida sites are protected by Haida Watchmen, who are based at camps at Skedans, Sgan Gwaii, Windy Bay, Tanu and Hotspring island. The Watchmen programme is funded by Parks Canada and the Watchmen are all volunteers, trained by means of classes which take place over the winter and involve not only record keeping and visitor skills but also traditional crafts such as drum making and spruce root weaving. Watchmen are intended not just to guard the site but also to act as culture brokers and interpreters, a programme which is both successful with visitors and highly regarded by the Haida themselves. This replaces the former *ad-hoc* system where potential visitors had to personally approach Haida officials for permission to go to a site. Haida Watchmen have constructed traditional log cabins and maintain a watch rota, as well as a visitors book which acts as a record of all who have come to the sites. They often take time to explain social and technological aspects of Haida culture using oral histories. Visitors to the Reserve are able to get a good idea of what life was originally like for the powerful and successful Haida communities although the existing wood carvings and totem poles visible at Haida sites are only a fraction of what was there originally. A famous photograph of Skedans taken by the Geological Survey in 1878 (ten years before the villagers left for good) showed fifty-six totems and twenty-seven houses. Today, only a small number remain, survivors of looting by individuals and institutions including most of the world's major museum collections. There is even a prime example in the British Museum.

Anthony Island (Skungwai)

The Kunghit Haida

The most southernmost group of Haida included the Kunghit people who lived on Skungwai, or Anthony Island, which is small, approximately 138 ha in extent and shaped like a bird in flight. It can only be reached by the sea with most visitors either arriving by sea kayak or by an inflatable boat to which they have transferred at Rose Harbour from a seaplane out from Skidegate. Rose Harbour, 160 km of private land inside the Reserve boundary, is located some 15 km from Anthony Island and represents its nearest neighbour. It offers some limited guest-house accommodation and acts as a transit point for visitors to the main Anthony Island site of Ninstints who have come south by floatplane (taking about one hour) or by boat (one day). Any tour operators within Gwaii Hanaas National Park/Reserve need to be licensed and form part of a small group of Haida Gwaii tour operators, strongly committed to protecting wilderness and heritage values. Most operate only in the Queen Charlottes, employ only local people and have well-developed environmental policies, usually promoting kayaking as the lowest-impact activity which produces less noise to disturb seabirds and mammals.

Skungwai originally supported several hundred Haida whose world changed for ever in 1787 when they met, and traded sea-otter pelts with, the British Captain George Dixon and his crew of the *Queen Charlotte*. Other traders soon arrived, attracted by the news of such valuable furs. The wealth they brought both to Skungwai and other islands supported the Haidas' first professional artists. Unfortunately, this contact with Eurpeans brought plague as well as profit. Later visits included mutual hostilities and raids, with contemporary accounts stressing the warlike nature of the Haida although the brutal violence of the white traders and sailors was probably just as significant.

During the decades which followed more stable relationships developed between Haida and white settlers, with many Kunghit moving to Masset and Skidegate to become wage labourers in the mining and forestry industries. Small-pox arrived at Ninstints in 1863 with a series of epidemics over the next decade. About 1840 there were 308 Haida living at Ninstints but forty years later that number had been reduced to thirty. Most had died of smallpox and other diseases from a wave of epidemics which started in 1862. The remaining Kunghit left their village at Ninstints for Skidegate on Graham Island while their houses and monuments steadily fell into ruins, not helped by a fire at the southern end of the village started in 1892 by Koskimo Indians and the crew of a sealing schooner.

Ninstints Village

The Kunghit Haida had several dozen villages scattered throughout their terri-tory, including that of Ninstints on the most secluded and protected location on a sheltered bay on the eastern side of Skungwai. There is a single, narrow naviga-ble channel providing access to the bay at high tide. Early census data (Swanton, 1909) suggests that the village had twenty houses, details being provided by a daughter of the chief who lived there at the time of its abandonment. The main house row straddled a natural terrace bordering the bay with the houses punctu-ated by memorial and mortuary totem poles (Figure 11.2). Each house had an evocative name. House Eleven was 'Driving a Weasel House' and House One 'People think of this house even when they sleep because the master feeds every-one who calls House'. The houses were complex heavy timber constructions, home to between thirty and forty individuals from the same extended family and clan. More than two dozen of the great totem poles which were dotted through-out the village still stand at Ninstints, in a quietly magical setting of great solem-nity, recalling the stone monoliths (*moai*) of Easter Island, set in an enchanted forest of many-coloured moss, giant tree ferns and seemingly endless varieties of trees. This is by far the world's most impressive collection of totem poles still in place on their original village, although the cedar poles are bleached by the weather, rotting and tilting towards each other, and mixed up with the remains of seventeen houses. Glimpses of the carved faces and figures of beavers, bears, dogfish and thunderbirds stare out from the the moss-covered remains. Ninstints feels like a sacred place, often referred to as a natural cathedral, full of Haida ancestral forests spirits surviving in a green world of unchanging silence. So powerful is this impression that otherwise staid historians and archaeologists have

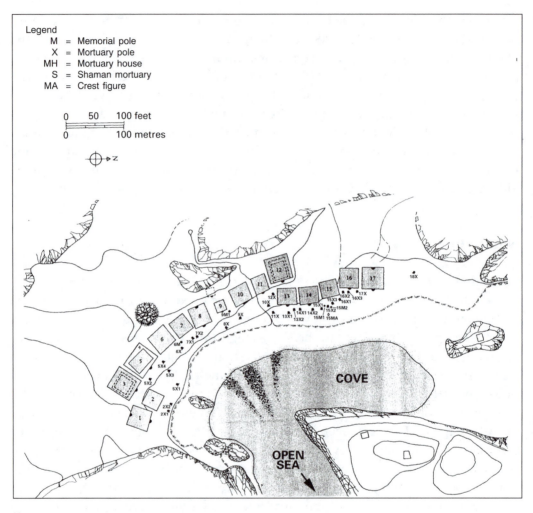

Legend

M = Memorial pole
X = Mortuary pole
MH = Mortuary house
S = Shaman mortuary
MA = Crest figure

Key

House 1	People Think of This House Even When They Sleep Because the Master Feeds Everyone Who Calls
House 2	Cloudy House
House 3	Thunder Rolls upon it House
House 4/5	Grease House
House 6	House That Is Always Shaking
House 7	No name recorded
House 8	No name recorded

House 9	No name recorded
House 10	People Wish to be There House
House 11	Driving a Weasel House
House 12	Mountain House
House 13	No name recorded
House 14	No name recorded
House 15	No name recorded
House 16	No name recorded
House 17	Raven House

Figure 11.2 Plan of Ninstints Village

been known to refer to Ninstints as one of Canada's holiest places (e.g. MacDonald, 1983a, p. 1).

Many of the portable artefacts from Ninstints were taken to Skidegate by the surviving Haida and some sold to collectors. Other pieces were removed from abandoned houses and burial caves. Concern was being expressed about the need to preserve the heritage of Ninstints, particularly its monumental carvings, way back into the nineteenth century, when Charles Newcombe made a photographic inventory between 1897 and 1913. Some poles were removed in 1938 and taken to Prince Rupert and in 1957 a major salvage expedition was underwritten by Walter C. Koerner, a Vancouver lumber baron and native-art collector, who removed eleven of the best-preserved poles, some 16 m tall, which were brought to the Museum of Anthropology in Vancouver and the Royal British Columbia Museum at Victoria. The village was mapped, archaeological excavations were carried out. This and subsequent systematic work was used to support the application for World Heritage status made to UNESCO, together with estimates of factors which could delay the deterioration of the poles and ensure a long-term management plan for both scholars and visitors. The carvings are fragile and continuous careful removal of seedling roots is necessary with careful cleaning by conservators to prevent further damage by root growth. Much conservation work took place in the late 1970s accompanied by pilot studies of new poles outside the UBC museum in Vancouver. The process of vegetation growth on the poles was documented by over 80 years of photographs and excavations carried out to examine decay rates. Some poles have been X-rayed to determine their strength and an on-site conservation programme initiated.

Visitor management

Ninstints can only be reached between July and September and receives less than 1000 visitors per year. Although no precise breakdown of visitors is available 50 per cent are thought to come from British Columbia, 15 per cent from the USA, 10 per cent from the rest of Canada and the remainder from overseas, mainly from Germany and France. There are no visitor facilities, except the interpretation provided by the on-site Watchmen, no catering, marketing or signs. Visitors must land on the beach at high tide, register with the Watchmen and then walk around the abandoned village of Ninstints. Watchmen sometimes offer to take visitors to the other six Haida sites on Skungwai (including two burial caves) if they have time, and may welcome visitors into their longhouse for a chat and a cup of tea.

Ninstints is arguably the most remote tourist attraction in Canada. The isolation of the site, its perfect quietness and the necessity for arriving by sea, as its original inhabitants did, usually make a profound impression on the visitor. Because of its remote location only one group of visitors may arrive per day, permitting a tranquil and satisfactory experience.

Contemporary Haida people view Ninstints as their most sacred site, to be preserved at all costs. During the 1990s they successfully lobbied for helicopter flights and floatplane landings to be banned so that all visitors must come by water, by either inflatable boat or sea kayak. A more ambitious project involving the reconstruction of a Haida war canoe with which to transport visitors from Rose Harbour has not, as yet, come to fruition. The current watchmen programme is funded by Parks Canada. Watchmen keep a visitor-utilization record and have the powers to limit visitors to twenty at a time, and to evict or exclude the unwelcome.

Conclusions

In 1988 after a long period of unrest in the Queen Charlottes the National Parks Review from Parks Canada produced a new agreement between provincial authorities and federal government which excluded the Haida, resulting in even worse unrest and a rash of land claims. Today's co-management system in Gwai Hanaas is the result of the partial settling of this dispute, sharing land and visitor management between the Haida nation and Parks Canada (an agreement also implemented at Head-Smashed-In-Buffalo-Jump, another Canadian Native American cultural site, in Alberta).

The management of visitors to Ninstints is a surprisingly delicate issue. No World Heritage Site plaque or memorial exists at the Site and most Haida are unaware of the World Heritage designation. Others resent it, saying that Ninstints is a sacred Haida site so only Haida should determine its future and that the Canadian authorities had no right to submit the site to UNESCO in the first place. However, World Heritage designation was instrumental in setting up the management plan and getting the former South Moresby joint management board moving to develop a new strategic plan for the site. Parks Canada made a very substantial contribution of $C106 million (approximately £53 million) to establish the Parks Reserve, although in the future it will compete with other sites for central funding resources. Old arguments over whether Ninstints should or should not be a World Heritage Site have largely been forgotten and it is now clear that the existing management plan is satisfactorily controlling visitor numbers by empowering the Haida themselves, via the Watchmen programme.

There are no visible tourism impacts at Ninstints and today's visitor will see the site looking much as it did at the time it was abandoned, albeit rather more weathered. Instead, one of the major problems is conservation of the red cedar poles which have now been exposed to the elements for a hundred years. Some have been preserved by being removed, others given on-site first aid. None have suffered at the hands of visitors. The preservation of their ancient sites and controlling access to them is of both cultural and religious significance to the Haida. Despite their opposition to the World Heritage designation, the new management plan has acted as an impulse for conservation, and enabled many young Haida, whose culture is currently experiencing a major national revival, to see the homes of their ancestors. Ninstints is the focus of Haida nationalism, a memorial to days of greatness and a living symbol of the former power and wealth of the Haida people. The Haida welcome visitors to their ancient sites, since this provides an opportunity not only to educate the visitor but also to raise their own consciousness and awareness of the extent of what has been lost. Today's visitor to Gwaii Hanaas is surrounded by manifestation of a Haida cultural re-emergence, from the excellent museum near Queen Charlotte City to the flourishing and successful world of Haida art. With the exception of the Inuit, the Haida are the only Native American people who are actively developing their ancient arts and crafts as major players in the international art market. Contemporary Haida silversmiths, argillite carvers and print makers create works valued by collectors all over the world, keeping alive and promoting the culture and traditions of their people. Archaeological sites like Ninstints do the same thing, with the addition that the visitor to Ninstints has the benefit of the almost tangible presence of Haida ancestors, an experience perhaps unique, certainly unsettling but (hopefully) sustainable.

References

Barbeau, C. M. *Totem Poles* (2 volumes), Ottawa: The Queen's Printer

Florian, M.-L., Beauchamp, R. and Kennedy, B. (1982) 'Haida Totem Pole conservation: Ninstints Village, Anthony Island, British Columbia', *Proceedings of the ICOMOS Wood Committee Fourth Symposium*, Ottawa: Icomos

MacDonald, G. F. (1983a) *Haida World Heritage Site*, Vancouver: University of British Columbia Press

MacDonald, G. F. (1983b) *Haida Monumental Art; the villages of the Queen Charlotte Islands*, Vancouver: University of British Columbia Press

Swanton, J. R.(1909) *Contributions to the Ethnology of the Haida*, Washington, DC: Memoirs of the American Museum of Natural History, Volume 5

12 Conclusions – visitor management at cultural World Heritage Sites

Myra Shackley

The World Heritage Sites described in this collection of case studies are immensely varied. Some are isolated, others form part of a complex of buildings. The inaccessibility of some (like Ninstints) contribute to low visitor numbers of 1000 visitors per year and no management problems. At the other extreme the Valley of the Kings at Thebes (Egypt) sees 3000 visitors per day and has appalling management problems compounded by difficult conservation requirements and dire traffic congestion. The same techniques useful for the management or interpretation of small, nodal sites such as Biertan are not applicable to complex linear features situations such as Hadrian's Wall which stretches 117 km across northern Britain and includes forts, milecastles, earthworks, ditches and museums apart from the Wall itself. The level of non-tourist use is also highly varied. Lalibela is a living museum in active daily use for Christian worship whereas Ninstints is abandoned. Hadrian's Wall is in a living and working landscape with its central sector dominated by agricultural activity and less than 10 per cent of the Wall managed purely for conservation. Some sites are immensely complex; Cracow, for example, includes 300 historic town houses, fifty-eight churches, 6000 historic buildings and thirty museums. However, despite these immense differences World Heritage Sites do present a series of common management problems associated with their visitors.

A spirit of place?

One of the criteria for nomination to the World Heritage List is that the site must be unique. Such sites are frequently powerful cultural symbols, and should present the visitor with an evocative experience by creating a visitor environment within which the original spirit of place is retained while still creating adequate facilities and providing sufficient information for visitors. This is notoriously difficult to do, unless the site is extremely remote. Ninstints remains a holy place, but it is on a remote island with no road or shore facilities. Visitor numbers are kept low, restricted to one group per day and the quality of the experience is maintained by ensuring that visitors arrive quietly by sea. The opposite is true at the Valley of the Kings where any spirit of place is destroyed by the proliferation of boats on the Nile and diesel fumes on the quay, with the visitor who arrives by water sometimes needing to clamber over thirty to eighty 'floating hotels'. The visual impact of the spectacular rock-cut churches at Lalibela in Ethiopia is spoiled by obvious signs of decay in both fabric and artefacts, as well as by intrusive scaffolding and tin roofs. The chaos of the Giza plateau where the Pyramids and Sphinx are surrounded by a miscellany of poorly constructed modern buildings, defunct power cables and electricity substations detracts from any sense of place. Attempts to artificially reconstruct this feeling seem doomed to failure. The creation of a pedestrian area at Bukhara has not reproduced the bustling central Asian market scene that was there at its heyday but instead a sterile stage-set with magnificent buildings connected by lifeless walkways in the middle of a seemingly permanent building site. Although there seems to be no precise formula for retaining this elusive spiritual quality that creates a magnificent visitor experience at a World Heritage Site, Easter Island seems to come close. Here the experience is enhanced by the knowledge that one is standing on the most remote inhabited place in the world, even though the 'mystery' of Easter Island has been generated partly by marketing and partly by public reluctance to accept relatively boring archaeological information when fantasy is more romantic (a phenomenon also seen at the Pyramids).

Guides and interpretation

Most visitors to cultural World Heritage Sites are (obviously) motivated by and interested in the history, development and significance of the site. To a large extent the success of their visit will depend on the availability of information, and that information may be obtained in a variety of ways of which the two most common are the printed word (maps, guidebooks, pamphlets) and verbal information given by a guide. Other means of interpretation, including signage, storyboards or audiovisual displays are conspicuous by their absence at most of the sites considered here. In an ideal world guide and guidebooks should be complementary ways for visitors to obtain information. At these sites they are generally alternatives and there are immense variations in the quality (and quantity) of such information. Some guides have been through excellent training programmes and are able to greatly enhance the quality of the visitor experience. The Haida Watchmen of Ninstints, for example, spend their winters at training courses organized by Parks Canada which teach them not only to function as culture brokers but also to relearn many traditional crafts. A visitor to Thebes will have the option of utilizing an official Egyptian guide who will have qualified in both Egyptology and tourism as well as a foreign language. But such guides may be under immense pressure, generated by the need to control huge parties of visitors on a very tight timetable and will therefore lose opportunities to influence visitor behaviour (for example, by preventing the touching of inscriptions) and can sometimes actively increase visitor congestion. Their services are indispensable since no on-site information is available. Child 'guides' are a problem at Lalibela in Ethiopia and children may start as young as ten years old, approaching visitors without an official guide and removing business from the thirty official adult guides who have had some training and are registered with the Ethiopian Guides Association. Children are unlikely to provide accurate information which is important since no maps or on-site information is available, but at least their work improves their language skills and may enable the child to contribute a substantial amount to his or her household. On Easter Island the guides are excellent though self-trained, and many speak up to six foreign languages.

Bukhara has inherited twelve outstanding guides who were the product of the old Soviet Intourist guide training system, outfitting them with high levels of technical and interpersonal skills. But how will the next post-Soviet generation of guides be trained, and, moreover, equipped with the skills needed to cope with small groups and individuals rather than mass tours? The existing Bukharan guides are innovative; coping with a large party of Japanese tourists arriving by a charter flight by utilizing the sensible policy of dividing the party into small groups and starting tours from different parts of the city, thus avoiding overcrowding. This simple but effective strategy could well do to be copied by sites (particularly the two examples from Egypt) where much overcrowding is the direct result of poor tour scheduling.

Some sites (such as Biertan) possess no guides, interpretation or information for visitors (except a small entrance notice written in German) but they are the exception. However, all sites share problems with insufficient information provision and many are developing plans to cope. Even the best-presented sites (such as

Hadrian's Wall) are proposing to build orientation centres, gateway sites and more visitor information points as part of a network of information provision designed both to educate and inform. The lack of even the simplest information provision at Giza is to be addressed by the construction of three visitor centres related to key attractions on the plateau, which follows the currently accepted good practice of locating tourist facilities at a reasonable distance from the main attraction.

Economic impact

Throughout the world heritage tourism is experiencing a period of rapid growth, and it is inevitable that World Heritage Sites should be viewed by national governments as major potential generators of funding from heritage tourism, and by private-sector tourism operators as having unlimited potential for merchandising, retail and service operations. Bearing this in mind, it is quite surprising to find that the on-site level of economic exploitation of World Heritage Sites discussed here is, in general, quite low, although they are all, in their own ways, pivots of their national tourism industries. This is particularly the case in countries such as Egypt where high levels of unemployment and vast cultural resources have made heritage tourism a major contributor to the economy. But even in developed countries such as the UK heritage tourism is of very substantial economic significance with 67 million visits made to historic properties in 1995, generating more than £200 million in revenue. The relationship between tourism and other economic activities is often complex; on the Queen Charlotte Islands, for example, the growth of interest in abandoned Haida sites like Ninstints is closely related to both a resurgence of interest in Native American culture and a decline in commercial logging as part of the management plan for the protected area. This produced economic hardship and unemployment, with the result that former loggers moved into the tourism business and heritage tourism is seen as a means of survival for the islands. Some economies relatively new to large-scale tourism (like that of Ethiopia) have developed tourism products structured around their cultural resources. Others (such as Easter Island) have no viable alternative to heritage tourism which makes them economically extremely fragile.

Another economic point emerging from these case studies is how seldom the revenues from visitors to World Heritage Sites are returned (even in part) to conservation and the provision of visitor facilities, which can be a costly business. The development costs of the new National Trail at Hadrian's Wall are estimated to exceed £5 million, just for a long-distance footpath, and there is never any question of the costs of new visitor centres such as those proposed for Giza being met from visitor revenues. Not all World Heritage Sites charge for entry and even when a charge is made it may apply to only part of a complex site (as at Cracow or Bukhara). The more complex the site, the more likely it is to consist of some paid elements (museums or specific attractions) and many unpaid elements, some of which will also be utilized by local people. Not surprisingly, visitor numbers at free sites tend to grow faster than numbers at sites where a charge is made. At some sites (e.g. Ninstints and Lalibela) the imposition of a direct admissions fee would be delicate bearing in mind the sacred nature of the site. Even where a charge is made (such as the US$10 to enter the National Park on Easter Island) only 60 per cent is returned, generating a mere US$60 000 per year towards the management of the park and its archaeological sites. This sum must support ten park rangers but is insufficient to provide them with adequate resources, a point amply demonstrated in the 1996 severe fire. CONAF, the Chilean Forestry Department, who manage the Park, double the visitor revenue to US$122 000 from their funds, but it has been estimated that more than a million dollars is required urgently for essential maintenance and stabilization.

In order to maximize economic benefit from World Heritage Sites there is a need to maintain a highly satisfactory visitor experience. This is particularly so in view of the cultural significance of the sites and the high costs of reaching many of them. Although this type of high-prestige cultural tourism is often not price sensitive it seems probable that some locations have nearly reached an acceptable price ceiling, as at Easter Island where the already astronomical prices charged for accommodation and transport double during the annual cultural festival. Within transitional economies (such as those of Romania or Uzbekistan) the newly emerging private-sector tourism industries are frequently chaotic with a proliferation of private-sector enterprises, generally poorly controlled yet vital for the development of the tourism sector.

Arts and crafts

All major cultural sites generate souvenirs but it is remarkable (at least from the cases examined here) how little merchandise is actually sold on-site, either by the deliberate imposition of legal controls over trading or because little is available. This is not the case, however, at very well-established tourist sites such as Giza or Thebes where the visitor will be pestered to buy small objects. The major monuments in Bukhara such as the Nadir Divanbegi madrassa have handicraft and souvenir stalls inside, though with little pressure to buy. Most sell items not specifically developed for the tourist trade and there is some evidence that the development of a market economy in Uzbekistan and more international visitors has stimulated the revival of ancient crafts such as the manufacture of silk carpets and textiles and a revival of silver and coppersmithing. The Haida renaissance of interest in traditional arts and crafts has included the production of very high quality prints, carvings and metalwork which are not sold on the sites but in shops, although a less reputable development of Haida art (such as the production of miniature totem poles) is also available although not produced by Haida craftsmen.

Transport

Getting visitors to and around World Heritage Sites presents many difficulties, resulting from the need to provide adequate access while preserving sensitive landscapes and vulnerable buildings. Many different solutions have been suggested here, some of which are currently being tried. Transport problems can not only have a serious effect on the quality of the visitor experience but can also actively damage monuments. This is the case at a number of sites such as Bukhara and Giza, with the internal transport chaos of Luxor being especially difficult to sort out. The proposed pedestrian walkways of Giza and continuous bus shuttle service between three new visitor centres is an admirable solution, enabling visitors to reach individual monuments without crossing sensitive archaeological areas, but it will be extremely expensive and will meet with opposition both from local people whose right to provide any transport they choose will be challenged and from some visitors who feel that they should be able to arrive at the gates of even the most remote sites by motor transport.

This curious mentality is amply demonstrated at Cracow. Visiting Cracow is helped by the fact that many of individual attractions are grouped within walking distance in the city centre. Serious traffic congestion at peak times has been helped by a park and ride system but the banning of coach entry to the Old City has meant that visitors are concentrated into a relatively small area near the car park. The provision of electric chauffered buggies helps but the ban on coaches has also meant that tour groups must stay in hotels outside the Old City. With urban centres the creation of pedestrian zones is not without its perils, as at Bukhara where the pedestrian zone effectively minimized traffic vibration and pollution but has created a sterile, characterless area. Perhaps the most effective way of controlling visitor access is at Ninstints where helicopter and seaplane landings are banned and visitors are compelled to arrive quietly by sea, although the second stage of this plan (the recreation of a 23 m Haida war canoe to transport visitors from Rose Harbour) has not yet got off the drawing board.

The effect of World Heritage designation

It is frequently assumed that any site awarded World Heritage status will immediately receive a marked increase in visitors. However, this is not necessarily the case and visitor numbers depend on a number of factors including the way in which the site is marketed and issues connected with access. World Heritage designation for Biertan, for example, has contributed no increase in visitors since the site is hardly known. Easter Island, on the other hand, is so famous that most people would have expected it to be a World Heritage Site anyway. Official designation in 1996 seems likely to have no appreciable effect on visitor numbers which are entirely dependent on the LanChile Airline monopoly and the frequency of cruise-ship visits.

A more consistent result of World Heritage designation is the contribution that such designation makes to the development and implementation of protection and conservation measures. Of course, this is reciprocal since the status is dependent upon the submission of a detailed management plan. The Hadrian's Wall Military Zone was recognized as a World Heritage Site in 1987 but until 1996 its boundaries, necessary for the development of a management plan, were not really defined but only loosely described. The precise recognition of these boundaries was both a benefit of, and requirement for, World Heritage status. The new management plan aims to balance the conservation of sites with the needs of a living and working landscape, managing public access and visitor experience and maximizing the contribution that the site makes to both the national and the regional economy.

The island of Ninstints is included within the Gwaii Hanaas Reserve which includes 15 per cent of the Queen Charlotte Islands. Here earlier mapping and archaeological work was available to support World Heritage designation, including a long-term conservation management for the totem poles and their visitors.

Despite the fact that the Haida people themselves had not been keen (and were probably not consulted) about the World Heritage application for Ninstints (a fact reflected in the lack of a commemorative plaque), it is undeniable that the nomination was instrumental in setting up the existing management plan and Reserve status making the Haida co-managers with Parks Canada, with a £53 million initial funding input from the latter. A similar problem recurred on Easter Island where some militant Rapa Nui felt that the island should be reclaimed by them from Chile and resented any outside interference. However, the designation facilitated access to the World Monument Fund which provided cash for the conservation of Orongo as well as an excellent map (produced in conjunction with CONAF) which carefully omits the location of fragile lesser-known archaeological sites to assist with their conservation. In theory World Heritage designation should not affect the way in which local people use their island although it was opposed by those who resented the fact that it would prohibit construction or anything that modified the present environment. However, many Rapa Nui applauded the nomination for exactly that reason, planning to continue with existing management practices that restrict settlement and visitor services to Hanga Roa.

As is common with heritage sites, many of the problems encountered in coping with visitors to the world's cultural heritage are worsened by difficulties with ownership and balancing the requirements of visitor and visited. At Lalibela in Ethiopia, for example, the site is owned by the Ethiopian Orthodox Church but without properly determined boundaries. Tourism provides vital revenues to support (among others) 560 priests and deacons, paying for salaries, festivals and the upkeep of churches. No records are kept. At Hadrian's Wall more than thirty private and public sector organizations are involved in managing the Wall and its visitors, who have formed themselves into a Consultative Committee which has developed a strategy and policy framework.

Many complex and interrelated factors combine to determine the effect of World Heritage designation. At Cracow, one of the first twelve sites ever to receive World Heritage nomination (in 1978) the key issue is now the protection and preservation of its heritage at the time of transition to a market economy which was not the case at the time of designation. After the designation of Cracow the National Government created a fund specifically to restore its monuments, a fund which currently stands at US$10 million per year and has provided an important resource to protect and improve the Old City and to provide tourist amenities. At the time of nomination it would have been assumed that most visitors would go to the Old City, but today (partly as a result of the filming of *Schindler's List*) many visitors wish to see the old Jewish quarter of neighbouring Kazimierz which has no special funds and where there is a lack of clarity about property ownership. At Bukhara World Heritage designation was also the key to obtaining conservation funding and implementing a visitor management scheme. This both enabled and encouraged extensive restoration of areas such as the Shrakristan and many of the city's original multi-domed bazaars but most of the latter stand empty with rents too high for locals and a decline in visitor numbers. At Biertan restoration work which had encountered financial difficulties towards the end of the 1970s was resumed in 1993 after World Heritage designation brought new sponsors and new roads making access easier.

Visitor management

Almost all the case studies in this book stress the difficulty of getting accurate information about visitors and at some sites (such as Bukhara) there is considerable difficulty in defining visitor and tourist. At Lalibela international visitors are small in number but economically significant, yet many of the problems on the site are compounded by the huge numbers of domestic tourists and pilgrims arriving for religious festivals, about whom no records are available.

Site records may either not be kept at all (Biertan) or may be published in combination with other sites (Ninstints) or may (in the majority of cases) be simply unreliable. How do you count how many people have visited a free open-access site? Many site managers resort to guesswork. Two things are clear: at almost all sites visitor numbers are increasing and most sites have strong seasonal visitation patterns. Another consistent pattern seems to be that visitor arrival patterns at a micro level (during the course of a week or even during the course of a day) are determined by the schedules of tour operators which seldom take into account crowding, visitor experience quality or visitor preference. Visits are timed to fit in with tour itineraries with little variation in routine or timetables despite seasonal opening hours, often creating both traffic and people jams as on Fridays at the Valley of Kings where 3000 people arrive.

Sheer pressure of numbers at peak times creates problems of safety, reduces the pleasure of the visit and adversely affects the fabric of monuments and buildings. At Thebes, for example, the size of the tombs theoretically constrains capacity levels but limitations on numbers are not enforced by guardians. A calculation done by the Getty Institute at the Tomb of Nerfertari suggested that 125 people for one hour produces the equivalent of 12 litres of water poured on the walls. Access is supposedly limited to 150 per day by special tickets sold directly at the quay ticket office to bypass ticket touts and a time limit of ten minutes per visit has been imposed. Observations suggest that these precautions are not being enforced and that some recommendations (such as the wearing of masks and shoe covers) have never been started. Footwear is a common problem and much erosion at Lalibela is caused by visitors in heavy boots who can walk everywhere. The solution must be to restrict access, also necessary because of the need to preserve the sanctuary function of the Lalibela churches and to create areas for quiet prayer.

The duration of the visit to a site may (theoretically) be predetermined by some regulation, as at Nerfertari's tomb, but is far more likely to result from the constrictions imposed by tour operators' schedules or lack of interpretation. Giza receives 1.25 million visitors per year to probably the most famous World Heritage Site in the world yet visitors only stay 90 minutes since there are no visitor facilities, interpretation or information. On the other hand, the unpredictability of visitor arrivals may cause problems; Easter Island gets 10 000 visitors each year but these arrive in bursts depending on flights. A single cruise ship can generate 10 per cent of annual arrivals in just one hour, creating great pressure on all shore facilities.

The impact of visitors

It would probably be true to say that the negative impacts of visitors at most World Heritage Sites pale into insignificance when considered against natural conservation problems, although visitor pressure can exacerbate such issues. The monuments of Thebes, such as Nerfertari's tomb, are threatened by rising water levels, saline intrusion and continuous archaeological activity as well as tourism since their unstable limestone is affected by moisture and vibration. At Lalibela threats to both fabric and artefacts are extremely worrying; handcrosses, manuscripts, prayer sticks, drums, robes and carpets are simply wearing out due to handling by priests, tourists and local people and there are problems with theft and illegal sales. Domestic visitors and Muslim pilgrims to Bukhara remove tiles or pieces of plaster as souvenirs from holy places, but this is a minor matter compared with the problems the city's historic buildings are experiencing with saline groundwater, air pollution and traffic.

Management plans designed to minimize visitor impact are only as effective as their enforcement. At Easter Island, for example, problems with graffiti and vandalism have all but disappeared but archaeologists are still very concerned about the natural erosion of the stone *moai*. The archaeological remains of Hadrian's Wall are physically unprotected and frequently climbed on; some argue that this should be allowed in order for the visitor to get a feel for what the Wall would originally have been like. Poor visitor behaviour at Giza also includes climbing on monuments, casual damage, wall climbing, litter, souvenirs, grafitti and urination against the limestone structures. Visitors walk over the burial regions around the Pyramids ignorant of their significance, a factor entirely attributable to lack of interpretation or information. At Cracow the worst problem is poorly placed and inappropriate advertising with clusters of signs and banners testifying to private enterprise but distracting from visual amenity.

The future

We have already seen the emergence of some common factors which influence the quality of the visitor experience at World Heritage Sites, and the complex inter-relationship between conservation and visitation that World Heritage status implies. Tourism is a highly dynamic industry and, although the future of heritage tourism at present looks extremely rosy the precise implications of policy and practice changes at particular destinations can never be fully determined. An infinite number of 'what if?' scenarios are possible. What if the LanChile monopoly on travel to Easter Island is broken and tourist numbers triple? What effect will the new walking trail at Hadrian's Wall have on the erosion of the monument? What will happen to visitor numbers if a feature film is made at a World Heritage Site? We already have some examples of this last possibility including the three-mile sector of Hadrian's Wall which is heavily eroded by visitors seeking the location of a sequence used in the 1991 film *Robin Hood – Prince of Thieves* starring Kevin Costner. The 1992 film *Schindler's List* which dealt with the destruction of Cracow's Jewish community has generated a new tourism industry tempting international visitors away from the Old City of Cracow to the adjacent district of Kazimierz containing the old Jewish quarter. Local tour operators offer *Schindler's List* tours to Kazimierz although many of the real events portrayed in the film took place elsewhere. Visitors still prefer to see the film sets.

Other cultural issues determining the future of visitation include political change, evidenced by the move here by Poland and Uzbekistan towards a market economy with a consequent expansion in the tourism industry and proliferation of small businesses. The role and rites of indigenous people at World Heritage Sites are also likely to be increasingly significant and this book includes two examples (Ninstints and Easter Island) where there was considerable opposition to the designation from local people resenting outside interference. World Heritage Sites can be a focus for nationalism, whether for the revival of national culture (as at Ninstints), a reaffirmation of religious identity (Lalibela) or a reinforcement of identity (the Polynesian culture on Rapa Nui). A site may change its function or gain a new market, as at Bukhara whose monuments are being visited by increasing numbers of Muslims in a country which is gradually recovering its Islamic faith. The possession of a World Heritage Site and the development of cultural tourism can create a (spurious) image of long-term stability and the basis for establishing a national identity (as at Bukhara) or may become the focus for a new nationalism (as at Ninstints). World Heritage Sites have the highest visibility of any cultural attractions in the world, and possess a symbolic value which may be disproportionate to their size or beauty. They are symbols of our history, cultural icons whose importance transcends their current political status. Visitors to such sites deserve to receive an experience that is something special, something unique, an order of magnitude better than anything they have visited before. Large visitor numbers, poor interpretation, little available information, crowds, congestion and pollution affect the quality of that experience, a quality which can, unfortunately, only be maintained at a high cost. At present only a fraction of that cost is derived from visitors, yet the value of the experience should be beyond price and is certainly, and more prosaically, price inelastic. The future of the world's built heritage and its visitors has to be closely related to the willingness of visitors to pay, as well as to the willingness of the many authorities involved both to derive and to enforce regulations and management plans.

Appendix 1: The World Heritage List

(December 1996)

The World Heritage Committee has inscribed the following properties on the World Heritage List. The List, arranged alphabetically by nominating country, is current as of December 1996.

Albania
1992 Butrinti

Algeria
1980 Al Qal'a of Beni Hammad
1982 Tassili N'Ajjer
1982 M'Zab Valley
1982 Djémila
1982 Tipasa
1982 Timgad
1992 Kasbah of Algiers

Argentina
1981 Los Glaciares
1984 Iguazu National Park

Argentina and Brazil
1984 Jesuit Missions of the Guaranis: San Ignacio Mini, Santa Ana, Nuestra Senora de Loreto and Santa Maria Mayor (Argentina), ruins of Sao Miguel das Missoes (Brazil)

Armenia
1996 The Monastery of Haghpat

Australia
1981 Great Barrier Reef
1981 Kakadu National Park
1981 Willandra Lakes Region
1982 Tasmanian Wilderness
1982 Lord Howe Island Group
1987 Uluru-Kata Tjuta National Park
1987 Central Eastern Australian Rainforest
1988 Wet Tropics of Queensland
1991 Shark Bay, Western Australia
1992 Fraser Island
1994 Australian Fossil Mammal Sites (Riversleigh/Naracoorte)

Austria
1996 The Historic Centre of the City of Salzburg
1996 The Palace and Gardens of Schönbrunn

Bangladesh
1985 Historic Mosque City of Bagerhat
1985 Ruins of the Buddhist Vihara at Paharpur

Belarus/Poland
1992 Beloveshskaya Pushcha/Bialowieza Forest

Belize
1996 Belize Barrier-Reef Reserve System

Benin
1985 Royal Palaces of Abomey

Bolivia
1987 City of Potosi
1990 Jesuit Missions of the Chiquitos
1991 Historic City of Sucre

Brazil
1980 Historic Town of Ouro Preto
1982 Historic Centre of the Town of Olinda

1984 Iguacu National Park
1985 Historic Centre of Salvador de Bahia
1985 Sanctuary of Bom Jesus do Congonhas
1987 Brasilia
1991 Serra da Capivara National Park

Bulgaria
1979 Boyana Church
1979 Madara Rider
1979 Rock-hewn Churches of Ivanovo
1979 Thracian Tomb of Kazanlak
1983 Ancient City of Nessebar
1983 Srebarna Nature Reserve
1983 Pirin National Park
1983 Rila Monastery
1985 Thracian Tomb of Sveshtari

Cambodia
1992 Angkor

Cameroon
1987 Dja Faunal Reserve

Canada
1978 L'Anse aux Meadows National Historic Park
1978 Nahanni National Park
1979 Dinosaur Provincial Park
1981 Anthony Island
1981 Head-Smashed-In Buffalo Jump Complex
1983 Wood Buffalo National Park
1984 Canadian Rocky Mountain Parks*
1985 Quebec (Historic Area)
1987 Gros Morne National Park
1995 Lunenburg Old Town

*The Burgess Shale Site, previously inscribed on the World Heritage List, is part of the Canadian Rocky Mountain Parks.

Canada and the United States of America
1979 Tatshenshini-Alsek/Kluane National Park/Wrangell–St Elias National Park
and Reserve and Glacier Bay National Park
1995 Waterton Glacier International Peace Park

Central African Republic
1988 Parc National du Manovo-Gounda St Floris

Chile
1995 Rapa Nui National Park

China
1987 The Great Wall
1987 Mount Taishan
1987 Imperial Palace of the Ming and Qing Dynasties
1987 Mogao Caves
1987 Mausoleum of the First Qin Emperor
1987 Peking Man Site at Zhoukoudian
1990 Mount Hungshan
1992 Jiuzhaigou Valley Scenic and Historic Interest Area
1992 Huanglong Scenic and Historic Interest Area
1992 Wulingyuan Scenic and Historic Interest Area
1994 The Mountain Resort and its Outlying Temples Chengde
1994 Temple of Confucius, Cemetery of Confucius, and Kong Family Mansion
in Qufu
1994 Ancient Building Complex in the Wudang Mountains
1994 The Potala Palace, Lhasa
1996 Lushan National Park
1996 Mount Emei and Leshan Giant Buddha

Colombia
1984 Port, Fortresses and Group of Monuments, Cartagena
1994 Los Katios National Park
1995 Historic Centre of Santa Cruz de Mompox
1995 National Archaeological Park of Tierradentro
1995 San Agustin Archaeological Park

Costa Rica/Panama
1983 Talamanca Range–La Amistad Reserves/La Amistad National Park

Côte d'Ivoire
1982 Taï National Park
1983 Comoé National Park

Croatia
1979 Old City of Dubrovnik
1979 Historic Complex of Split with the Palace of Diocletian
1979 Plitvice Lakes National Park

Cuba
1982 Old Havana and its Fortifications
1988 Trinidad and the Valley de los Ingenios

Cyprus
1980 Paphos
1985 Painted Churches in the Troodos Region

Czech Republic
1992 Historic Centre of Prague
1992 Historic Centre of Cesky Krumlov
1992 Historic Centre of Telc
1994 Pilgrimage Church of St John of Nepomuk at Zelena Hora
1995 Kutna Hora – the Historical Town Centre with the Church of Saint Barbara
and the Cathedral of our Lady at Sedlec
1996 The Lednice–Valtice Cultural Landscape

Denmark
1994 Jellings Mounds, Runic Stones and Church
1995 Roskilde Cathedral

Dominican Republic
1990 Colonial City of Santo Domingo

Ecuador
1978 Galapagos National Park

1978 Old City of Quito
1983 Sangay National Park

Egypt
1979 Ancient Thebes with its Necropolis
1979 Islamic Cairo
1979 Memphis and its Necropolis – the Pyramid Fields from Giza to Dahshur
1979 Nubian Monuments from Abu Simbel to Philae
1979 Abu Mena

El Salvador
1993 Joya de Ceren Archaeological Site

Ethiopia
1978 Rock-hewn Churches of Lalibela
1978 Simien National Park
1979 Fasil Ghebbi, Gondar Region
1980 Aksum
1980 Lower Valley of the Awash
1980 Lower Valley of the Omo
1980 Tiya

Finland
1991 Old Rauma
1991 Fortress of Suomenlinna
1994 Petäjävesi Old Church
1996 Verla Groundwood and Board Mill

Former Yugoslav Republic of Macedonia
1979 Ohrid Region, including its cultural and historical aspects, and its natural environment

France
1979 Chartres Cathedral
1979 Decorated Grottoes of the Vézère Valley, including the Grotto of Lascaux
1979 Mont-St Michel and its Bay
1979 Palace and Park of Versailles
1979 Vézelay, Church and Hill

1981 Amiens Cathedral
1981 Chateau and Estate of Chambord
1981 Cistercian Abbey of Fontenay
1981 Palace and Park of Fontainebleau
1981 Roman and Romanesque Monuments of Arles
1981 The Roman Theatre and its Surroundings and the Triumphal Arch of
Orange
1982 The Royal Saltworks of Arc-et-Senans
1983 Place Stanislas, Place de la Carrière, and Place d'Alliance, Nancy
1983 Church of Saint-Savin-sur Gartempe
1983 Cape Girolata, Cape Porto, Scandola Natural Reserve, and the Piano
Calanches in Corsica
1985 Pont du Gard (Roman Aqueduct)
1988 Strasbourg, Grande Isle
1991 Paris, Banks of the Seine
1991 Cathedral of Notre-Dame, former Abbey of Saint-Remi and Tau Palace,
of Reims
1992 Bourges Cathedral
1995 Historic Centre of Avignon
1996 Le Canal du Midi

Georgia
1994 The City-Museum Reserve of Mtskheta
1994 Bagrati Cathedral and Gelati
1996 Upper Svaneti

Germany
1978 Aachen Cathedral
1981 Speyer Cathedral
1981 Würzburg Residence, including the Court Garden and Residence Square
1983 Pilgrimage of Church of Wies
1984 The Castles of Augustusburg and Falkenlust at Brühl
1985 St Mary's Cathedral and St Michael's Church, Hildesheim
1986 Roman Monuments, Cathedral and Liebfrauen-Church in Trier
1987 Hanseatic City of Lübeck
1990 Palaces and Parks of Potsdam and Berlin
1991 Abbey and Altenmünster of Lorsch

1992 Mines of Rammelsberg and the Historic Town of Goslar
1993 Town of Bamberg
1993 Maulbronn Monastery Complex
1994 The Collegiate Church, Castle, and old Town of Quedlinburg
1994 Völklingen Ironworks
1995 Messel Pit Fossil site
1996 Cologne Cathedral
1996 The Bauhaus and its sites in Weimar and Dessau
1996 The Luther Memorials in Eisleben and Wittenberg

Ghana
1979 Forts and Castles, Volta Greater Accra, Central and Western Regions
1980 Ashante Traditional Buildings

Greece
1986 Temple of Apollo Epicurius at Bassae
1987 Archaeological Site of Delphi
1987 The Acropolis, Athens
1988 Mount Athos
1988 Meteora
1988 Paleochristian and Byzantine Monuments of Thessalonika
1988 Archaeological Site of Epidaurus
1988 Medieval City of Rhodes
1989 Archaeological Site of Olympia
1989 Mystras
1990 Delos
1990 Monasteries of Daphni, Hossios Luckas and Nea Moni of Chios
1992 Pythagoreion and Heraion of Samos
1996 The Archaeological Site of Vergina

Guatemala
1979 Antigua Guatemala
1979 Tikal National Park
1981 Archaeological Park and Ruins of Quirigua

Guinea and Côte d'Ivoire
1981 Mount Nimba Strict Nature Reserve

Haiti
1982 Citadel, Sans-Souci Palace, and Ramiers National Historic Park

Holy See
1984 Vatican City

Honduras
1980 Maya Site of Copan
1982 Río Platano Biosphere Reserve

Hungary
1987 Budapest, including the Banks of the Danube with the district of Buda Castle
1987 Hollókö
1996 The Millenary Benedictine Abbey of Pannonhalma and its Natural Environment

Hungary and Slovakia
1995 Caves of Aggtelek and Slovak Karst

India
1983 Ajanta Caves
1983 Ellora Caves
1983 Agra Fort
1983 Taj Mahal
1984 Sun Temple, Konarak
1985 Group of Monuments at Mahabalipuram
1985 Kaziranga National Park
1985 Manas Wildlife Sanctuary
1985 Keoladeo National Park
1986 Churches and Convents of Goa
1986 Group of Monuments at Khajuraho
1986 Group of Monuments at Hampi
1986 Fatehpur Sikri
1987 Group of Monuments at Pattadakal
1987 Elephanta Caves
1987 Brihadisvara Temple, Thanjavur
1987 Sundarbans National Park
1988 Nanda Devi National Park

1989 Buddhist Monastery at Sanchi
1993 Humayun's Tomb
1993 Qutb Minar and its Monuments, Delhi

Indonesia
1991 Komodo National Park
1991 Ujung Kulon National Park
1991 Borobudur Temple compound
1991 Prambanan Temple compound
1996 Sangiran Early Man Site

Iran
1979 Persepolis
1979 Tchoga Zanbil Ziggurat and Complex
1979 Meidan Emam, Esfahan

Iraq
1985 Hatra

Ireland
1993 Archaeological ensemble of the Bend of the Boyne
1996 Skellig Michael

Italy
1979 Rock Drawings in Valcamonica near Bresica
1980 Church and Dominican Convent of Santa Maria delle Grazie with 'The Last Supper' by Leonardo da Vinci
1982 Historic Centre of Florence
1987 Venice and its Lagoon
1987 Piazza del Duomo, Pisa
1990 Historic Centre of San Gimignano
1993 I Sassi di Matera
1994 The City of Vicenza and the Palladian Villas of the Veneto
1995 Historic Centre of Siena
1995 Historic Centre of Naples
1995 Crespi d'Adda
1995 Ferrara, City of the Renaissance
1996 Castel del Monte

1996 The Trulli of Alberobello
1996 The Early Christian Monuments and Mosaics of Ravenna
1996 The Historic Centre of the City of Pienza

Italy/Holy See
1980 Historic Centre of Rome, the properties of the Holy See in that city enjoying extraterritorial rights, and San Paolo fuori le Mura

Japan
1993 Himeji-jo
1993 Buddhist Monuments in the Horyuji Area
1993 Yakushima
1993 Shirakami-Sanchi
1994 Historic Monuments of Ancient Kyoto (Kyoto, Uji and Otsu Cities)
1995 Historic Villages of Shirakawa-go and Gokayama
1996 Hiroshima Peace Memorial (Genbaku Dome)
1996 Itsukushima Shinto Shrine

Jerusalem
1981 The Old City of Jerusalem and its Walls (site proposed by Jordan)

Jordan
1985 Petra
1985 Quseir Amra

Lao People's Democratic Republic
1995 Town of Luang Prabang

Lebanon
1984 Anjar
1984 Baalbek
1984 Byblos
1984 Tyre

Libyan Arab Jamahiriya
1982 Archaeological Site of Leptis Magna
1982 Archaeological Site of Sabratha
1982 Archaeological Site of Cyrene

1985 Rock-art Sites of Tadrart Acacus
1988 Old Town of Ghadamès

Lithuania
1994 Vilnius Historic Centre

Luxembourg
1994 The City of Luxembourg, its old quarters and fortifications

Madagascar
1990 Tsingy Bemaraha Strict Nature Reserve

Malawi
1984 Lake Malawi National Park

Mali
1988 Old Towns of Djenné
1988 Timbuktu
1989 Cliffs of Bandiagara (Land of the Dogons)

Malta
1980 City of Valetta
1980 Megalithic Temples
1980 Hal Saflieni Hypogeum

Mauritania
1989 Banc D'Arguin National Park
1996 The Ancient Ksour of Ouadane, Chinguetti, Tichitt and Oualata

Mexico
1987 Historic Centre of Mexico City and Xochimilco
1987 Pre-Hispanic City and National Park of Palenque
1987 Pre-Hispanic City of Teotihuacan
1987 Historic Centre of Oaxaca and the Archaeological Site of Monte Alban
1987 Historic Centre of Puebla
1987 Sian Ka'an
1988 Historic Town of Guanajuato and adjacent mines
1988 Pre-Hispanic City of Chichén-Itza

1991 Historic Centre of Morelia
1992 El Tajin, Pre-Hispanic City
1993 Whale Sanctuary of El Vizcaino
1993 Historic Centre of Zacatecas
1993 Rock Paintings of the Sierra de San Francisco
1994 The Earliest Sixteenth-Century Monasteries on the slopes of Popocatepetl
1996 The Prehispanic Town of Uxmal
1996 The Historic Monuments Zone of Querétaro

Morocco
1981 Medina of Fez
1985 Medina of Marrakesh
1987 Ksar of Aït-Ben-Haddou
1996 The Historic City of Meknes

Mozambique
1991 Island of Mozambique

Nepal
1979 Kathmandu Valley
1979 Sagarmatha National Park, including Mount Everest
1984 Royal Chitwan National Park

Netherlands
1995 Schokland and its surroundings
1996 The Defence Line of Amsterdam

New Zealand
1990 Te Wahipounamu – South-West New Zealand (Westland/Mount Cook National Park and Fiordland National Park, previously inscribed on the World Heritage List, are part of this site)
1990 Tongariro National Park

Niger
1991 Air and Ténéré Natural Reserves
1996 'W' National Park

Norway
1979 Urnes Stave Church
1979 Bryggen
1980 Røros Mining Town
1985 Rock Drawings of Alta

Oman
1987 Bahla Fort
1988 Archaeological Sites of Bat, Al-Khutm and Al-Ayn
1994 Arabian Oryx Sanctuary

Pakistan
1980 Archaeological Ruins at Moenjodaro
1980 Buddhist Ruins at Takht-i-Bahi and Neighbouring City Remains at Sahr-i-Bahlol
1980 Taxila
1981 Fort and Shalamar Gardens at Lahore
1981 Historic Monuments of Thatta

Panama
1980 Fortifications of Portobelo and San Lorenzo
1981 Darien National Park

Paraguay
1993 Jesuit Missions of La Santisima Trinidad de Parana and Jesus de Tavarangue

Peru
1983 City of Cuzco
1983 Historic Sanctuary of Machu Picchu
1985 Chavin (Archaeological site)
1985 Huascarán National Park
1987 Manu National Park
1988 Chan Chan Archaeological Zone
1990 Rio Abiseo National Park
1991 Historic Centre of Lima
1994 The Lines and Geoglyphs of Nasca and Pampas de Juma

Philippines
1993 Baroque Churches of the Philippines
1993 Tubbataha Reef Marine Park
1995 Rice Terrasses of the Philippines Cordilleras

Poland
1978 Historic Centre of Cracow
1978 Wieliczka Salt Mines
1979 Auschwitz Concentration Camp
1980 Historic Centre of Warsaw
1992 Old City of Zamosc

Portugal
1983 Central Zone of the Town of Angra do Heroismo in the Azores
1983 Monastery of the Hieronymites and Tower of Belém, Lisbon
1983 Monastery of Batalha
1983 Convent of Christ in Tomar
1988 Historic Centre of Evora
1989 Monastery of Alcobaça
1995 Cultural Landscape of Sintra
1996 The Historic Centre of Oporto

Republic of Korea
1995 Sokkuram Grotto and Pulguksa Temple
1995 Haiensa Temple Changgyong P'ango, the Depositories for the Tripitaka Koreana Woodblocks
1995 The Chongmyo Shrine

Romania
1991 Danube Delta
1993 Biertan and its Fortified Church
1993 Monastery of Horezu
1993 Churches of Moldavia

Russian Federation
1990 Historic Centre of St Petersburg and related groups of monuments
1990 Khizi Pogost
1990 Kremlin and the Red Square

1992 Historic Monuments of Novgorod and surroundings
1992 Cultural and Historic Ensemble of the Solovetsky Islands
1992 The White Monuments of Vladimir and Suzdal
1993 Architectural Ensemble of the Trinity Sergius Lavra in Sergiev Posad
1994 The Church of the Ascension, Kolomenskoye
1995 Virgin Komi Forests
1996 Lake Baikal
1996 Volcanoes of Kamchatka

Senegal
1978 Island of Gorée
1981 Djoudj National Bird Sanctuary
1981 Niokolo-Koba National Park

Seychelles
1982 Aldabra Atoll
1983 Vallée de Mai Nature Reserve

Slovakia
1993 Vlkolinec
1993 Spissky Hrad and its Associated Cultural Monuments
1993 Banska Stiavnica

Slovenia
1988 Skocjan Caves

Spain
1984 The Historic Centre of Córdoba
1984 Alhambra, Generalife, and Albayzin, Granada
1984 Burgos Cathedral
1984 Monastery and Site of the Escurial, Madrid
1984 Parque Güell, Palacio Güell and Casa Mila, Barcelona
1985 Altamira Cave
1985 Old Town of Segovia, including its aqueduct
1985 Churches of the Kingdom of the Asturias
1985 Santiago de Compostela (Old Town)
1985 Old Town of Avila, including its Extra Muros churches
1986 Mudejar Architecture of Teruel

1986 Historic City of Toledo
1986 Garajonay National Park
1986 Old Town of Caceres
1987 Cathedral, the Alcazar and Archivo de Indias, Seville
1988 Old City of Salamanca
1991 Poblet Monastery
1993 Archaeological Ensemble of Mérida
1993 Royal Monastery of Santa Maria de Guadalupe
1993 The Route of Santiago de Compostela
1994 Doñana National Park
1996 The Historic Walled Town of Cuenca
1996 'La Lonja de la Seda' of Valencia

Sri Lanka
1982 Sacred City of Anuradhapura
1982 Ancient City of Polonnaruva
1982 Ancient City of Sigiriya
1988 Sinharaja Forest Reserve
1988 Sacred City of Kandy
1988 Old Town of Galle and its fortifications
1991 Golden Temple of Dambulla

Sweden
1991 Royal Domain of Drottningholm
1993 Birka and Hovgården
1993 Engelsberg Ironworks
1994 Rock Carvings of Tanum
1994 Skogskyrkogården
1995 Hanseatic Town of Visby
1996 The Church Village of Gammelstad, Luleå
1996 The Laponian Area

Switzerland
1983 Convent of St Gall
1983 Benedictine Convent of St John at Müstair
1983 Old City of Berne

Syrian Arab Republic
1979 Ancient City of Damascus
1980 Site of Palmyra
1980 Ancient City of Bosra
1988 Ancient City of Aleppo

Thailand
1991 Thungyai-Huai Kha Khaeng Wildlife Sanctuaries
1991 Historic Town of Sukhothai and associated historic towns
1991 Historic City of Ayutthaya and associated historic towns
1992 Ban Chiang Archaeological Site

Tunisia
1979 Amphitheatre of El Djem
1979 Site of Carthage
1979 Medina of Tunis
1980 Ichkeul National Park
1985 Punic Town of Kerkuane and its Necropolis
1988 Medina of Sousse
1988 Kairouan

Turkey
1985 Historic Areas of Istanbul
1985 Göreme National Park and the Rock Sites of Cappadocia
1985 Great Mosque and Hospital of Divrigi
1986 Hattusha
1987 Nemrut Dag
1988 Xanthos-Letoon
1988 Hierapolis-Pamukkale
1994 City of Safranbolu

Uganda
1994 Bwindi Impenetrable National Park
1994 Rwenzori Mountains National Park

Ukraine
1990 Kiev: St Sophia Cathedral and related monastic buildings, and Lavra of Kiev-Pechersk

United Kingdom

1986 The Giant's Causeway and Causeway Coast

1986 Durham Castle and Cathedral

1986 Ironbridge Gorge

1986 Studley Royal Park, including the Ruins of Fountains Abbey

1986 Stonehenge, Avebury and associated sites

1986 The Castles and Town Walls of King Edward in Gwynedd

1986 St Kilda

1987 Blenheim Palace

1987 City of Bath

1987 Hadrian's Wall

1987 Palace of Westminster, Abbey of Westminster, and St Margaret's Church

1988 Henderson Island

1988 The Tower of London

1988 Canterbury Cathedral, St Augustine's Abbey, and St Martin's Church

1995 Old and New Towns of Edinburgh

1995 Gough Island Wildlife Reserve

United Republic of Tanzania

1979 Ngorongoro Conservation Area

1981 Ruins of Kilwa Kisiwani and Ruins of Songo Mnara

1981 Serengeti National Park

1982 Selous Game Reserve

1987 Kilimanjaro National Park

United States of America

1978 Mesa Verde National Park

1978 Yellowstone National Park

1979 Everglades National Park

1979 Grand Canyon National Park

1979 Independence Hall

1980 Redwood National Park

1981 Mammoth Cave National Park

1981 Olympic National Park

1982 Cahokia Mounds State Historic Site

1983 Great Smokey Mountains National Park

1983 San Juan National Historic Site and La Fortaleza

1984 The Statue of Liberty

1984 Yosemite National Park
1987 Monticello, and the University of Virginia, Charlottesville
1987 Chaco Culture National Historic Park
1987 Hawaii Volcanoes National Park
1992 Pueblo de Taos
1995 Carlsbad Caverns National Park

Uruguay
1995 Historic Quarter of the City of Colonia del Sacramento

Uzbekistan
1990 Itchan Kala
1993 The Historic Centre of Bukhara

Venezuela
1993 Coro
1994 Canaima National Park

Vietnam
1993 Hué (Complex of Monuments)
1994 Ha Long Bay

Yemen
1982 Old Walled City of Shibam
1988 Old City of Sana'a
1993 Historic Town of Zabid

Yugoslavia
1979 Natural and Culturo-Historic Region of Kotor
1979 Stari Ras and Sopocani Monastery
1980 Durmitor National Park
1988 Studenica Monastery

Zambia/Zimbabwe
1989 Victoria Falls/Mosi-oa-Tunya

Zimbabwe
1984 Mana Pools National Park, Sapi and Chewore Safari Areas

1988 Great Zimbabwe National Monument
1988 Khami Ruins National Monument

The World Heritage List was established under terms of The Convention Concerning the Protection of World Culture and Natural Heritage adopted in November 1972 at the 17th General Conference of UNESCO. The Convention states that a World Heritage Committee 'will establish, keep up-to-date and publish' a World Heritage List of cultural and natural properties, submitted by the States and considered to be of outstanding universal value. One of the main responsibilities of this Committee is to provide technical cooperation under the World Heritage Fund for the safeguarding of World Heritage Sites to States Parties whose resources are insufficient. States Parties can request international assistance under the Fund for expert missions, training of specialized staff, and supply of equipment when appropriate; they can also apply for long-term loans and, in special cases, non-repayable grants. Requests must concern work necessary for the preservation of cultural or natural sites included in the World Heritage List or assistance to national or regional training centres. Emergency assistance is also available under the Fund in the case of properties severely damaged by specific natural or man-made disasters or threatened with imminent destruction.

As of December 1996, 147 Member States had ratified the Convention, the United States being the first to do so. As of December 1996, the number of sites on the World Heritage List stood at 506. The Committee named twelve sites in 1978, forty-five in 1979, twenty-eight in 1980, twenty-six in 1981, twenty-four in 1982, twenty-nine in 1983, twenty-three in 1984, thirty in 1985, thirty-one in 1986, forty-one in 1987, twenty-seven in 1988, seven in 1989, seventeen in 1990, twenty-two in 1991, twenty in 1992, thirty-three in 1993, twenty-nine in 1994, twenty-nine in 1995, and thirty-seven in 1996. Small discrepancies in numbers may be due to different methods of numbering sites, and overlapping of sites into two countries. Enquiries should be sent to:

UNESCO World Heritage Centre
7 Place de Fontenoy
75352 Paris 07 SP, France
wh-info@unesco.org

http://www.unesco.org/whc/heritage.htm
December 1996

Appendix 2:
Teaching notes

Chapter 2 Bukhara

Context

Bukhara is an ancient city with major significant monuments and with Central Asia's only inhabited, intact historic core. Its significance was recognized in 1993 when the whole of the Old City was designated as a World Heritage Site. With neighbouring cities of Samarkand and Khiva it forms part of an Uzbekistan heritage tourism 'milk run'. It also has a central position on the ancient Silk Road which linked China with Europe. During the seventy years in which it was a Republic of the Soviet Union tourism to Uzbekistan developed as part of a centrally planned, command economy. Visits to the ancient cities formed a key part of this tourism. Current tourism services and facilities reflect this Soviet legacy. At the same time, restoration and planning was carried out to protect the ancient sites and create the effect of an open-air museum. As a result, despite the splendours of the buildings the Bukhara experienced by the tourist has a lifeless atmosphere. As Uzbekistan moves towards a market economy, following independence in 1991, it is seeking to develop its tourism sector and within this the ancient monuments and cities are playing a major role. However, the legacy of the Soviet period and the dislocation of the years since independence are creating some obstacles to the successful development of tourism. This case highlights the situation of tourism in Bukhara in the mid-1990s after a start has been made on the development of tourism in a market economy building upon the attractions and legacy of the past.

Open-air museum

The major attraction of Bukhara, its historic core, has been heavily restored and protected. As a result, it presents a sterile, lifeless atmosphere. Does this provide an adequate basis for the development of tourism?

Other attractions

Most of the attractions of Bukhara are based on its historic core. This has important implications for the length of stay and seasonality of visits. Is there scope and is it desirable for Bukhara to widen its attractions base?

The 'milk run' and the Silk Road

There is a strongly developed 'milk run' in Uzbekistan of which Bukhara is an important component. The city is also on the much more extensive Silk Road which the World Tourism Organization has identified as an important tourism product. What issues are raised about the impact of 'milk run' tourism and the associated short length of stay in individual destinations?

Restoring connections with the global tourism market

In the past tourism in Uzbekistan was organized and controlled through Moscow. This meant that contact with the global tourism markets was handled by Soviet organizations, notably Intourist, and international travellers arrived in Uzbekistan via Moscow. After 1991 the newly independent country has had to establish its own links and also create a separate identity in the tourism marketplace. Why was it necessary to set up an airline and tourist offices as well as creating marketing images?

The Soviet legacy

The tourist facilities and services, particularly in the hotels, strongly reflect the Soviet legacy. Setting aside differences in quality which are now being addressed with the opening of new hotels, the accommodation stock was most suitable for large, standardized tour groups. This raises an important question about whether these are suitable for modern forms of tourism.

Chapter 3   Biertan

Context

Biertan is an old Transylvanian village which stands as key evidence of the centuries-old German colonization of the Romanian territories. Its fortified church, which was once the most important Protestant Episcopal centre in Transylvania, was designated as a World Heritage Site in 1993. The designation had a major impact on the restoration of the monument, bringing sponsorship and foreign expertise which enabled essential conservation of the structure and its contents. A new guest-house was build in Biertan in order to accommodate and attract more tourists to the site and emphasis is currently put on improving the quality of services provided. The World Heritage designation was also instrumental in drawing the attention of the new Romanian leadership to the importance of protecting heritage sites. The new government had elaborated a tourism strategy until the year 2000 which has in view financial contribution to the conservation of Romanian heritage sites, but the legacy of the previous Communist regime currently sets cultural and legislative barriers to the development of these tourist attractions.

National and international importance of Biertan

The fortified church of Biertan and the traditional German village where Romanians and Germans cohabited for centuries are extremely well conserved. They offer domestic and international tourists and visitors the unspoilt beauty of the integration of two different cultures. Does this site have the natural resources for attracting more domestic and international tourists and visitors in the future?

Fortified churches – a new visitor destination in Romania

Approximately 300 similar fortifications were built in Romania. They originate in the Dacian fortresses built during the Roman domination and are a testimony to medieval knowledge of architecture, religion, astronomy and the science of war. How should fortified churches be promoted as visitor destinations?

The quality of tourist services at Biertan

Apart from the tourists who come to Biertan on organized tours, independent domestic and international visitors encounter difficulties understanding the culture of the village and the historic significance of the church, due to the lack of guiding, signs, maps or on-site information. How can the quality of the tourist experience at Biertan be improved?

The Communist legacy

The quality of the services throughout the Romanian tourism industry suffer from the imprints of the Communist legacy. In the past years, the accommodation available catered mainly for mass tourism, therefore small tourism businesses are very much in their infancy. Should more small businesses be encouraged by the new government policies?

Chapter 4   Cracow

Context

Cracow is a former capital of Poland and is the coronation and burial site of Polish kings and heroes. It is also the site of many important Polish institutions such as the Roman Catholic Church and the Jagiellonian University, which is Poland's oldest and leading seat of learning. Pope John Paul II was a former Cardinal Archbishop of Cracow. Given this background, it is a kind of national shrine for Poles and a visit to Cracow is an important part of the education of Polish children. During its long history Cracow has been invaded and influenced by many foreign powers from the Mogul invasion of the Middle Ages to the Nazi occupation from 1939 to 1945. During the latter time the city's thriving Jewish population was largely destroyed although the buildings in the Old City itself were undamaged.

Today, the city contains monuments, artefacts and reminders of all the periods of its history with 6000 historic buildings and monuments and thirty museums containing more than 2 million exhibits. The Old City is particularly attractive with a compact, geometric, medieval design set around one of the largest market squares in Europe. The Old City is circled by a ring of parkland which marks the site of the old defensive walls.

Cracow is becoming an increasingly attractive town for tourist visits both by Poles and by foreigners. Most of the visitors want to see the major sites which are contained in the relatively small area of the Old City and the adjacent Wawel Hill which contains the Royal Castle and Royal Cathedral. Some are now also making their way to a nearby part of the town called Kazimierz. This contains the former Jewish quarter and provided the location for the film *Schindler's List*. This recorded the tragic fate of the Cracow Jews under the Nazi occupation. Although the locations used in the film are mainly in Kazimierz, most of the events that are recorded in the film took place in another part of the town. Typically tourists to Cracow stay for only one or two days. During this time they try to see the Old City, sometimes Kazimierz plus a visit to the nearby salt mine at Wieliczka and the former concentration camp at Auschwitz–Birkenau.

Following the fall of Communism in Poland in 1989 the country has made a speedy and generally successful transfer to a market economy. In tourism in Cracow the growing private sector has been relatively successful in developing and providing services and facilities to meet and attract tourists. Small businesses running restaurants, bars, souvenir shops, and tourist visits have been set up and most of the hotels are now operated privately. However, this development is creating some conflicts and problems because the planning and control mechanisms are not always able successfully to meet the problems created by tourism. As a result, there are problems of tourist congestion and unattractive signs which detract from the appearance of the town.

Visitor management

At present most of the visitors want to see the same sites all of which are in a relatively small area in the Old City. This creates over-crowding at some of the pressure points. What techniques could be used to manage the flows of visitor more effectively?

Length of stay

Tourists to Cracow stay for a relatively short period of time. The average stay for international visitors is 1.79 nights and for Polish visitors is 2.02 nights. The foreign visitors are often on tours of Poland and sometimes tours of a number of countries. Cracow is only one of the places that they visit. Is it important to extend the length of stay and what measures could be used to achieve this?

Planning in a market economy

Under Communism the Poles experienced forty-five years of living under a planned economy. After 1989, with the move to a market economy, Poles have successfully responded to the needs of the market. In Cracow, bars, restaurants and other tourist facilities have been created and the individual enterprises have put up advertising signs to encourage customers. At the same time large companies, such as McDonald's and Pizza Hut, have been looking for sites in the Old City. Is there a need to control these developments in a heritage city like Cracow and how can this be achieved?

Schindler's tourism

The world-wide success of the film *Schindler's List*, which records the fate of the Jews of Cracow under the Nazi occupation, has meant that many visitors to the town now want to visit the scenes shown in the film. For centuries the Jews lived in a part of Kazimierz which is an area of Cracow. However, after the Nazi invasion they were forced to move into a closed ghetto across the river. From there many were moved to concentration camps and were killed. The events shown in the film did not generally take place in Kazimierz but for artistic reasons many of the locations used in the film were based there. An increasing number of tourists have been drawn to Kazimierz to see where *Schindler's List* was filmed. Tourist routes have now been created to see both the locations shown in the film and where the actual events occurred. This development raises a number of important questions. Are locations of tragic events of the recent past suitable for exploitation as tourist attractions? Is it necessary or desirable to clarify the confusion in the tourists' minds between film and reality in a site such as Kazimierz?

5 Easter Island

Context

The *moai* statues of Rapa Nui, Easter Island, are universally famous and act as the pegs of a tourism industry on which the economy of the small island is entirely dependent. Rapa Nui is a small subtropical island half-way between Chile and Tahiti, forming the most remote land mass in the world. It is home to nearly 3000 people, only 30 per cent of whom are native Rapa Nui, many being mainlanders brought in for roadbuilding projects. Although formerly heavily wooded, Rapa Nui has no indigenous trees. The island was formerly covered in dense woodland, cut down to facilitate moving the giant statues.

Rapa Nui landscapes are bleak, grassy and windswept and the island is circled by dramatic cliffs, 300 m high in places. There is no natural deepwater harbour so that ships must offload passengers and freight into small boats up to 1 km from shore. Rapa Nui was colonized by Polynesians from the west (and ultimately from Asia) between AD 400 and 700 with the peak of statue construction at AD 1200–1500. By that time the population may have reached as high as 10 000, far exceeding the resource capacity of the small island's ecosystem. Scarce resources, destruction of lush palm forests both for agriculture and to transport the massive stone *moai* probably plunged a thriving and complex society into decline, culminating in civil war and cannibalism. Local chaos replaced centralized government and by 1700 the population had crashed and clans had started to topple their rivals' statues. Some *moai* were seen upright by the first European visitors in 1773 but all had been torn down by the islanders themselves by 1864.

Around 1000 *moai* seem to have been made, 200 of which once stood on coastal *ahu* platforms, facing inland and carved from volcanic tuffs with coral eyes and red topknots. Another 700–800, in varying stages of completion, were abandoned in the quarry or along the ancient roads between quarries and the coast. Most of the erected statues came from a single quarry (Ranu Raraku) and were transported as far as 8 km despite heights of up to 11 m and weights of up to 82 tons.. The perennial fascination of the island is the 'mystery' of who carved the statues and how they were moved, an issue made especially interesting by the barren, desolate nature of the island. Rapa Nui came under Chilean military rule until the mid-1960s but now has local self-government although many islanders are still dissatisfied with the Chilean presence. Complaints include neglect by the Chilean government, who clearly regard the island as of peripheral significance, poor health and education services, deficient transport and scarce farmland increasingly pressured by a rising population who are forbidden to utilize National Park land. Some militant Rapa Nui pressure groups feel that the island should be returned to their ownership and resent outside interference, including World Heritage designation. The islanders' Polynesian identity is still very strong, preserved in traditional wood carvings, tapa crafts, tattooing, music and dance.

Some 10 161 visitors went to Rapa Nui in 1995, of whom 3181 were cruise passengers who came on just three large ships and remained on the island for only four to six hours. Tourism is seasonal with its capacity almost totally constrained by the airline monopoly of LanChile. The island has at least 700 tourist bedspaces with accommodation providers able to charge extremely high prices. Local transport is minimal but the tourism industry on the island is managed in an effective low-key way with all facilities confined to Hanga Roa and minimal intrusive signage or on-site interpretation. Rapa Nui's tourism industry is managed by the Rapa Nui people themselves but is highly import intensive. Moreover, not all the entry fees to the National Park which occupies 70 per cent of the island and protects its statues are returned for conservation. Only eight rangers are employed, their lack of funding being highlighted in December 1996 when the single ranger on duty had to walk twenty miles to Hanga Roa to report a serious fire, since he had no radio.

Tourism to Rapa Nui is growing at roughly 10 per cent per year but there is cause for concern about the impact of cruise-ship visitors, the lack of funding for archaeological and conservation work and a possible diminution in the quality of the visitor experience. Rapa Nui is inevitably an expensive destination since it is unique, but care must be taken to ensure the survival of the monuments on which the entire economy of the island is now based.

Rapa Nui highlights the fragility of an island economy now based entirely on tourism and served by a single airline monopoly. Its success depends on providing a unique visitor experience.

The site and its setting

Rapa Nui is the most remote inhabited place on earth and its tourism industry is highly dependent upon the airline monopoly of LanChile. What might be the consequences for the tourism industry of the island if this monopoly is removed?

Tourism economics

Nearly the whole population of Rapa Nui is partly or entirely dependent on a tourism industry which is seasonal and highly import intensive. Are there any methods for reducing the dependency on imports or diversifying the tourism product?

Tourism management

Tourism on Rapa Nui is managed unobtrusively by SERNATUR (the Chilean State Tourist Office) and CONAF (the Forestry Department) but the number of rangers employed is small and they are poorly equipped. These deficiencies were emphasized by the recent fire which damaged many of the statues. Only a fraction of tourism revenues is returned to finance management and conservation programmes. How could this be increased and what should be done?

Visitor facilities

The arrival of large numbers of cruise-ship passengers puts immense short-term pressure on island resources. What environmental, cultural and economic impacts, if any, is this likely to have in the short and medium term?

A unique resource

Rapa Nui is both inaccessible and unique and as such is bound to be a very expensive destination to visit. It is not a price-sensitive destination; should there be any price controls for accommodation providers or should they be allowed to charge whatever the market will bear? If the market changes (perhaps as a result of increased air access) what changes will be seen in the nature of Rapa Nui tourism?

Chapter 6   Giza

Context

The Pyramids and monuments of the Giza Plateau were officially recognized as a World Heritage Site in 1979, since when degradation levels have been deemed unacceptable by UNESCO who commissioned a Masterplan for management of the site in 1992. Significant portions of the site have been degraded both by tourists, due to unsuitable siting or lack of facilities, and local people – by the encroachment of Cairo onto the site fringes. This is compounded by the little amount of site interpretation available. The Pyramids dominate the landscape while less visible – but important- features are trampled underfoot.

GIS may play a role in the implementation of the Masterplan by helping to check the validity of proposals, monitor the effects of those in place and model potential new developments. Additionally, technology such as 'Virtual Reality' could be used to aid in site interpretation, giving an overview of the area, and allowing its exploration as a 'fly-through' model. This would allow visitors to identify the historical significance of site features by showing how their appearances have been affected by time. The case highlights the current problems facing the Giza Plateau, and suggests ways in which IT (particularly GIS) can support the Giza Masterplan.

Degradation

Significant areas of the site have been degraded. Why are the problems so bad, and what factors have contributed to the negative impacts?

Interpretation

It is suggested, that many negative impacts are caused because tourists do not understand, or are not aware of, features of the site. Better interpretation could increase the quality of visitor experience. How might this be achieved?

Uses of information technology

IT can be used for both monitoring and managing the site, and aiding in site interpretation. What other potential roles could also be linked in when considering the wider demands of tourism (e.g. promotion/marketing/sales)?

Conflicts

To what extent does the Masterplan address conflicts between users of the site (tourists/local people/tour operators)? What potential conflicts are there?

Chapter 7 Hadrian's Wall

Context

As the northern frontier of the Roman Empire Hadrian's Wall has been dubbed the most important monument left behind by the Romans during their occupation of Britain, and is thus of great archaeological significance. However, it was not merely the Roman Wall that received World Heritage status in 1987; rather, Hadrian's Wall Military Zone, comprising an assemblage of Roman sites and fortifications, and their setting. Management of the Zone is made more difficult by the sheer size and physical dispersal of the remains, with the Wall stretching from Wallsend on the Tyne in the east to Bowness on Solway in the west. In addition to the rural situation of the central section, the line of the wall and existing remains pass through the urban centres of Newcastle and Carlisle. This living and working landscape places additional pressures on the fragile remains as conflicts arise from multiple use. The Military Zone is owned and managed by numerous individuals, organizations and interest groups, with the recent *Management Plan*, authored by English Heritage, an attempt to address the need for one vision. Less than 10 per cent of the Wall is managed purely for the purposes of conservation.

Access to the site and its setting are of great consequence to the sustainable future of the site, providing opportunities for financial gain, education and appreciation. Visitors walk nearby rights of way and visit a plethora of free and paid-entry sites, though pressure is greatest in the central section. With visits to paid-entry sites in decline for more than twenty years, and visits to free sites increasing, Hadrian's Wall faces visitor management challenges with regard to managing the behaviour and impact of visitors to sites where direct economic benefits are not received. However, visits to free sites are necessary to foster an appreciation of the Wall and its setting. Furthermore, adequate interpretation of the site and its context is essential if visitors are to realize the significance of seemingly lifeless monuments and artefacts. The case highlights the complexities of managing access and visitor experience at Hadrian's Wall, in view of the multiple use and multiple ownership of the site and its setting.

The site and its setting

Hadrian's Wall Military Zone, stretching the breadth of England, is situated within modern urban and agricultural landscapes, with such living and working environments creating pressure from multiple use. What visitor management challenges might arise as a result of multiple use?

Ownership and responsibility

The site and its setting are owned and managed by numerous individuals, organizations and interested parties. In the central section it is the balance of conservation with access and agricultural concerns which must be met. What are the implications of multiple ownership with regard to visitor management and the future of Hadrian's Wall?

Access and impact

In enabling expansive views of Hadrian's Wall and its rural setting, free sites in the central section are crucial to a comprehensive and rewarding experience of the site. However, decreasing visits to paid-entry sites and increasing visits to free sites potentially lead to increased adverse impact in those areas where visitors are more difficult to control and manage. What might be done to ensure adequate and appropriate visitor management at free sites?

Interpretation

If visitors are to leave a Roman site with a reasonable level of understanding and appreciation the remains must be effectively interpreted – setting the monuments and remains in their historical context while providing relevant information about Roman ways of life. However, such interpretation must always be sympathetic to the resource so as not to trivialize its cultural significance; and, in addition, it must not create visual pollution. English Heritage are proposing to link exhibitions and other interpretative facilities into an overall interpretation strategy. What techniques of interpretation might be appropriate?

The future

In the light of recent planning initiatives and the visitor management challenges facing Hadrian's Wall, consider the future for those paid-entry sites in the central section. What might be done to improve visitor experience, and thus the financial returns, of these gateway sites?

Chapter 8   Kakadu

Kakadu National Park is a World Heritage Park with both environmental and cultural significance. An area of 20 000 km² in the Northern Territory, Australia, it has been the site of human occupation for over 50 000 years. It represents the world's largest single source of rock art, and for the current Aboriginal people it is a living place.

The Park has over 200 000 visitors a year, drawn by its biodiversity and by an opportunity to experience elements of Aboriginal culture. The Kakadu is owned by the Aboriginal peoples and leased to the Australian National Parks and Wildlife Service (ANPWS) who manage the Park in consultation with the traditional owners. The Service has thus to meet the concerns of a people seeking to maintain a traditional culture, the conservation needs associated with a major location of often unique wildlife, the wants of tourists, and also to permit in some areas, mining activities.

Visitor management

Given the need to conserve natural habitats and maintain sacred places, what visitor management strategies can be pursued by the Park Authorities?

Demand and pricing structures

To what extent can visitor demand be satisfied, but conservation needs (both natural and cultural) be met by adopting price structures that may not inhibit a growth of numbers but might reduce duration of stay?

Sacred sites

Is it a correct policy to permit visitation to sacred sites? Does it help visitors to a better understanding of Aboriginal culture or does it impinge upon the exercise of traditional beliefs? Is there any comparison with allowing visitors to cathedrals in Western Europe?

Aboriginal control

Aboriginal control of tourism is important and a major purpose of the Park is to allow the traditional way of life outside Western commercial work patterns to continue. What, then, is the purpose of limiting the number of Aboriginal people living in Kakadu?

Visitor numbers

Should visitor numbers to the Yellow Waters be permitted to increase? How should visitors be catered for – more small boats or a smaller number of large ones?

Chapter 9   Lalibela

Context

The case describes how tourism to the historic rock-cut churches of Lalibela in Ethiopia has developed throughout a history of Imperial government, civil war and famine up to the present day. Lalibela now forms part of a heritage tourism 'milk run' that is becoming economically significant for Ethiopia. However, the complex church site hosts large numbers of domestic visitors (many on pilgrimage or attending religious festivals) as well as increasing numbers of international visitors. Both fabric and artefacts are becoming heavily eroded and there are some problems with theft. Poor restoration and conservation has left unsightly construction works and social concerns have emerged such as the role of untrained 'child guides' and gender issues related to tourism employment.

Religion and tourism

The site of Lalibela is owned by the Ethiopian Orthodox Church although the boundaries are poorly defined. Tourism is necessary to support priests, services and festivals but to what extent should the Church be involved in a commercial enterprise such as tourism?

Benefits to the community

What lessons can Lalibela learn from other similar World Heritage Sites in rural areas where some groups in the host population are on the poverty line? How can vulnerable groups such as women, farmers and children be included in the tourism equation?

Conservation of the churches

Considering the fragility of the churches and the pending increasing pressure from expansion in tourism development how can the carrying capacity of the churches be measured and put into practice? To what extent should conservation and preservation change a historic site when its importance as a religious centre will inevitably be disturbed?

Social responsibility

A code of ethics for tourist activity in Lalibela and the impact of the activity on the host community needs to be assessed and developed. What other forms of education would be useful for the host community if tourism is going to be an ongoing feature in Lalibela?

Visitor information and experience

There is a need for further information for the visitor. As there is no museum or exhibition, the quality of visitor experience is sometimes reduced for those who wish to seek more knowledge than just seeing the churches. What form of interpretation could be used for Lalibela in order to assist in this?

Chapter 10   Luxor

Context: traffic and visitor flow management

Luxor, the town at the centre of Thebes tourism, is one of the most historically important areas in Egypt, as well as being a major heritage tourism destination and departure point for cruises along the Nile corridor of Upper Egypt. The ancient monuments of Thebes have attracted international interest from archaeologists, Egyptologists and visitors since the nineteenth century and official recognition came in 1979 when the temples of Karnak and Luxor and the Necropolis and Mortuary Temples of the Pharaohs were designated by UNESCO as a World Heritage Site. Since then considerable tourism development has taken place with strong support from the Egyptian government, although political unrest has deterred tourists at times. Perceptions of risk have now declined and visitor numbers are once again rising to record numbers, with the consequence that tourism in Luxor is generating peak arrivals of visitors to the antiquities sites. This density of visitors causes particular problems at the tombs which are susceptible to increases in humidity and vibration and in the recently opened tomb of Nefertari the authorities are restricting entry in order to preserve the decorated inscriptions and limit the damage to the tomb. However, measures are also needed to protect other tombs and other Theban sites which should include better information for visitors who are ill-informed about conservation needs. As a majority of visitors are part of guided tour groups, travelling in large modern coaches, and with similar schedules, there are frequent problems of congestion, over-crowding and queues. Such large numbers of vehicles and floating hotels which dock at Luxor have an impact on the environment, both in the levels of air pollution from diesel fumes and river pollution from oil and refuse, which may have the effect of impairing the quality of the tourist experience.

   This case study assesses the visitor management issues of traffic and visitor flows within the heritage site of Thebes and identifies some of the impacts of tourism which pertain to the area.

Partnerships between government and private tourist operations

Public- and private-sector partnerships have proved successful in stimulating tourism demand, and for developing tourism in Luxor. How should these organizations approach the formulation of visitor management strategies for Thebes tourism, considering the specific conditions which prevail in Luxor?

Conflict or balance

Indicators of the physical impacts on the monuments from environmental factors, archaeological activity and the volume of visitors, requires a response. How can a balance be found between the economic needs for tourism and the preservation of the monuments? In a developing country such as Egypt, economic growth is a priority for a government struggling against the demands of a rising population. Why are strategies required for conservation? The monuments have existed for thousands of years, why should they need protecting now?

Employment benefits

Current transport arrangements for visiting Thebes' sites provide employment opportunities which could decline when operators use the new bridge to visit the West Bank. What traffic management schemes could be introduced that would alleviate problems without jeopardizing the employment benefits for those involved?

Implications of mass tourism

International tour operators representing the mass tourist market are becoming increasingly involved in heritage tourism and cruises; Luxor offers both products in an equable climate during the winter 'off-season'. What are the implications of mass tourism to heritage destinations such as Luxor?

Dependence on tourism

Luxor's dependence on tourism became evident during 1993 when the slump in demand brought considerable hardship. What measures can be taken to sustain Luxor's tourism in the long term?

Information and interpretation

Visitor information and on-site interpretation in minimal in Luxor. What improve-ments are possible, and how could they be implemented?

Gateway centre

The idea for a gateway centre on the corniche in Luxor could have improved the tourist experience and helped to regulate the flow of visitors to the West Bank sites. How and where should this visitor management scheme be implemented and what are the factors required to ensure its success?

Visitor impacts

In addition to the physical and environmental visitor impacts identified in this study what possible economic and social impacts of Thebes tourism are likely to occur?

Advantages/disadvantages of World Heritage status

Discuss the implications of World Heritage status for the Thebes site.

Role of tour guides

Tour guides play an important role in visitor management at most historic sites, and their level of income often depends on their performance. How could their role be adapted to enhance the visitor experience while giving consideration to the preservation of the ancient monuments?

Chapter 11   Ninstints

Context

This case examines tourism to the abandoned Haida village of Ninstints on Skung-wai (Anthony Island), the southernmost of the Queen Charlotte Islands off the coast of British Columbia, Canada. Ninstints is the most significant of a series of Haida villages whose inhabitants, the coastal Haida people, were largely wiped out by diseases transmitted by contact with European traders and sailors in the nineteenth century. Today, the surviving Haida who live in the Queen Charlotte Islands are experiencing something of a cultural renaissance, and it has become essential for them to preserve and interpret their ancestral sites for a new generation. External interest in Haida sites is growing, too, partly as a result of the successful marketing of high-quality modern Haida works of art. At the same time, tourism to the Queen Charlottes is flourishing, partly because of the opportunity to visit Haida sites but also for sea kayaking and wilderness visiting.

Ninstints lies in the remotest tip of the Queen Charlottes and can only be reached by sea, from a kayak or inflatable boat. Visitors can see the collapsed remains of log houses and an extraordinary collection of intricately carved but heavily weathered totem poles, the world's largest assemblage still *in situ*. The inaccessible site and its spectacular location has the ability to generate a powerful spirit of place, and it is this ability, combined with the stories underlying the abandonment of the sites told by the Haida Watchmen who act as guide/ interpreters, which are bringing increasing numbers of visitors. The Watchmen programme is funded by Parks Canada as part of a complex deal which led the management of the entire Gwaii Hanaas Park Reserve (in which the site is located) being shared between the Canadian federal government (via Parks Canada) and the Haida nation. This was mainly the result of Haida pressure against intrusive logging within the area, but the current management plan for Gwaii Hanaas was undoubtedly helped by the announcement of World Heritage status for Ninstints in 1981, although many Haida objected to the nomination.

Today, Ninstints receives less than a thousand visitors a year with tourism carefully controlled by on-site Haida Watchmen who live in a modern replica of a Haida longhouse. Visitation is highly seasonal due to rough seas for nine months of the year and the Haida successfully campaigned to have helicopter or floatplane landings banned at what they consider to be a sacred site. In many ways Ninstints is the heart of the Haida nation, the careful control of visitors helped by its remote location. The major threat to Ninstints is no longer people but the environment itself, with the surviving carved poles and house fragments becoming heavily eroded, though being closely monitored by conservators. Their survival is essential for the Haida and desirable for the rest of the world, as a memorial to the rich but largely unknown culture of the formerly powerful Haida nation.

This case stresses the significance of partnership in visitor management strategies, and underlines the relationship between accessibility, visitor numbers and site erosion.

The site and its setting

Ninstints is probably Canada's least accessible tourist attraction but one of its most significant sacred sites. Visitor numbers are also restricted by seasonality and ensuring arrival by sea. Do you agree with this policy or feel that it is elitist?

Ownership and responsibility

The Gwaii Hanaas Reserve is now managed by a partnership between Parks Canada (a branch of the federal government) and the Haida nation themselves. What would the different implications be for the future of the site if this partnership was dissolved leaving control with only one organization?

Access and impact

Visitors to Ninstints pay no fee, leave no impact and receive no facilities. This has been decided upon as the most suitable management strategy for a sacred site with low visitor numbers. What is the connection between the absence of fees and the absence of impact. Do you feel that a fee should be charged to develop visitor facilities or contribute funds for conservation or the Watchmen programme?

Contemporary culture

The growing interest in Haida sites is part of a general resurgence of interest in different North American First Nations. Contemporary Haida craftsmen are famous for their artworks utilizing ancient motifs from Haida myths and legends. In what way does this relate to the need to preserve Haida heritage sites?

World Heritage designation

Designation of Ninstints as a World Heritage Site in 1981 was achieved without the consent of many of the Haida people although many have become reconciled to the designation after seeing its benefit for the development of a better management plan. However, should the Haida have the right to ask for the designation to be withdrawn if they wish to do so, or should that right be vested only with the Canadian government?

Index